ORTEGA AS PHENOMENOLOGIST

The Genesis of *Meditations on Quixote*

ORTEGA AS PHENOMENOLOGIST

The Genesis of *Meditations on Quixote*

Philip W. Silver

New York   Columbia University Press   1978

Library of Congress Cataloging in Publication Data
Silver, Philip W.
    Ortega as phenomenologist.

    Bibliography: p.
    Includes index.
    1. Ortega y Gasset, Jose, 1883–1955.
2. Phenomenology.   3. Ortega y Gasset, Jose,
1883–1955. Meditaciones del Quijote.
4. Aesthetics.   I. Title.
B4568.074S56   196'.1   78-667
ISBN 0-231-04544-1

Columbia University Press
New York   Guildford, Surrey

Printed in the United States of America

To my Daughters,
Pamela, Anna, Edith,
with much love.

CONTENTS

Preface   ix
1. Introduction: The Invisible Philosophy   1
2. Spain, Marburg, and European Science   15
3. Philosophy as Rigorous Science: Marburg and Beyond   31
4. Ortega and Transcendental Phenomenology, 1912–1914   58
5. Toward a Mundane Phenomenology: The Life-World,
   The Reduction   88
6. *Meditations on Quixote* as Mundane Phenomenology   115
7. *Meditations on Quixote*: The Cervantean Perspective   131
8. Postscript: On Remembering the Past   150
   Bibliography   163
   Index   169

PREFACE

So many books have been written about the Spanish philosopher, José Ortega y Gasset, that a word seems justified to explain the need for the present one. *Ortega as Phenomenologist* is essentially a retracing of the steps that led Ortega to his surprisingly early philosophical maturity. As such it manages to do three things: (1) it gives the first complete picture of the crucial stage of Ortega's philosophy of vital or historical reason; (2) it places his emerging philosophy for the first time in its proper European context, the movement known as existential phenomenology; and (3) in showing that Ortega's principal philosophical discovery was contemporary with *Meditations on Quixote* (1914), it explains Ortega's unfailing loyalty to his first book. The fact that the present study deals almost exclusively with Ortega's writings prior to World War I, and is yet concerned with his mature philosophy, is a function of the thesis developed here. I show, in other words, that a mundane phenomenology is already operative in *Meditations on Quixote*, and this is why it is the focus of my study.

Although what I demonstrate here—that Ortega reached philosophical maturity with the writing of his first book—is no more than he himself claimed, this view has never enjoyed much sympathy with his critics. In fact, with rare and honorable exceptions, even his immediate disciples seem not to have realized what an original philosopher he was. This may account for the fact that until recently his pre-*Meditations* work has received little serious non-literary attention.

Yet close scrutiny of Ortega's writings from this early period has paid dividends. It had been assumed that before 1914 Ortega was influenced only by his Neo-Kantian teachers at Marburg. In truth, as C. Morón Arroyo and others have pointed out, Ortega was also unusually familiar with the early writings of Edmund Husserl and Max Scheler. It is also certain that he knew the work of Brentano on Aristotle, the research and writings of the experimental phenomenological psychologists of Göttingen, Jaensch, Katz, and Rubin, and the Würzburg School's studies of imageless thought. This more detailed knowledge of Ortega's reading in the years before he completed his first book has opened the way for a reexamination of its contents. From within this new perspective of what he could and did know, it is clear that by the time he finished *Meditations*, Ortega had evolved something very like that phenomenology of origins of which Merleau-Ponty spoke on several occasions. Of course, this is not to say that all of Ortega's philosophy is in his first book, but rather that what is not there was left out on purpose. Still, by placing Ortega's early work in the context of the phenomenological movement, I have been able to explain his repeated claim to have written, in *Meditations*, an original and preemptive book. Moreover, where my explanation touches on Ortega's sotto voce disagreement with Heidegger, what emerges is new and surprising. It turns out that Ortega's philosophical journey begins, as does Heidegger's, with Franz Brentano's *On the Several Senses of Being in Aristotle*.

Let me say finally that the present study is an essay in "intentional history" rather than philosophy. No brief is held here for the fairness of Ortega's readings of other philosophers, suggestive though many of these readings may have been. Instead, I begin with a single text, a footnote to his posthumous work, *The Idea of Principle in Leibniz and the Evolution of Deductive Theory*, and attempt to extract the meaning from both its words and its silences. But the same conclusions could have been reached by beginning with Ortega's frequent employ, early and late, of the Spanish words semantically related to the Greek *energeia*.

Now philosophers may wish to pay a more specialized attention to Ortega's work, developing comparisons of his phenomenology with that of later exponents in the movement. Even though it was not my primary purpose to offer such comparisons, because I wanted to mark out a position for Ortega between early, transcendental, and later, existential, phenomenologists, I refer to Ortega's philosophy as a mundane phenomenology, as well as employing terms—vital reason, historical reason—that he himself coined.

While the shortcomings of this book are no one's fault but my own, I should like to thank Manuel Durán, E. Inman Fox, Edmund L. King, Vicente Lloréns Castillo, and Elias L. Rivers for inviting me to lecture on work-in-progress. Without friends such as these scholarship would be a strange undertaking indeed. Special thanks are also due to Richard M. Zaner and Edith Helman, who were generous enough with their time to read and comment on earlier drafts, to José Ferrater Mora and Ciriaco Morón Arroyo, who carefully read later, more final ones, and to Manuel Asensio, Jaime Salinas, Juan Marichal, David Young, Ian Gibson, Bill Capitan, Francisco Ayala, Juan Goytisolo, Ramón Xirau, Madeleine Fletcher, F. Javier Sádaba Garay, and Fernando Ariel del Val, whose enthusiasm for literature, philosophy, and history, has encouraged and nurtured my own. I am also deeply indebted to Gloria Adelman and to Sal Calomino for patiently deciphering the manuscript; and I herewith acknowledge as well a long overdue debt of gratitude to the John Simon Guggenheim Foundation, whose munificence allowed me to spend a year in Madrid in 1966–67 when this project began, and to the American Council of Learned Societies for a Grant-in-Aid in 1974 to help bring it to an end.

Madrid–Bass Harbor, Me.　　　　　　　　　　Philip W. Silver
June 1976

ORTEGA AS PHENOMENOLOGIST

"One thinks that one is tracing the outline of the thing's nature over and over again, and one is merely tracing round the frame through which we look at it."

—L. Wittgenstein, *Philosophical Investigations*, I, 114.

"At a time when only a few copies of Brentano's book on the multiple meanings of Being in Aristotle circulated in Europe, Ortega called attention to this point as one of the central themes of philosophy."

—Xavier Zubiri, "Ortega, teacher of philosophy," *El Sol*, 8, III, 1936

[1]

INTRODUCTION
THE INVISIBLE PHILOSOPHY

Con la grande polvareda
Perdimos a Don Beltrane.
Spanish Comic Ballad

ORTEGA'S dictum that we comprehend only what we have seen being born is nowhere more clearly illustrated than in the case of his own philosophy. What occurred between Ortega and his immediate disciples, why most have remained relatively silent about his work, can perhaps never be known for certain. But the unfortunate result is that Ortega's philosophy, so often explained, systematic or not, continues to elude us. In this study, I want to describe that philosophy *in statu nascendi*, to make this process, as it were, visible again, and so establish publicly a more or less precise moment following which it can be said that Ortega had his philosophy substantially in hand.

To do this, it will be necessary to examine what Ortega learned at Marburg, weigh the significance of Scheler, Husserl, and Brentano in his development, and thereby reexamine his encounter with phenomenology, for this last is the *positio quaestionis* that will allow us to locate Ortega's discovery for the first time in its proper context.

Once this has been done, and once Ortega's own thesis has been described and dated, it will then be an easier task to explain what he did and did not mean in successive programmatic works such as *Meditations on Quixote, The Dehumanization of Art,* and *The Revolt of the Masses.* In stressing a difference between thesis and program in Ortega's philosophy, I want to introduce here a new way of looking at his development, one that notices a moment of origination and another of implementation. This working distinction is implicit throughout the present study.

My claim in this essay is that Ortega came into possession of his phi-

1

Introduction

losophy between 1911 and 1914 as a result of his training at Marburg, his reading of Brentano and Aristotle, Scheler and Husserl, and his extraordinary knowledge of what passed at the time for philosophical or psychological phenomenology. It is true that this claim contradicts the gradualist view of Ortega's philosophical coming-to-maturity, one holding that "Renan" (1909) and "Adam in Paradise" (1910) are the first important steps, but that the final steps are not in evidence until 1929 (*What is Philosophy?*) and 1935 ("History as a System"). Since the earlier of these essays were written before Ortega began to "seriously study" Husserl in 1912, the gradualists are thus able to play down the Spanish philosopher's relationship to the phenomenological movement. At the same time, Julián Marías, who first suggested the importance of the 1910 essay, seems also to imply in his *History of Philosophy* and in his *Ortega: Circumstances and Vocation, I*, that Husserl and phenomenology did play a role in Ortega's philosophical development, albeit a minor one. For my part, I have tried to decide the argument along lines suggested by Ortega himself in "Preface for Germans." That is, instead of Ortega's criticism of idealism in the person of Husserl being merely a by-product of Ortega's developing philosophy, something like the reverse is true, and his philosophy in fact crystalized in the process of that criticism. Moreover, I think that the *apparent* gradualness with which Ortega made his philosophy public can in part be explained as the result of a weighing of the possibilities for success that was forced on him in the course of a lifelong service to Spain. But only in part. What I have called the *apparent* gradualness was also due to a failure of *vision* on the part of his contemporaries, one which was itself a tribute to the acuity of Ortega's perception of Spain's problem.

If Ortega had been what he was not, a European philosopher, our elucidation of his work would take an entirely different form, or would even be unnecessary. Instead, he was a philosopher and a Spaniard, and in 1914 this meant being a "philosopher *in partibus infidelium*" (*Meditations on Quixote*). That is, the very conditions which made his philosophy possible and necessary also guaranteed that it would remain virtually invisible, and that it would not be so much misunderstood as overlooked. But if we keep in mind that Ortega's primary goal was to bring Spain into the twentieth century, and was not to write a *Critique of Practical Reason,* we have a better chance of penetrating the confusion surrounding the genesis of his work. The reasons for this confusion are neatly stated in Ortega's own words when, at the behest of an editor, he reflected on his career. On the one hand, he was a philosopher who, he said, had placed his life at the service of a philosophically indigent country:

My vocation was thinking, a longing for clarity with respect to things. Perhaps it was this constitutional fervor that quickly allowed me to see that one of the characteristics of my circumstances was a lack of what inner necessity required that I be. And naturally my own inclination toward philosophy and the firm conviction that this was a service to my country became fused. For this reason all my work and my whole life have been a service to Spain. (VI, 350–51)[1]

On the other hand, as a philosopher Ortega realized that his message and its medium were so consubstantial with his life as to be barely distinguishable from it:

Works that are more abstract, separate by intention and style from the life in which they arose, are more easily assimilated since they require less labor of interpretation. But each of the pages collected here sums up my whole life down to when it was written, and, placed together, they convey the melody of my personal destiny. (VI, 347)

When Ortega wrote these words in 1932 for the preface to the first edition of his *Works,* he believed he had at least brought Spain abreast of Europe. Except that now, as had been the case for at least the last decade, Europe itself was in crisis: "Someday people will realize how, when Spain was just about to take wing again after centuries of indolence, she was stopped by a great unsettling wind that blew in from Europe" (VI, 353).

Now the battle must be joined on European soil and so it was that Ortega announced a shift in emphasis from the medium of the newspaper to that of the book. This meant, as Ortega was the first to recognize, that he must enter a special plea for understanding at this decisive juncture of his career. As we have seen, he also acknowledged that his plea

[1] All references to Ortega's works, unless otherwise noted, are to the *Obras Completas* (Madrid: Revista de Occidente, 1963), vols. I–XI. Wherever possible I have corrected and used the existing Norton translations.

Introduction

might be in vain. In calling attention to this shift from the publication of articles in newspapers like *El Imparcial, El Sol,* and *España,* to the publication of books, Ortega also was acknowledging the impact on his disciples of Heidegger's *Sein und Zeit.* Ortega, after working quietly on Spain's behalf for over twenty years, was provoked into demanding *visibility* for his labors and so allowed his *Works* to be collected and published in 1932. In retrospect, we can see how ill-timed this was. Because he suddenly demanded visibility on the heels of Heidegger's epoch-making work, he garnered a reputation in Spain as a mere popularizer of German philosophy. And his staunchest defenders reacted with a counter-claim of so much originality that his work was uprooted from the only context that could have made it intelligible to European and American philosophers. The immediate and continuing result has been that the two opposing schools of exegetes have given us a strangely inanimate view of Ortega's philosophical development. From his detractors, who see him as a kind of ventriloquist's dummy for twentieth-century German philosophy, we receive a confused impression of begrudging admiration at what they must consider inspired plagiarism. While his defenders, in their turn, give so little attention to his philosophical context that his philosophy ceases to be a historical event. What each group has to say about the genesis of Ortega's philosophy follows from the position it takes up initially. The detractors offer us a philosophical trend-follower; the defenders, a too original prodigy. For the first group, *Meditations on Quixote* is still Neo-Kantian; For the latter, it is "ratio-vitalistic" in everything but name. But whichever perspective we adopt, Ortega's philosophical development remains tentative and gradual *until we reject the model of a gradual public development* and substitute instead the model of two "moments," one of origination and another of implementation, that I mentioned above. Like Sartre and Merleau-Ponty, who turned from their work of origination in *Being and Nothingness* and *Phenomenology of Perception,* to the programmatic implementation of their respective philosophies in the journal *Les Temps Modernes,*[2] so we must also allow for an initial moment of origi-

[2] Hubert L. Dreyfus and Patricia Allen Dreyfus, "Translators' Preface," in Maurice Merleau-Ponty, *Sense and Non-Sense* (Evanston, Ill.: Northwestern University Press, 1964), p. ix.

4

nation in Ortega, followed by a second moment of implementation in successive works like the projected series of *Meditations,* of which only one was published; the series, *The Spectator,* in eight volumes; and such expository efforts as the lectures *The Modern Theme* [*The Theme of Our Time*] (1921) and *What is Philosophy?* (1929).

But if, following this model, *Meditations on Quixote* belongs to our moment of implementation and not of origination, where are we to find in the Ortega canon the systematic works that are analogous to Sartre's *Being and Nothingness* and Merleau-Ponty's *The Structure of Behavior* and *Phenomenology of Perception?* The answer is simply that there are no works such as these, unless it be the posthumously published *The Idea of Principle in Leibniz and the Evolution of Deductive Theory.* Yet, even if Ortega's moment of origination is invisible, his period of implementation, reaching from 1914 until his death, encompasses such an extraordinarily large body of essays as to make him not only the most prolific but the most complete of all the existential phenomenologists.

Unfortunately, however, the invisibility of Ortega's first period confronts us with a problem in hermeneutics, for, with the displacement forward of *Meditations,* there is no major text to mark the moment of origination and, as we already know, no *central* text in the canon as a whole. This is usually taken to mean that the canon itself is *not* whole. And since there is no single text to explain ("create") the whole, there is no whole context in terms of which to explain any single text. Faced with this vicious circle, both readers and critics alike have tried to make *Meditations on Quixote* say more than it can say and have overlooked a constellation of earlier texts that stand in lieu of a major text at the crucial moment of origination. The invisibility of this constellation of earlier essays has placed such a heavy interpretive burden on *Meditations* that its original *programmatic* purpose has been lost sight of. Like the introductory essays in *The Spectator, I,* it is really in the nature of a convocation of potential *philotheamones.* Although *Meditations* is a somewhat elliptical work, this must not be taken to mean that it contains all of Ortega, even though most of his later work seems implicit there. The truth is that *Meditations* is not primarily doctrine, but the cornerstone of a program designed to deal with specific problems, and if

Introduction

so much of Ortega's doctrine or *thesis* seems already implicit there, it is not because it lies in the future but in the past. Since *Meditations* belongs to the period of *implementation*, it naturally presupposes the philosophy that has gone before. *Meditations* seems enigmatic only because it is constantly looking back over our shoulder to a point we cannot see.

If *Meditations*, like the political speech "The Old and the New Politics," was part of a stratagem to bring Spain abreast of Europe through the implementation of an already discovered philosophical thesis, then Ortega could not, given the philosophical "level" in Spain in 1914, have done otherwise. Although it was an article of faith with him that philosophy must be as rigorous as science, since Spain could not absorb too much philosophy, he was obliged to write especially designed (philosophical) essays instead. In *Meditations on Quixote* he writes:

These *Meditations*, free of erudition—even in the best sense of the word—are propelled by philosophical desires. Nevertheless I would be grateful if the reader did not expect too much from them. They are not philosophy, which is science. They are simply essays. The essay is science, minus the explicit proof. For this writer it is a point of intellectual honor not to write anything susceptible of proof without possessing the latter beforehand. But it is permissible for him to eliminate from his work all apodictic appearance, leaving the verifications merely indicated in ellipse, so that whoever needs them may find them and so that they do not hinder, on the other hand, the communication of the inner warmth with which the thoughts were conceived. (p. 40)[3]

Incredibly, this important paragraph from *Meditations* has never been taken literally. No one has ever inquired as to the precise nature of the apodictic evidence which Ortega, with untoward asceticism, chose to leave out. Instead, this principal clue to Ortega's philosophical intentions has been considered no more than a rhetorical flourish. But from the vantage point of our origination-implementation hypothesis about his philosophical development, these key words take on new meaning. The systematic thesis or doctrine is nowhere, not only for practical reasons, such as that no Spaniard in 1914 was aware enough of the

[3] José Ortega y Gasset, *Meditations on Quixote*, ed. Julián Marías, trans. Evelyn Rugg and Diego Marín (New York: Norton, 1961). Unless otherwise described, all references to *Meditations on Quixote* are to this edition.

questions to understand the answers, but for philosophical reasons as well. When Ortega speaks in *Meditations* of a longing philosophy has often expressed to reduce itself to a single proposition, his point is subtler than it seems. The phrase "The Idea is the Absolute" does not *contain*, Ortega says, Hegel's *Logic*; rather, once we have read the *Logic* and think the phrase, then "the whole treasury of its significance bursts open suddenly and it illuminates for us at once the enormous perspective of the world." Philosophy, therefore, longs to return to its own place of origin through a momentary flash of comprehension, compared with which the writing of philosophy is an anticlimax. Ortega's omission of proof is therefore an essential part of his readers' seduction. It allows each reader in turn to think himself back to this moment of maximum illumination. Here is one reason why Ortega is merely offering his work "*modi res considerandi*, (as) possible new ways of looking at things." But there is also additional support for our hypothesis here, as the reader familiar with *Meditations* will have noticed. For the famous phrase ("I am 'I' and my circumstances") that was intended to condense and relate Ortega's own doctrine immediately follows his mention of Hegel's. And how could it be expected to produce in us the desired philosophical *frisson* if it condensed nothing?

For these and other reasons, Ortega's work nowhere offers us the intellectual *points d'appui* of systematization that Sartre and Merleau-Ponty were moved to produce even in the teeth of the German occupation. But if it is true, as García Morente wrote, that in 1910 "philosophy did not exist in Spain," Ortega himself was soon of the opinion that this might even be an advantage, since the Modern Age itself was at an end in both philosophy and science. So that if Spain were philosophically indigent by the old standards, this might yet be her secret strength. At least this very indigence, this "constitutional prejudice in favor of the real," had been one of Ortega's strengths against an idealism that reached from Descartes to Husserl. And if this also meant he had no one to write philosophy for, so that he could never enjoy the luxury of recording his own moment of maximum illumination, like Cervantes before him Ortega still could not refrain from calling attention in *Meditations on Quixote* to what he had forsworn. Yet, ironically, even this deference to his Spanish readers was turned against him. When, follow-

Introduction

ing the publication of *Sein und Zeit,* Ortega called attention to what he *had* written in *Meditations,* it was only acknowledged that he had a gift for hindsight. This is why we must investigate the nature of the apodictic evidence missing, like a piece of mosaic, from *Meditations,* and, beyond that, reveal the invisible moment of origination of Ortega's philosophy, when in 1912 or 1913 he began to study phenomenology seriously.

An obvious point of departure, then, for our study, is the question, Has not Ortega's relationship with Husserl and phenomenology already been examined? To which the only answer is that it has and has not been. Julián Marías, Jean-Paul Borel, Fernando Salmerón, Paulino Garagorri, and most recently, C. Morón Arroyo have all alluded to Husserl, as Ortega himself did in later years. Yet none of these critics has made Ortega's relationship to phenomenology a matter of *primary* concern, with the result that the whole question must be examined anew.

We can best begin by being as precise as possible about what Ortega himself had to say on the subject. This is not hard since in both "Preface for Germans" and *The Idea of Principle in Leibniz* he offers detailed and similar critiques of Husserl's notion of pure consciousness and the transcendental reduction. The most closely reasoned of these, and the most significant because of its context, is in *The Idea of Principle in Leibniz,* in the form of a long footnote to a discussion of Heidegger's "catachresis" of the concept of Being (VIII, 271–72). Not only is Ortega in fundamental disagreement with Heidegger on this question, as he says, but he himself proposed, as early as 1925, a revision of the problem of Being, to be based on four premises: (1) the traditional problem of Being must be completely reexamined; (2) this must be done by employing the phenomenological method to the extent that it is, and only to that extent, *"a synthetic and intuitive thought* and not merely a conceptual-abstract thought like the thought of traditional logic" [Ortega's italics]; (3) to the phenomenological method must be added a dimension of systematic thought; and (4) in order to achieve "a systematic phenomenological thought," it will be necessary to "start with a phenomenon that *is itself* systematic" [Ortega's italics]. This systematic phenomenon is "human life and we must start with its intuition and analysis. In this way I abandoned Phenomenology at the very moment of encountering it" (VIII, 273). The last sentence quoted is not logically a conclusion to the fourth point, but stands as a kind of summary of the long footnote on Husserl appended to the sentence before it. Notice that while Ortega declares he abandoned "Phenomenology" at the moment of his first encounter with it, he still describes here what he refers to elsewhere as the philosophical method of Vital or Historical Reason as "a systematic *phenomenological* thought" [italics mine]. Notice, too, that this method is to proceed by "intuition" and "analysis." Ortega does *not* mean, therefore, that he dispensed with phenomenology, but merely that he abandoned a particular form of it. In our turn, we ought now to examine the footnote itself to ascertain what Ortega's declared differences with Husserl, as distinct from Heidegger, were. That Ortega did not make himself understood on this point, or that what he says is liable to misinterpretation, is demonstrated by the fact that on the one hand Julián Marías sees an essay of 1913—"On the Concept of Sensation"—as the first overcoming of phenomenology and the idea of consciousness, while, on the other, Ciriaco Morón Arroyo holds the opinion that between 1914 and 1916 Ortega, along with Husserl and Scheler, maintained a "peasant's faith in the idea of consciousness."[4] What Ortega says, however, is:

Since 1914 (see my *Meditaciones del Quijote, Obras Completas,* Vol. I) *the basis of all my philosophical work* has been the *intuition* of the phenomenon "human life" [italics mine]. At that time I formulated it—in order to explain Husserl's phenomenology in several university courses—, correcting especially his description of the phenomenon "consciousness of . . ." which, as is well known, is in its turn the basis of his doctrine. (VIII, 273, n. 2)

This, as it stands, is clear enough, but there is more. In later years, Ortega continues, when he finally met Husserl, the latter was old and infirm, so that it was to Dr. Eugen Fink, Husserl's current assistant, that he was obliged to offer his "liminary objection to phenomenology":

Consciousness in its character as phenomenon is thetic ("*Setzend*"), something which Husserl recognizes and calls the "natural attitude of consciousness." Phe-

[4] Ciriaco Morón Arroyo, *El sistema de Ortega y Gasset* (Madrid: Ediciones Alcala, 1968), p. 213. Julián Marías, *La escuela de Madrid* (Buenos Aires: Emece Editores, 1959), 257–64.

Introduction

nomenology consists in describing this phenomenon of natural consciousness from the vantage point of a reflexive consciousness which looks upon natural consciousness "without taking it seriously," without its positings ("*Setzungen*"), but suspending its executant quality ("*ejecutividad*") [in an *epoche*]. To this I object on two counts: (1) that to suspend what I have called the executant character (*vollziehender Character*) of consciousness, its thetic or actualizing character, is to eliminate what is most basic to it and hence to *all consciousness*; (2) that we suspend the executant character of one from the vantage point of another, the reflexive consciousness, which Husserl calls "penomenological reduction," without its having any superior right to invalidate the primary consciousness reflected upon; (3) on the other hand, the reflexive consciousness is allowed to retain *its* executant character, and to posit the primary consciousness as *absolute being*, which is called *Erlebnis* or *vivencia* ("lived-x"). This shows precisely that *every* consciousness has executant validity and it makes no sense for one consciousness to invalidate the other. We can discount an act of our consciousness with a subsequent thought, as always happens when we correct an error; as, for example, an optical illusion: but if we counterpoise, without intermediate thought, the "deluded" consciousness and the "normal" consciousness, the latter does not invalidate the former. Hallucination and perception have as such inherently equal rights.

The consequence of these objections was that from 1914 on, I set forth the description of the phenomenon "consciousness of . . .," pointing out, *against all idealism* [italics mine], that it is a hypothesis and not *pure* description to say that an act of consciousness is real while its object is *merely* intentional; therefore, unreal. A description that attended strictly to the phenomenon—I said then—would state that in a phenomenon of consciousness like perception we discover the *coexistence of myself and some thing*, that, therefore, the coexistence is not ideality or intentionality, but very reality. So that in the "fact" of perception what we have is: on the one hand, myself, "being-to" the thing perceived, and on the other, the thing "being-to" me; that is to say, there *is* no phenomenon "consciousness of . . ." as a general form of the mind. Instead there is a reality that I am, opening out on, and undergoing, the reality that my surroundings are; and the supposed description of the phenomenon "consciousness" becomes description of the phenomenon "real human life" as the coexistence of myself and the things around me or my circumstances. *The result, therefore, is that there "is not" this consciousness as phenomenon, and that consciousness is a hypothesis, the very one we inherited from Descartes.* This is why Husserl turns back to Descartes. (VIII, 274–75, n.)

Although the question at issue in the text, as opposed to this footnote, is whether it was Ortega or Heidegger who first called for a reconsideration of the traditional problem of Being, the real issue, that closest to Ortega's heart, is who was the first to arrive at the method to be employed in that revision; in short, did Heidegger announce his analysis of *Dasein* before Ortega had come upon the phenomenon "human life." This is the reason for the footnote. In it Ortega asserts that this fundamental thesis was *formulated* by him as early as 1914 when he began lecturing on Husserl in university courses and offering for the first time in public his fundamental objection to Husserl's description of the phenomenon "consciousness of . . ." The parenthetical reference to *Meditations on Quixote* (1914) must be taken to mean that the phenomenon "human life" was already, in 1914 (and in that work), the basis of his thought, though, of course, it was not given a *discrete* formulation there as it was in the university lectures. If we now take the footnote as a reflection of the *explicit* formulation of the university courses, available at least as early as 1914, we avoid doing Ortega the injustice of calling the *substance* of the footnote the product of hindsight—post-*Sein und Zeit* hindsight—or of supposing that once he had criticized Husserl's description of "consciousness of . . .," he had achieved that only, and then had to wait until 1927 to discover, or *realize* he had discovered, the phenomenon "human life." In fact, as Ortega himself implies with the footnote, sometime before he made public his fundamental criticism of Husserl he stepped neatly through the looking glass of idealism and into his own philosophy as if it were there waiting for him. Actually, here as elsewhere, Ortega has left several important steps out. Nevertheless, as we shall discover later on, the immediate context in which this criticism of Husserl appears—that is, in the midst of a discussion of Heidegger's alleged misreading of Aristotle—is an essential clue to what the missing steps are. For as ontologists, both Ortega and Heidegger took their departure from Franz Brentano's *Von der mannigfachen Bedeutung des Seienden nach Aristotles*, even if their respective notions of the meaning of Being turned out to be diametrically opposed.

What Ortega is saying, then, on the subject of Husserl, as distinct from Heidegger, is (1) that his encounter with Husserl's phenomenology was brief, but is linked to his discovery of the phenomenon "human life"; (2) that the latter was first *formulated* in the process of lecturing on

11

Introduction

Husserl's description of the phenomenon "consciousness of . . ." i.e., *intentionality;* (3) that since acts of consciousness succeed one another in time, one cannot invalidate or cancel another and be awarded a preferred ontological status, so that the transcendental reduction is impossible and Husserl's phenomenon "consciousness of . . ." as "a general form of the mind" is a mere hypothesis; and, finally, (4) a more rigorous description of the phenomenon reveals instead *"the coexistence of myself and some thing"* [Ortega's italics]. What is not clear in the footnote is precisely what else went into (2), and just how (3) and (4) necessarily amount to the discovery of (1). Without apparent transition, Ortega moves from a technical account of his objections to Husserl's description of "consciousness of . . ." (*Bewusstsein von*) to a discussion, apparently on an empirical level, of "a phenomenon of consciousness like perception"; and at the same time he changes to the mode of speech that we associate with the "vitalistic," that is, non-mentalistic, discourse of works such as *Meditations on Quixote*. It is because of this change of diction and apparent direction that Ortega becomes liable to misinterpretation, for he speaks both of a more rigorous description of consciousness than Husserl's, while at the same time terming consciousness a mere hypothesis and seeming to deny it any philosophical status at all. In the light of this apparent contradiction, it would seem we must either agree with Julián Marías that in 1913 an "overcoming" of phenomenology and consciousness did take place, but without it being clear how this led to the thesis of "human life," or we must side with Ciriaco Morón Arroyo, who says that Ortega believed in consciousness between 1914 and 1916, as did Husserl and Scheler, and that, therefore, no such "overcoming" *could* have taken place.

Fortunately, there is a third alternative that will enable us to explain, among other things, the apparent contradictions of this important footnote.

In the first place, it would be unwise to decide the question of whether or not Ortega had gone beyond phenomenology, of whether he believed in consciousness or not, on the basis of any single text. It is true that on the rare occasions when Ortega discusses Husserl in detail, as in "Preface for Germans" or in the present footnote, he invariably returns to the question of Husserl's description of the phenomenon "consciousness of . . ."; but it is just as important to notice that his specific critique of Husserl is only one element, albeit a crucial one, in a larger critique directed against idealism—as though it were the only part of a general argument against idealism that had to be formulated in a detailed way. And, in a sense, this is probably true. At least, what we may call Ortega's argument against idealism (actually an argument against both realism and idealism), with the two exceptions I have mentioned, invariably takes the form of a *historical*, one could also say, a dialectical, presentation of his own philosophy of Vital Reason. The dialectical presentation receives its classic form in the public lectures of 1929 entitled *What is Philosophy?* and in the ex cathedra lectures of 1932–33, published as *Some Lessons in Metaphysics*. But it was also the substance of his ninth and final lecture, first series, given in Buenos Aires in 1916, under the auspices of the Spanish Cultural Institute with the title "The Three Great Metaphors," and its *form* is implicit in the 1913 lecture, "Sensation, Construction, and Intuition," delivered at the IV Congress of the Spanish Association for the Advancement of Science. What I mean to suggest, in calling Ortega's presentation historical, is that in each case, because of the nature of his audience, he never found it appropriate to exhibit the analytical process by which he had arrived at his own philosophy. What he invariably offers instead is a general (historical) argument that moves from a critique of realism and idealism to a schematic presentation of his own philosophy of Vital or Historical Reason. That is, Ortega never exhibited more than the public face of his philosophy. But this must not be taken to mean that the public face conceals nothing; Ortega offered his repeated historical account for two related reasons: (1) his audiences, which were always large, could simply not have followed the intricacies of a more compressed version, and (2) the historical presentation, *itself* a species of philosophical *epoche*, had a special meaning for Ortega, inasmuch as with it he saw himself achieving a breakthrough in philosophy comparable to Einstein's revolution in physics. Later, in the course of this study, we will examine the several elements of his historical account. But we can do this only in the course of uncovering each and every one of the philosophical steps that led Ortega to his philosophy.

What we need in order to substantiate what I have called the third al-

ternative is not another review of the public side of Ortega's philosophical achievement, but an explication of what underlies his usual
presentations of it. This will entail four things: (1) an examination of
Ortega's training at Marburg; (2) some knowledge of his encounter with
Scheler's early writings, with Brentano's *Psychology*, and with his studies
of Aristotle; (3) attention to Husserl's thought as it developed from the
Logical Investigations through the *Ideas* of 1913; and (4) a reconstruction of the way in which (1) and (2) prepared Ortega for his partial rejection of (3) and the conception of his own philosophy.

This revival of the stages of Ortega's textual biography is, it seems to
me, the only way to comprehend finally the genesis of his philosophy;
especially since Ortega never deemed it appropriate to set out or explain—even to his intimates—the analytical steps involved. Thus, what
we must do presently is give an account of the development of the phenomenological movement itself, and then describe Ortega's reaction to,
and partial rejection of, it. At least the historical period with which we
have to deal is a brief one. To judge from the indications in Ortega's
important autobiographical essay, "Preface for Germans," written in the
early thirties, this stretches from 1911 to 1914, the period during which
his reported "overcoming" of Husserl took place. Actually, to come to
grips with what occurred between Ortega and phenomenology in that
compressed span of time, we must first answer the question: Who was
Ortega when the encounter with phenomenology took place? That is,
Why had Ortega gone to Germany and Marburg to study in the first
place? Or, and it amounts to the same thing, What was it like to have a
vocation for philosophy in Restoration Spain?

[2]

SPAIN, MARBURG,
AND EUROPEAN SCIENCE

Spain is only possible in the perspective of Europe.
Ortega y Gasset (I, 138)

To judge by his speech, "Our National Problems and the Youth," given before the Madrid Ateneo in 1909, the Tragic Week in Barcelona, the rioting, the failure of a general strike, and the government's cruel repression, had a special meaning for Ortega. It was not a case of an awakening to the social and political realities of his day such as the night of San Daniel had been for Galdós in 1865, or the Carlist bombardment of Bilbao for the young Unamuno. Instead, the revolutionary temper of the Spanish *pueblo* and the government's repression had quickened Ortega's already urgent sense of a mission to be accomplished. The meaning of the revolution, he told his audience, was that the people's cause was just, but the acts of violence by rioters and government alike were equally criminal. Some restraining force, perhaps in the form of viable political parties, must be applied to both sides. For what, Ortega wondered, would be the outcome for Spain if the next revolution succeeded? Although this speech to his Ateneo audience ended with a brave reference to education—"Europe, gentlemen, is science above all: friends of my generation, study!" (x, 118)—his vivid allusions to the bloody dungeons of Montjuich show that he himself wondered if formulas such as these could lay the specter of violent revolution to rest.

The following year, in 1910, when he expounded the foundations for a political program to the "El Sitio" Club in Bilbao, in a speech entitled "Social Pedagogy as a Political Program," Ortega again betrayed some of his own feelings when he said: "The fact that I should be addressing you here today may seem to you insignificant; but to me it is

15

a sad fact, I admit it freely" (I, 503). He then went on to explain a sadness that seemed to border on resentment. It was tantamount to a national disgrace, Ortega said, that a young Spaniard like himself, "without fame or glory," should be called on to address such a distinguished gathering; moreover, it could mean only one thing. Spain in 1910 was at such a low ebb that she must borrow against her future: "The only way I can explain my presence here at this time is with the thought that the supply of men graced with complete spiritual and intellectual maturity is so small in our country that it has been quickly exhausted, and you have been forced to turn to the crucible of the nation's soul, to the still unformed, to what is at most a preliminary sketch, a project, a possibility, a hope" (I, 503–04).

In 1910, one year after his speech in the Madrid Ateneo, instead of uncertainty his attitude seemed to be one of impatience. He felt that he was being asked for too much too soon, that he would rather be elsewhere, that if his immediate elders had fulfilled their historic mission, his generation would not have had to leave its laboratories for the public arena at all. For all the national soul-searching since the disastrous 1898 war with the United States there had been no change, except that now Ortega's own contemporaries had begun to repeat the same empty clichés as everyone else.

By 1913, however, Ortega felt he had reason to voice some confidence and optimism. At least he himself now felt equal to the task at hand. The Generation of 1868, in helping sire the first Spanish Republic, had authored what he termed an honorable mistake. Only the Generation of 1898 had betrayed its mission. As for Ortega's own generation, that of 1914, which reached political awareness in 1898, maturing just as the Restoration ground to a halt, what else could it have done, with no illusions about Spain, but turn to Europe? As Ortega put it: "Since Spain did not exist, (we) had to invent an ideal nationality in which to conduct an imaginary existence. (We) had to evolve an ideological homeland, since the faults of others had deprived (us) of our real one. This homeland of desires has been the idea of the Europeanization of Spain, and our patriotism has had to take the form of a critique of our Spanish past" (X, 227).

What were the reasons—the non-philosophical ones—for this change in Ortega's attitude from a seeming reluctance to be called in 1909 to an exemplary optimism in 1913? In the realm of politics there was the fact that the King, Alfonso XIII, now seemed to have heeded the program Ortega had outlined before "El Sitio" in 1910. In royal audiences with Azcárate, President of the Institute for Social Reforms, with the President of the Council of Post-Graduate Education, and with the Director of the Education Museum, his Highness had spoken of the need to Europeanize Spain. Although his royal decree founding the Council of Post-Graduate Education and Scientific Research had been signed by Alfonso XIII on February 11, 1907, it finally seemed, as Ortega wrote in *El Imparcial*, that in meeting not just with the leader of the Republican party but with "technocrats" as well, the King was at last ready to make "history" and not just "politics." In placing more emphasis on the educational part of this event than on the King's flirtations with republicanism, Ortega showed himself to be closer in spirit to the founder of the Institución Libre de Ensenanza than was his own contemporary Manuel Azaña. Although Ortega occupied the center of the political arena for many years more, like Giner de los Ríos he was not so much interested in men of action who knew how to gain power, as in spiritual leaders with the requisite vision to legislate wisely. But in order to understand what lay behind this fundamental difference between Ortega and Azaña, in order to understand why Ortega, while remaining a philosopher, should wish to be spokesman for his generation, we must examine the advantages and responsibilities that were his and that moved him to make his laconic remark about having been "born on a printing press."

In its original context there is more *noblesse oblige* in his remark than would appear from the form in which it is usually quoted. Actually, the remark comes from a 1920 article in *El Sol*, entitled "Sr. Dato, Guilty of an Infraction of the Constitution," and the title itself is a measure of the extraordinary impunity that Ortega's social and professional status allowed him to enjoy. Since in the text he recalls that he has founded several magazines and newspapers, and may wish, *pace* Sr. Dato, to found several more, he is really calling attention to the fact that, journalistically speaking, he was born with a silver spoon in his mouth. But in other ways this was also true.

Spain, Marburg, and European Science

Ortega was born in Madrid on May 8, 1883, near the end of Alfonso XII's reign, and his maternal grandfather, Eduardo Gasset Artime, a liberal monarchist, was the founder of *El Imparcial*, the quasi-official paper of the Liberal party in 1887. This meant that Ortega had grown up in the heart of the Restoration establishment. His own father, the journalist José Ortega Munilla, was a writer, academician, and a contemporary of Menéndez Pelayo, Leopoldo Alas, and Pardo Bazán. Somewhat more liberal and a good deal more bohemian than his wife's family, Ortega's father had opened the literary supplements of *El Imparcial* to some of the Restoration's most outstanding critics. This liberal policy brought members of the Generation of 1898 into the *Imparcial* family, and the young Ortega into close and admiring contact with men like Unamuno, Azorín, Baroja, Benavente, the Machados, Zuloaga, and Maeztu.

Ortega had studied with the Jesuits in Málaga, received his degree of *bachiller* in 1897, and took the examinations for his first year of university studies at Salamanca, where Unamuno was one of his examiners. From that year until 1902 he attended the University of Madrid, where he studied Philosophy and Letters as well as Law, finally giving up the latter. In 1902 he received his *licenciatura* and in 1904 became a doctor in Philosophy with a thesis entitled "Terrors of the Year One Thousand: Critique of a Legend." On the evidence of articles that he began publishing in *El Imparcial* in 1902, he seems to have had contact with no other German thought than that of Nietzsche, who had become fashionable in Spain under the aegis of the Generation of 1898. But then, in 1905 (what prompted his decision is not clear), Ortega went off to Leipzig to study.

Besides learning German, he decided to study Comparative Philology and to continue Greek and Latin. In addition, it is interesting to note, he took Anatomy and Histology, so as later to be able to study Physiology and Physiological Psychology. A remark in a letter to his friend "Pepe" Navarro Ledesma gives perhaps the best explanation for Ortega's having chosen Leipzig at all. When his German was fluent enough he would study experimental psychology because, as he said, "My mind is already too dried out with intellectual pursuits for me to be able to dedicate myself to the study of a physical science." He accepted, as did all his generation and their predecessors, the view that philosophy ("We men of noble stripe were born especially to be philosophers and no other thing") was a scientific undertaking, and that a philosopher must also be no stranger to the natural sciences.[1] Although Wundt's name does not appear in the published letters, Ortega probably had him in mind. The fifth edition of his *Physiologische Psychologie* had appeared in 1902–03, and four years after his arrival in Leipzig in 1875 the great German psychologist and philosopher had established "the very first formal psychological laboratory in the world." Moreover, between the second and third editions of his *Physiologische Psychologie*, Wundt had published a *Logik*, an *Ethik* and in 1889 his *System der Philosophie*.[2] At the same time, Ortega insists, he will also begin Sanskrit with the patriarchal Brugmann. But Ortega remained in Leipzig for one semester only, returning to Madrid to compete for a government stipend to pay for more studies abroad.

When he returned to Germany, he studied briefly in Berlin and next went on to Marburg, where he remained from November of 1906 until the late summer of 1907. Then he again returned to Madrid where he wrote the paper entitled "Descartes and the Transcendental Method," which he delivered in October of 1908 at the Zaragoza Congress of the Spanish Association for the Advancement of Science. That same year, 1908, he won a Chair at the Escuela Superior de Magisterio in Madrid and was shortly confirmed there as Professor of Psychology, Logic, and Ethics by royal decree. Why had he chosen Marburg this time instead of Leipzig? According to his plans as he relayed them to Navarro Ledesma, Marburg was the obvious choice. Marburg was the home of the most powerful Neo-Kantian school in Germany, and a place where philosophy had everything to do with the exactness of science. Here, in Hermann Cohen (1842–1918), the principal figure of the Marburg School, and in Paul Natorp (1854–1924), Ortega found the teachers he had been seeking. His accounts of these years at Marburg, most of them written much later, suggest that he

[1] "Cartas inéditas a Navarro Ledesma," Leipzig, May 16, 1905, *Cuadernos*, November 1962, pp. 6–7.

[2] See Edwin G. Boring, *A History of Experimental Psychology*, 2nd ed. (New York: Appleton-Century Crofts, 1950), pp. 326, 323–24.

Spain, Marburg, and European Science

dealt with Hermann Cohen almost as an equal. This cannot have been the case, unless, of course, Ortega is referring to the second full year he spent there, in 1911, when he already occupied the Chair of Metaphysics at the University of Madrid and Cohen himself would retire to Berlin the following year. But Ortega's first year in Marburg must have been very different, perhaps not unlike his experience of Leipzig in 1905, where he had had a first "hand-to-hand encounter" with Kant's *Critique of Pure Reason*. In Marburg, with ten or twelve hours a day given over to reading, Ortega's first year was spent devouring the classics of philosophy and listening to Cohen's subtle and original extension of critical philosophy or Natorp's lectures on the pedagogy of Plato and Pestalozzi.

As it turned out, both Cohen and Natorp had a decisive effect on him, but unlike Ernst Cassirer, his near contemporary at Marburg, Ortega quickly passed beyond the unitary Neo-Kantian view of the natural, cultural, and exact sciences. Not only that, but by a happy coincidence—according to his account of his final year at Marburg—he, Nicolai Hartmann, and Heinz Heimsoeth all reached philosophical maturity just as Husserlian phenomenology hove into view. It came naturally to their attention. In a review, Paul Natorp had urged Husserl to adopt his own concept of the Pure Ego, and so influenced the latter's *Ideas*.[3] In a word, Marburg was not the isolated philosophical school that Ortega makes out; while he has said that he began to study phenomenology seriously only in 1912, he recalls discussing Franz Brentano's work with Cohen as early as 1911, and he was probably familiar with Scheler's earliest published work and with Meinong's *Gegendstandstheorie* before he ever read Husserl. At any rate, the rapidity of Ortega's philosophical development after 1911, the year of his first contact with Scheler, Brentano, and Husserl, suggests that we leave further mention of the phenomenological movement for the next chapter. First we must examine the problems Ortega confronted in Spain when he began to apply what he had learned on his first visit to Marburg in 1906–07, problems of method and content which, as he would soon find, phenomenology alone was equipped to solve.

[3] Fritz Kaufmann, "Cassirer, Neo-Kantianism, and Phenomenology," in *The Philosophy of Ernst Cassirer*, ed. Paul Arthur Schilpp (New York: Tudor Publishing, 1949), p. 823.

Spain, Marburg, and European Science

The best way to measure Marburg's pre-1911 impact on the young Ortega, and at the same time contravene the present artificial separation of his essays in political and philosophical volumes, will be to examine "Social Pedagogy as a Political Program," his Bilbao lecture, together with the philosophical essay "Adam in Paradise." Both date from the year 1910.

In a curious way, it would not be incorrect to hold that Paul Natorp's "Sozialpädogogik" was ultimately responsible for the creation in 1913 of the League for Spanish Political Education by Ortega and Azaña. This is abundantly clear from even a quick examination of Ortega's speech before "El Sitio" in Bilbao. In addition, our juxtaposition of the speech and the essay will also help explain what has been labelled the period of Ortega's Objectivism,[4] that is, roughly, the philosophical position evident in Ortega's polemics with Unamuno and Maeztu during the years 1904–13. On this question of "objectivism," or what Juan Marichal sees as a characteristic of Azaña and all the Generation of 1914, even closer study will show that in Ortega's version it was less a function of his personality than a program of social pedagogy learned in Marburg from Paul Natorp.[5]

As we saw, Ortega already had his heart set on being a philosopher when he arrived in Leipzig; but, perhaps following in the steps of Ramón y Cajal, he was equally dedicated to the formula "work with scientific precision," and the goal of his vocational undertaking was to educate Spain. Yet until he heard Natorp lecture at Marburg, Ortega had no systematic, supra-individual view of education itself. Added to what he studied with Cohen, and in addition to the systematics that were so much a part of the Marburg School, in Natorp's lectures on psychology and pedagogy Ortega found "a moral system of which education was the fundamental feature."[6] While Cohen was more concerned with the epistemological limitations of Kant's system and their extension and modification, Natorp stressed "the place of feeling and the social life of

[4] José Ferrater Mora, *Ortega y Gasset: An Outline of His Philosophy*, new rev. ed. (New Haven: Yale University Press, 1957), pp. 9–22.

[5] Juan Marichal, *La vocación de Manuel Azaña* (Madrid: Editorial Cuardernos para el Diálogo, 1971), pp. 62–63, 75–77.

[6] Robert McClintock, *Man and Circumstances: Ortega as Educator* (New York: Teachers College, Columbia University, 1971), p. 51.

Spain, Marburg, and European Science

mankind as determining factors in knowledge and religion."[7] Nor can Ortega have been indifferent to the fact that Natorp's vision of pedagogical reform was a major contribution to the Neo-Kantian Marxism of Marburg. At the same time we must remember that Natorp's "moral system," like Cohen's views on Logic and Ethics, was framed in terms of the cardinal division in Kant's system between phenomena and noumena. Thus the crux of both was "the relation of the fictional world of thought to the factual world of things." Although in contrast with the contemporary "Sensationists," Mach and Ziehen, the Marburg men were "Constructionists," Natorp especially dealt with the mind-body problem, not "as a question of epistemology, but as an opportunity for the education of character."[8] And while members of the Marburg School were forced to accept, together with Kant's anti-metaphysical bias, his separation of "all there is" into a phenomenal, material world over against a conventional (because logical), hypothetical and ideal one created by man's intellect,[9] both Cohen and Natorp hypostatized Kant's moral philosophy so that Pure Will, in the Kantian sense of an End, came to have in their view "affinities with Plato's Idea of the Good and of God."[10]

In terms of education, this meant two things: in the first place, the "absolute" distance of the Will introduced a dynamics of infinite effort toward an ultimate goal; in the second, since the Will expressed itself in action, it was only in the realm of the State that morality became possible, that is, "the moral ideal could only be realized within a community."[11] All this was presupposed by Natorp's "theory of civic pedagogy";[12] and in the aggregate it provided the ground against which Ortega, at least in the years between 1905 and 1914, developed his own civic pedagogy.

---

[7] W. Tudor Jones, *Contemporary Thought of Germany*, I (New York: Knopf, 1931), 36, 42.

[8] McClintock, *Man and Circumstances*, pp. 56, 53, 54.

[9] McClintock, p. 54; see also José Ortega y Gasset, *Apuntes sobre el pensamiento*, 2d ed. (Madrid: Ediciones de la Revista de Occidente, 1966), p. 114.

[10] Jones, *Contemporary Thought*, p. 38.   [11] Jones, p. 38.

[12] McClintock, *Man and Circumstances*, p. 55. This is his translation of "*Sozialpädagogik.*"

Spain, Marburg, and European Science

Clearly, it is here we must seek the origin of the complex views in the two essays we are to examine. The anti-individual, anti-subjectivist, or objectivist, bias; Ortega's incipient and, as we now see, Platonically shaded *social* "idealism"; and the fundamental concern for a rapprochement of "science" and "life"; all these ultimately derive from the Neo-Kantians and their interpretation of the classics of philosophy; an interpretation Ortega had also used in his essay "Renan" of 1909. Therefore we must not imagine that the influence of Natorp and Cohen affected *only* his social pedagogy and, hence, his politics, or that, conversely, Ortega could not have been, philosophically, *after 1911*, his own person. The reader familiar with his *Meditations on Quixote* must not be misled by Ortega's Horatian credo of *"dulce et utile"* into thinking that the Platonic, and as we now see, Natorpian-Platonic, vehicle is the only message there. Although some of his disciples rather romantically confuse originality with the absence of influence, Ortega himself would certainly have quoted Hegel to the effect that there is no advance that does not conserve even as it destroys. We can see this very principle at work in one of Ortega's rare references to the content of Cohen's teaching: "The structure of life as futurity is the most frequent leitmotiv in my work, [and was] inspired by questions far removed from the problems to which I apply it, questions raised in Cohen's *Logic*" (IV, 403, n. 1). The truth of this remark can be understood only in the context generated above; nor should we look for an admission of any *immediate* influence by Cohen, except, perhaps, on the part of Ortega's *Meditations* that deals strictly with esthetics.

With this review of the ethical and pedagogical theories of Marburg in mind, let us turn to the rationale of "Social Pedagogy as a Political Program." Here, indeed, there *is* what can only be called the pervasive presence of Ortega's Marburg masters. They provide him with the systematic support he needed as he began casting about on his own. It was indeed a heady feeling, this life within the Kantian mind, and Ortega never quite freed himself from a certain nostalgia for it; for that closed, complete system of Marburg, with all human endeavor classified under the headings of Logic, Ethics, or Esthetics; or for what Kant himself had called "the inventory of all our possessions through pure reason, systematically arranged."

Spain, Marburg, and European Science

Ortega's first and fundamental essay in social or civic pedagogy is finely drawn; and although it follows Natorp's ideas on education closely, clearly it has an argument of its own. Beginning with the intentional display of self-indulgence to which we have referred, Ortega gives an example of how emotions serve as a motive force. Bitterness at Spain's decadence is viewed as a positive conditioner of action, and Spaniards are urged to reject all myths of their past and present in favor of an as yet unforeseeable ideal Spain. Their homeland is the problem and all must engage in useful politics, understood not as strategies for winning and keeping governmental power, but as the technique of governing well. It would be immoral, Ortega says, to win power without first having an idea of what the new Spain must be. And as a substitute for such mindless politics, Ortega recommends a view of education; first, he calls for the scientific determination of just what the pedagogic ideal is to be. This must then be followed by a search for the intellectual, moral, and esthetic means with which to propel the *educando* in the direction of the ascertained ideal. Such a mobilization on three fronts is the first, and certainly not the last, allusion to the idealistic system of Marburg; for we are asked at once to recall that, as Kant tells us, everything in nature, even human beings, behaves in accordance with laws. This brings the discussion to the subject of man, the centerpiece of both this and the next essay, and, of course, much more. Although education is usually concerned with the "individual," as Ortega acknowledges, here as in the case of "nature" a careful definition is called for; and thus the principal question at this juncture is what we mean by man. History, especially political history, has customarily dealt with this problem, and by way of illustration we are given a "perspectival" view of a Christ who is a different man to the Roman soldiers, to his own followers, and to Pontius Pilate. Obviously, we are being prepared for a critical philosophical definition of man. But man is not the biological individual, as the next section heading warns, not an anthropus, but instead an inner man, one who thinks, feels, and desires; who, in a sense, carries the whole world in his heart and in his head; in other words, man not as the subject of biology, but as its creator. In this way, Neo-Kantian man participates in, sharing with his fellows, the ideal "substances" of science, morality, and art. At the same time man is heir to private caprices and appetites. For this reason Ortega says he has, in fact, two I's: one as the creature of instinct, the wild man, and the other as one who shares art, science, and beauty, in short, culture, with others. And here Ortega cites Natorp: "The individual in isolation is no man: apart from society, the human individual does not exist; he is an abstraction" (I, 513). And Ortega uses an illustration from physics to clinch the point: "The simplest element of which matter is composed, the atom, is an abstraction." Likewise, man only exists in a family, the family in a quarter, in a city, and so out into history and beyond, to the outer reaches of the universe. In short, Ortega concludes, the "human individual can be said to exist only to the extent that he contributes to a given social reality and is conditioned by it" (I, 514). It follows that all individualism, that is, all subjectivism, is anti-scientific, an obstacle. As for education, how can it work if it takes place only between one master and one pupil, in their few hours together? Fortunately, Plato as well as Pestalozzi have an answer in their social pedagogy. The home and the public square are in fact the real pedagogical establishments. And thus social pedagogy or civic pedagogy replaces politics as the science of transforming societies. And what of society itself? It is to be a community of common rational interests and mutual labor. Men are to share certain ideas and a common potential for manufacture, for all can agree on both the ideas and the products. And what of the ethics implicit in this social pedagogy? "If every social individual is to be a worker in our culture, then each and every worker must be able to acquire a consciousness of our culture" (I, 518). In short, a *quid pro quo* is assumed. Spain, it is hoped, will become such a community, a single order of workers and a shared undertaking. Such was Ortega's hope and design in 1910; in outline it sounds very much like an ideal version of the Second Spanish Republic.

In the "El Sitio" speech we are presented with the rationale for just such a league of political education as Ortega founded, and as we see, it was based squarely on Natorp's own civic pedagogy. Of course, it is true, a Neo-Kantian systematization, the underpainting of Natorp's pedagogy, shows through on occasion. Of the glimpses we have of it, the most notable in view of the reversal of *Meditations*, is the notion that a human individual is an abstraction, a drop of water in the sea of culture.

Turning now to the longer and more awkwardly worked out "Adam in Paradise," the ostensible subject is an esthetics of painting, and the painter under consideration is significantly a member of the Generation of 1898, Ignacio Zuloaga. However, in this essay the philosophical substructure is so obtrusive that it adds an ironic overtone to Ortega's discussion of Zuloaga's work. This was never the case in the speech on social pedagogy; but in turning his attention to esthetics Ortega moved somewhat closer to the epicenter of the Neo-Kantian system and so became more tightly enmeshed in the "prison" of Kantian epistemology.

In examining "Adam in Paradise," we need not concern ourselves with whether Ortega has managed, as his alter ego Dr. Vulpius suggests, to produce an esthetics original to Spain, nor need we weigh the suggestion by Julián Marías that this essay constitutes the first formulation of the doctrine of Life.[13] Instead, our interest focuses on the activity beneath the surface of the essay; on any convincing evidence of an early attempt by Ortega to free himself from the constraints of Neo-Kantian epistemology, or at least a design for such an escape.[14] This problem of the constraints of Neo-Kantian epistemology which Ortega chooses now to pursue in the esthetic realm, concerns, of course, the hermetic purity of Cohen's system, which went so far beyond the last vestiges of empiricism in Kant as to hold that "the material of knowledge is not the brute stuff of sensation."[15] And García Morente, from their first conversations about Kantian philosophy in 1910, surmised that Ortega's "essential preoccupation" was already to "breach idealism."[16] This is certainly why, as we are meant to understand from the

[13] Julián Marías, *La escuela de Madrid: Estudios de filosofía española* (Buenos Aires: Emece Editores, 1959), p. 185.

[14] This seems not to be what he is attempting in "Descartes y el método transcendental" (1908), published in *Actas de la Asociación Española para el Progreso de las Ciencias* (Madrid, 1910), IV, 5–13.

[15] Ortega, *Apuntes*, p. 108.

[16] Manuel García Morente, *Ensayos* (Madrid: Revista de Occidente, 1945), p. 206.

anecdote with which "Adam in Paradise" ends, Ortega acknowledges the humor of relying on so elaborate a system as Cohen's to explicate Zuloaga's rather pedestrian paintings. Today we can see how Ortega had every reason for humor, inasmuch as throughout his subsequent development he was never obliged to give up that "systematic vision of the universe" (I, 493). Instead, once he solved the epistemological problem, he had only to turn Marburg's idea of system inside out.

This being the case, we can begin to examine "Adam" by recalling that just as Kant, in examining logic, studied the conditions for the production of thought, and in examining ethics, the conditions for the production of morality, so he also undertook to give a similar account of artistic objects, although he assimilated them neither to logic nor to ethics. Cohen explicates and follows Kant, and Ortega in writing about painting follows both. He begins by distinguishing between a kind of painting that is primarily mimetic and one that is inventive. In Zuloaga's paintings he finds what we would call representational elements, but he finds there a more important, virtual quality as well, an energy generated by the unity of the painting itself. This is essential, for Cohen's systematic esthetics is decidedly anti-mimetic, as was to be expected given the abject status accorded matter in Kantian epistemology. For, what "things" are there for representational painting to copy? There really is no immutable fixed reality at all. Instead, there are merely as many realities as observers. This means, since "each thing is a part of something larger, . . . is what it is because of the limitations and boundaries these impose on it" (I, 474), that each "thing" is just a relationship with other things, and, hence, only a value. Moreover, these values vary according to the system of valuation adopted: the approximate system of the farmer, or the exact one of the astronomer. The question for painting then becomes the following. What kinds of relations—since things are only relations—are the essentially pictorial ones? And what system of valuation should apply? Sociological? Literary? No, Ortega thinks: "We already know that the transcendent unity that organizes the painting will not be philosophical, mathematical, mystical, or historical, but purely and simply pictorial" (I, 476). This sounds as though Ortega were going to talk like the Modernist Roger Fry about organic form, but instead, as the sentence hints, he will double back:

the expression "transcendent unity" is the clue. Ortega will now retreat to the center of Kant's system before proceeding. Man, he says, has an enormous problem to solve, so enormous that he must divide it up in order to conquer. Thus Science will deal with the first part, Ethics with the second, and Art with what remains. But, since even that part of the problem assigned to Art is insoluble, Art itself must be subdivided into genres. But what is the momentous problem to be solved? Well, we read, it is life, yet not organic and inorganic life as lived; it is Adam in Paradise, that is, life as a problem.

This is far from clear and yet it sounds closer to a philosophical valuation than to a strictly pictorial one. And Ortega goes on to explain that all things live, that the life of a thing is its being (ser), and that its being is the totality of its relations with other things. Now we understand the enormity of the problem and why it has been divided and subdivided. Science attempts to discover this being of a thing that is its life, but it can never arrive at the sum of all possible relationships. Science can give only general laws about what things are; it can never descend to the particular, individual, the concrete stone to which, say, the law of gravity would apply. The life that science discovers (the being it discovers) is an abstraction, whereas by definition "what is living is concrete, incomparable, unique" (I, 482). But the same holds true for the science of ethics; it too speaks of sadness in general. Thus no science can ever produce specific determinations of the concrete particular. But while science abstracts and generalizes, art at least deals in the coin of the concrete and individual. Its realm is "pure life constructed by individuation." But, even here, if "life" is individual and concrete, it too is a totality of relationships. Art, then, also faces an impossible task. Except that, unlike science, it need give only a fictive totality, instead of "life" it offers "the form of life." And in addition its task is also to join matter and spirit, the two parts of life that science has separated. Thus, no reality *is* in the world but only in the painting. The totality of relations can only "be" as an idea in the artist's mind. No artist ever copies Nature, which at best is a scientific "idea"; instead he "realizes" his idea of the totality. And that "form of life" "in" the painting is a perfect description since a painting must give the illusion, as Kant would say, of real organic unity. As we read in Morente's book on Kant: "Life is precisely its own inner *telos*, a system of forms in which each part determines and is determined, in which each part engenders the whole and is in turn engendered according to the idea of the whole."[17] Finally, Ortega concludes his essay by answering a question he raised earlier: What is the "ideal theme" of painting? Ortega's answer clearly comes from Cohen's lectures on esthetics, for he says: "Man in Nature . . . Man as an inhabitant of the planet earth" (I, 492). In a word, Adam, which is to say, *life*.

It should now be clear just how wrong it would be to consider this essay the first formulation of Ortega's own thesis about "my life." Although Ortega has followed the contours of Pure Reason in the direction of Practical Reason, moving from the scientific where the individual is a case in a general law, to the esthetic where the individual has immediate value and is the decisive element, from beginning to end this essay cleaves to the "constructivist" epistemology of Cohen and Natorp. But beyond a general and specific armature, Adam, the main figural device in the essay, is a blatant stand-in for the Kantian Transcendental Unity of Apperception, and all the talk about the life of things being their Being is another way of saying that being for the Marburg School is a construction.[18] Adam is not just life as it exists in a world without consciousness of its existence; Adam is reflection. He is like the figure of Ortega's Parmenides at the beginning of philosophy: before he appeared there was, of course, Being, but no one to equate it with being thought. As Cassirer writes in the early pages of his *Philosophy of Symbolic Forms*: "The first point of departure for speculation is denoted by the concept of Being. The instant this conception articulates itself and a consciousness awakes of the unity of Being, as set over against the multiplicity and variety of being things, the specifically philosophical mode of regarding the world arises."[19] Certainly Ortega

[17]Manuel García Morente, *La filosofía de Kant: Una introducción a la filosofía* (Madrid: Librería General de Victoriano Suárez, 1917), p. 323.

[18]As Ortega explains in "Sensación, construcción, e intuición": "Neither the appearances, nor the relations that serve as principle *are*, in and of themselves. What *is*, truth, is in the actual adequation of principle and problem, of hypothesis and appearances." *Apuntes*, p. 111.

[19]Cited by Helmut Kuhn, "Ernst Cassirer's Philosophy of Culture," in *Ernst Cassirer*, ed. Schilpp, p. 550.

cannot really mean that the "ideal theme" of painting is man and his questioning after Being. And if he does not mean that, or *all* of that, he must instead mean something like the following. He has pursued the esthetic mode as far as it will take him in Kantian and Neo-Kantian terms. But the problem remains, here as in the case of science, whether as theory or as pure knowledge. The general, the universal, may be true in all cases, it may even be true in an absolute sense, but for this very reason it can never touch reality at any point.

Ortega dealt with this same problem in more human terms at the beginning of 1911, in a published review in which he expressed reservations about a book on politicians by the managing editor of *El Imparcial*. The author, Sr. Cuartero, holds that a politician is essentially an orator, and since this requires attention to one's immediate circumstances, it means in terms of what Ortega established in "Social Pedagogy," that the orator would be "a wild man," "a capricious self." Sr. Cuartero thinks this leads all orators into triviality. But Ortega, citing Kant, wonders rather if the alternative, a disregard for one's circumstances, is not the madman's way. In addition to the orator, Sr. Cuartero's man of circumstances, there is of course a man of deep convictions, Ortega's philosopher. Yet Ortega will not side with him *against* the orator. Instead he extends the circumference of the orator's circumstances outward. There are, he says, "orators who know how to expand the circumstantial until it blends with everything that is human: their voices are always resonant with eternal actuality" (I, 564).

Again Ortega has been brought up short by the same problem. It would seem that the only solution is to stretch the idea of circumstances outward until it becomes . . . something else.[20]

---

[20] I am indebted for this observation to the very useful book by Fernando Salmerón, *Las mocedades de Ortega y Gasset* (México: El Colegio de México, 1959), p. 118.

[3]

PHILOSOPHY AS RIGOROUS SCIENCE:
MARBURG AND BEYOND

Phenomenology is not a philosophy of culture in the sense that it takes orders from any canonic standard. It is free not only to criticize the actual state of our culture, but to delimit even the idea and claims of culture as such. It does not accept Cohen's identification of the subject, i.e., the unity of consciousness, with the unity of the (sic) human culture—an identification through which the objective mind comes to account for the whole sphere of the human spirit. [1]

I T is hard to imagine Ortega as an impecunious foreign student, ill at ease and bereft of language, but that is exactly how he felt when he first arrived at Leipzig in the cold spring of 1905; this much we know from his letters to Navarro Ledesma. Yet he not only studied with Professors Lipps, Mirsch, and Hild, but managed to read the *Critique of Pure Reason* during afternoon visits to the Leipzig Zoo. In addition, once his money was exhausted, he went back to Spain to sit for a competitive examination that would allow him to continue studying in Germany. The stipend he won required him to study the "Prehistory of Critical Philosophy" at the University of Berlin and read a paper, on his return, based on his researches abroad. The stipend, awarded by Royal Decree, would be disbursed from October 1, 1906, until September 30, 1907. Instead, Ortega spent only a few months in Berlin and appeared at the University of Marburg on November 17, where he studied until August 2, 1907. He was undoubtedly drawn to Marburg by the reputation of its Neo-Kantian school, since 1890 the major philo-

---

[1] Kaufmann, "Cassirer, Neo-Kantianism, and Phenomenology," in *Ernst Cassirer*, ed. Schilpp, p. 806.

sophical school in Germany.[2] During his winter semester Ortega registered for Kant's System, Ethics and Esthetics, and a Philosophy Seminar with Cohen, taking, at the same time, General Psychology and General Pedagogy with Natorp. In the summer semester he registered only for Cohen's History of Modern Philosophy.[3] Then in late 1907 Otega returned to Madrid to resume the diverse occupations that would occupy him until 1936. There in Madrid he founded, with others, the magazine *Faro* and continued writing articles for *El Imparcial*. And when, by Royal Decree, he was named to the Chair of Psychology, Logic, and Ethics as the Escuela Superior del Magisterio, it was in part because he had been nominated with an unusual show of unanimity by the Central Council for Primary Education, the Royal Academy of Political Science, the Ministry of Public Education, and the Faculty of Philosophy and Letters of the Central University.[4] Then, in October of the same year, Ortega participated in a Science Congress in Zaragoza, organized by the Spanish Association for the Advancement of Science. The paper he read was "Descartes and the Transcendental Method," one result of his governmental stipend of 4,500 pesetas, his year and a half in Germany, and especially, as was evident to everyone, at Marburg. In Madrid he taught his courses and wrote for the daily press, now praising Pablo Iglesias and Francisco Giner de los Ríos, now criticizing Unamuno and Menéndez Pelayo. In 1909 he helped found the magazine *Europa*, and in early March of 1910 he was invited to deliver the speech we have examined at the Club "El Sitio" in Bilbao. When Nicolás Salmerón died the same year, the Chair of Metaphysics fell vacant at the Central University, and Ortega sat for and won the competitive examinations for that post as well. Thus, a second Royal Decree, naming him to the Chair of Metaphysics, was issued on November 12, 1910; it also allowed the new *catedrático*, at his own request, to continue teaching at the Escuela Superior without salary. One of the most important Madrid papers—not his family's—called the

[2] Henri Dussort, *L'École de Marbourg*, ed. Jules Vuillemin (Paris: Presses Universitaires de France, 1963), p. 129.

[3] Salmerón, *Mocedades*, p. 35. [4] Salmerón, p. 36.

day of the appointment a "red-letter day for Spanish science and education." [5]

But then, having made the relatively small world of Madrid his own, in March of the following year he returned to Marburg—postponing assumption of his new Chair. This time he arrived in Germany with his wife of nine months and a grant from the Ministry of Public Education. Now they remained in Marburg until the following December, when he finally returned to occupy his Chair and begin teaching at the University, the Escuela Superior, and the Center for Historical Research. And when, in late June of 1913, he next read a paper before the Spanish Association for the Advancement of Science, it was entitled "Sensation, Construction, and Intuition" and was no longer written from a solely Neo-Kantian perspective. Instead it showed acquaintance with the new phenomenological movement, although the latter was barely known outside Germany.

From a distance of over sixty years it is difficult to realize that when Ortega won the Chair of Metaphysics at the age of twenty-seven, he had been studying philosophy for thirteen years, Kant for at least five years, and Neo-Kantian philosophy for three years, which is to say, Plato, Leibniz, Descartes, Hegel, Fichte, Schelling, Rousseau, *and* Kant. He had also read more than his share of histology, anatomy, classical and ancient languages, and physiological psychology. Thus, as Ortega well knew, when he won the Chair of Metaphysics at Madrid he was repeating what Julián Sanz del Río, founder of the Spanish Krausist movement, had done or tried to do when he returned from Germany in 1843. In his turn, Ortega brought Europe back to Spain with him, but this time it was the best that Europe had to offer, instead of a minor, quasi-mystical, pseudo-philosophy. Ortega, when he won his second Chair, was acclaimed by Federico de Onís as a Neo-Kantian philosopher; and indeed, as we have seen, he was at least that.

And yet, we must imagine, Ortega cannot have been entirely pleased at being considered Spain's leading Neo-Kantian philosopher. That may have characterized him in 1908 when he delivered the paper on Descar-

[5] Salmerón, p. 37.

tes, but by 1910 he was already attempting to be considerably more. As García Morente tells it, by then Ortega was extremely unhappy with the whole question of critical philosophy.[6] It seems reasonable to suppose, then, that when Ortega absented himself from Spain for the entire year of 1911, it was not to escape his clamorous fame or to enjoy a leisurely honeymoon abroad, but to win time for himself, and for his own—as distinct from his country's—spiritual development. Not surprisingly, he returned to Marburg, the citadel of critical, that is to say idealist, philosophy. It was as though, after five years, he was setting out again on a new voyage of discovery. Just when one would expect him to take his ease and begin to reap the benefits of his success in a Madrid where no doors were closed to him, no heights left to conquer, Ortega, quite abruptly, aborted his career as Spain's leading Neo-Kantian to return to Germany and Marburg.

Curiously, none of his critics seems to have noticed that in 1910 Ortega made what can only be called a false start. No one seems to have remarked on how his speech, "Civic Pedagogy as a Political Program," delivered in Bilbao in 1910 and his announced plan to publish a series of ten "Salvations" with the publisher Editorial Renacimiento that same year, perfectly parallels his Madrid Speech, "The Old and the New Politics," delivered in early 1914 and the publication of *Meditations on Quixote* that same spring, with the same ten "Salvations" of 1910 now promised as ten "Meditations."[7]

There is thus an extremely important hiatus in Ortega's development as a philosopher that must be filled in, and this, substantially, is the subject of the present and the next chapter. In what follows we will examine Ortega's fifth-column approach to the problem of idealism at Marburg, examine his weapons of defense and escape, and, as succinctly as possible, what in large measure we can only conjecture were

[6] Morente, *Ensayos*, p. 206.

[7] "Nota de esta edición," *Obras*, II (Madrid: Revista de Occidente, 1946), 101. This curious note begins: "It is appropriate to note here that Mr. Ortega y Gasset, in 1910, planned a series of essays to appear under the imprint of the publisher Renacimiento, the most important of the period. These essays, first entitled *Salvations* and later *Meditations*, bore the following titles that appeared on the first page of the first edition of *Meditations on Quixote* in 1914."

the philosophical blazes that led Ortega out of the dark forest of idealism. Finally, since this is the key to his "second voyage" of 1911–14, we will examine evidence of Ortega's early encounter with the new phenomenological movement.[8] Anyone who would underestimate the magnitude of Ortega's struggle with idealism at Marburg fails to understand what the School of Marburg stood for. It was, in fact, in a curious way, not the fortress of Neo-Kantianism, but of idealism entire, with but one member (Husserl) excluded. As Ortega wrote, referring to this crucial year of 1911: "All my devotion and gratitude to Marburg is more than made up for by the effort it cost me to breach it and win my way through to the open sea" (III, 433).

The articles that Ortega sent back to be published in Spain during his final year at Marburg show him defensively guarding his Spanish flank against local attacks, while at the same time seeking, in unconscious justification for his absence, to distinguish between his own current hopes and remedy for Spain and those of his spiritual mentors. They were, as we recall, not so much the members of the Generation of 1898, as the men of '69, as Ortega termed them in a necrology on the death of Gumersindo de Azcárate, a founder of the Reformist Republican party in 1912. Thus Ortega's generation, which included such luminaries as Manuel Azaña, Picasso, Américo Castro, Pedro Salinas, and Jorge Guillén, felt less close to what he called the Generation of the Restoration (the Generation of 1898) than to the earlier Republican followers of Krause. This was not because Ortega and his contemporaries found the first Spanish Republic attractive, but because they admired "their moral probity, their desire to gain knowledge and their sagacity" (III, 12). Ortega knew that "bringing Spain culturally close to Germany" had been attempted once before, but the reaction that defeated the *Krausistas* was now less aggressive than in the 1870's and, in addition, Ortega did not mean to make the mistakes of a Joaquín Costa, whose romantic historicism had kept him from correctly diagnosing the national problem. At the same time, Ortega insisted, he dissociated both himself and German culture from German politics; he was only

[8] Unique among Ortega's well-intentioned Spanish critics, Paulino Garagorri has been valiantly suggesting for years that an understanding of Ortega's philosophy must entail some serious examination of his encounter with Husserl.

concerned, he said, to "subject the heart and minds of (his) compatriots to German discipline" (I, 212). And he repeated more than once the formula: culture = science; science = German culture. Yet by 1911 this formula must have sounded something less than new, as Ortega's insistence seems to acknowledge. In a sense, then, his rearguard action in the Spanish press, together with his return to Marburg, was little more than a holding action to buy time. Moreover, this "audible pause" in Ortega's public development may be another indication of an ambivalence toward, if not an outright defection from, the orthodox Neo-Kantian ranks. In other words, since obviously he could not admit in Spain that the Marburg way was not supreme, his only means of escape was via a return to Marburg. Certainly no one who had garnered a reputation as a Neo-Kantian was likely to apply for a fellowship to go anywhere else. The simple fact is that Ortega was literally at sea. He could not go backward and he was unaware of what lay ahead; so in order to conceal his own bewilderment he filled the air with nostrums. Of course there was no way to disguise the fact that he had been repeating the same formulae at least since 1908 when he first defended public support of Spanish science in an article entitled "Congress for the Advancement of Science." This was why he must soon say something new and why, perhaps, he returned to Germany to study. As a Neo-Kantian he had begun to elaborate an esthetic for Spain as well as a political program, but the latter made him seem as much a gradualist as the men of the Restoration, and the former had foundered on the problem he faced squarely in "Annoyance with Orators," published early in 1911. This impasse, which may well have provoked Ortega's second year-long sojourn in Marburg, was by no means academic nor even solely philosophical. For Ortega could not yet bridge the gap between Spanish particulars and ideal science, between being an "orator" himself and a traditional philosopher.

Beyond that, in 1910, he had realized that while Cohen's esthetics could and had served in the analysis of what Spain was, it had nothing *particular* to say about what Spain must be, and this was after all what Ortega had to discover, both as a Spaniard and as a philosopher. Culture was more, he wrote in September of 1911, than just giving imperishable form to human passions and ideas as Chateaubriand, Barrés, Ingres, and Cézanne had done. It was also, and especially, the "creation of new passions and of new ideas" (I, 208). In the light of his recent decision to go forward in 1911, he could even be generous with the Generation of 1898, with whose members he had been in danger of being confused just the year before. Once Ortega had decided *not* to write his own "Salvations," he could remark with a touch of malice that the best Spanish literature in the last ten years was to be found in "the essays of salvation of humdrum village Worker's Clubs, of worn-out old crones, of faceless provincials, of the inns, and the dusty roads—composed by a very good writer who disappeared four years ago, and who signs his work with the name *Azorín*" (I, 200).

This apparently generous observation about *Azorín* suggests that part of our difficulty in understanding this period of Ortega's life arises not because he neglected to leave a careful record of his development—he was in fact careful to do so—but either because due consideration has not been given to the context out of which he spoke, or because his words have not been taken literally enough. But this is to remind ourselves that if, as Ezra Pound said, poetry should be at least as well written as prose, that our criticism of prose should be at least as carefully executed as our criticism of poetry. This is by way of suggesting that we may not have looked closely enough at what Ortega has said of his own philosophical development. To remedy this shortcoming, we must scrutinize and take seriously what Ortega himself says in his unusually detailed "Preface for Germans," written, but never published, as the preface for a 1934 German edition of *The Modern Theme*.

To summarize "Preface for Germans" in the briefest possible compass, one could say that it begins with an anecdote to the effect that all Ortega's works were written with Spain and Spanish America in mind, continues with a description of his philosophical studies in Germany that amounts to a detailed account of modern German philosophy, and ends by referring to *Meditations on Quixote* as his own reaction to this German experience. What is more, and it cannot have escaped anyone's notice, in this fundamental account he acknowledges directly and explicitly that phenomenology played an important part in his passage from the "Kantian prison" to his own philosophy of Vital Reason. We cannot, however, understand what these brief indications entail unless we examine just what Ortega found in Germany on his return there in 1911.

Since Ortega, in explaining his philosophical development to German readers, was bringing coals to Newcastle in a very real sense, he went to greater lengths than ever before, and expressed himself with more precision than on any previous occasion. He took great pains to give Germany her due, and at the same time explain why he had written newspaper articles instead of books, once he returned from his studies in Leipzig, Berlin, and Marburg. The short answer to this is that he wrote newspaper articles instead of books because as a Spanish philosopher he was obliged to do so. For, he said, a Spanish philosopher was obliged to be much else besides. It was not a question of money. In 1905 he had been amazed to discover that even Wundt was not munificently provided for by the German government, as he had supposed, but in fact earned no more than his friend Navarro Ledesma. Instead, as Ortega learned on his return to Spain, he had too much ground to cover as publicist, conversationalist, editor, philosopher, teacher, and politician to allow him the time he needed to write books. This would seem a rather lame excuse, but there is no need to consider it further now. Instead we should scrutinize Ortega's account of his years in Germany, in order to see how his reasons for going there dictated that he not remain an orthodox Neo-Kantian for long. As we already know, Ortega was interested in German culture and German science much more than in French civilization. We also know that he studied psychology and that this included experimental, although not clinical, psychology, as well as "armchair" or philosophical psychology. To use language more appropriate to 1911, he studied "genetic" or explanatory as well as descriptive psychology. But we must not imagine that he did this casually for one semester in Paul Natorp's course in General Psychology. From the first, from 1905 onwards, Ortega seems to have been a rapacious student who not only studied diligently for three years in Germany, but avidly before and after as well, so that he was later able to say that "In some of the sciences I know virtually everything written in Germany, both the important work and the unimportant. . . ."[9] Of course, during both his stays at Marburg, one supposes he mostly studied philosophy, and philosophy according to the orientation of the Marburg School, but it is by no means clear that this was all he studied during his second full year at Marburg in 1911. What else may he have studied? To begin to imagine an answer to this question, we must carefully weigh his appreciation of his Marburg teachers, Cohen and Natorp. For it is true that "studying something else" had a special meaning at Marburg.

First of all, as he says, life in Marburg—intellectual life—was like life in a fortress under attack. The commander of the fortress was Cohen, and the enemy was everything that was not Marburg: "Everyone outside was a mortal enemy: the positivists, the psychologistic logicians, Fichte, Schelling, Hegel. So much were they considered antagonists that they were not even read. In Marburg one read only Kant and, once translated into Neo-Kantian terms, Plato, Descartes, and Leibniz" (p. 34). Ortega is being selectively *un*generous here, but the point is well taken.

Since all contemporary schools of philosophy in 1911 were considered either positivistic *or* psychologistic by the Marburg School, no *contemporary* philosophers were read except Cohen and Natorp. This does not mean, however, nor does Ortega say, that other contemporary philosophers were *not* read. All he suggests is that he and his contemporaries, Nicolai Hartmann, Paul Scheffer, and Heinz Heimsoeth, were not encouraged to read other philosophers. The rest we are left to infer from the long historical account Ortega gives of several generations of German philosophers, including his Marburg teachers.

Following his own method of dating generations, Ortega speaks first of two generations of Neo-Kantian philosophers, those of 1840–55 and 1855–70: Cohen (1842), Riehl (1844), Windelband (1848), Natorp (1854), and Rickert (1863). While recognizing the importance of the Neo-Kantians, Ortega sets aside for special mention an even earlier generation, all of whose members were born around 1830, born, that is, in

[9] José Ortega y Gasset, *Prólogo para alemanes*, 2nd ed. (Madrid: Taurus Ediciones, 1961), p. 24. Page references hereafter given parenthetically in the text.

an era dominated by positivism. According to Ortega, these men had no philosophy of their own; they were profoundly influenced by French and English thought, and were yet "the most authentically German generation there has been so far" (p. 41). The members of this group were Sigwart (1830), Teichmüller (1832), Wundt (1832), Brentano (1838), and Dilthey (1833). Although none of these philosophers had a philosophy (they are in good company, for Ortega has said the same of Plato and Kant), two of them were names that "rushed to meet an enviable future" (p. 40). This was especially true of Dilthey, although, he says, "Brentano had several first-class insights that would prove extraordinarily fruitful" (p. 40). But Dilthey, he says, was the most important philosopher of the second half of the nineteenth century in Germany or anywhere else, even though he was never aware of the magnitude of his own philosophical discovery (p. 40).

Yet at this point the reader may wonder what intrinsic interest the philosophers of 1830 can have had for Ortega, for none seem as interesting as his own Neo-Kantian teachers. Why speak, then, of this Generation of 1830 at all? The answer seems to be that, different as they were, they nevertheless shared a repertoire of interesting themes, which, in the main, amounted to an empiricist and a holistic outlook. Ortega next lists eight of the views they shared: (1) unlike the next generation the philosophers of 1830 were rabidly anti-Kantian; (2) they tended to assert the priority of the whole over the parts; (3) they maintained that activity or process came before things or entities; (4) they said that nevertheless the whole and the process were "given" as facts and were not posited, so that the categorical was "empirical" and a fact; (5) they believed that idealism must be superseded; (6) for them the "psychical" was the primary datum on which to build a "world"; (7) they would therefore base all philosophy on psychology; but (8) on a psychology understood as a fundamental science, and thus chosen with an eye to its usefulness for philosophy (p. 42). Even if Dilthey and Wundt could not agree on the question of the whole or the parts, Dilthey's basic idea, and Wundt's "law of the *Schöpferische Synthese*" and his apperception or "voluntarism" were "two distinct ways of intuiting a completely new idea in the history of philosophy." What was new, Ortega says, was that for Dilthey and Wundt the totality, the synthesis was a single fact, while for Kant it had been "the very sign of what was not a fact, but an act on the subject's part, something subjective added to what was given as fact" (p. 42). Once he has singled out this 1830 generation of predecessors, Ortega returns to his Neo-Kantian teachers' generation: the very same teachers that he and his contemporaries at Marburg became dissatisfied with between 1907 and 1911. He returns to them because he is about to explain his personal debt to Marburg. But he first observes that the Generation of 1830, of Brentano, Wundt, and Dilthey, was closer in spirit to his own generation than the two Neo-Kantian generations of 1840–55 and 1855–70, which were, of course, closer to them in time. Their spiritual affinity with his generation, with Heimsoeth, Scheffer, Hartmann, and Ortega, lies in what he terms their un-German empiricism. Moreover, Ortega feels that the way in which Brentano and Dilthey were empiricists, especially the latter, is still the direction in which the future of philosophy lies (p. 41). At this point in the essay, apparently because its title is so apposite, there comes one of the few mentions of a specific work of philosophy not by Ortega's hand. It is amusing, he remarks, to think that "the swan of phenomenology was hatched from the hen's egg that was the admirable *Psychology from an Empirical Standpoint* ("vom empirischen Standpunkt") by Brentano" (p. 41). We are to understand that although Ortega sees Dilthey as the greater philosopher of the two, his remark on Brentano's major work is not meant to be unkind. Our author is remarking on an obvious fact: the organization of Brentano's *Psychology* seems almost random when compared, say, with that of Husserl's *Logical Investigations*. Ortega's remark about the hen's egg is philosophical chitchat, containing an esthetic judgment. Still, the title of Brentano's book is alluded to again later on, when Ortega reiterates that Brentano's and Dilthey's generation is spiritually closer to his own. The point made in this indirect manner is that he and his generation, in turning away—to a greater or lesser degree— from Neo-Kantian philosophy, had retrieved a torch left smoldering by the Generation of 1830, and were now, even as Ortega was writing in 1934, realizing a part of that future philosophy envisaged by Brentano and Dilthey; nor is the expression "the future of philosophy" unexpected here; it was in fact the title of a lecture delivered by Brentano in 1892 before the Philosophical Association of Vienna.[10] Now that Ortega has tied the Generation of 1830 to his own generation, and placed the latter at the center of the current philosophical scene, he might be expected to establish some specific causal link. Instead, at this point he only hints at the possibility of a real connection, saying: "it is unnecessary to point out that our philosophy would have to be called psychology if placed in the perspective of 1870" (p. 43). With these words Ortega turns to a discussion of Kant, the Marburg School, and its place in the history of modern German philosophy. This leads back, at last, to his own generation's dissatisfaction with Neo-Kantian philosophy's lack of veracity, and to a further mention of the importance of phenomenology for his generation as they began to emancipate themselves from Marburg and go their separate ways in 1911.[11] This historical section of the "Preface" then comes to an abrupt end. No further mention is made of psychology *or* the Generation of 1830, and while phenomenology and Dilthey are treated in the penultimate section, the reader is left wondering why psychology (or even Brentano) was mentioned at all. It is not even clear why so much time is spent in the penultimate section on phenomenology and Husserl. Ortega states that he and his generation were never phenomenologists, just as they were never really Neo-Kantians, and that for them phenomenology was more in the nature of an instrument—however precious—to be put to uses of their own. In Ortega's case we are told this meant guiding his steps as he moved from Neo-Kantian idealism to "the idea of life as the fundamental reality." For this reason alone the space given over to the phenomenological view of pure consciousness seems justified, inasmuch as Husserl's description of consciousness, we learn, allowed Ortega to see the chink in idealism's armor. And, working backward, it now seems that the mention of Brentano is also explained since his

[10] Antos C. Rancurello, A *Study of Franz Brentano: His Psychological Standpoint and His Significance in the History of Psychology* (New York and London: Academic Press, 1968), p. 141.

[11] The 1912 Ateneo lectures, mentioned at the beginning of "Sobre el concepto de sensación," speak only of "positivism" and "idealism," not of Neo-Kantian philosophy or phenomenology.

Psychology hatched the swan of phenomenology. What is nowhere made clear is the precise nature of the inferred direct connection between Ortega's generation at Marburg and the Generation of 1830, a connection that enables Ortega to claim the latter as his spiritual ancestor, even though the only clear lineage established—via phenomenology—is an instrumental, if not a frankly negative, one. In what sense, indeed, can it be said that Ortega and his generation at Marburg were closer to the 1830 generation than to their own Neo-Kantian teachers, if in fact they reacted in some sense against both?

Rather than an inconsistency, there is here a misunderstanding due to our different perspectives on the phenomenological movement itself. We forget how much time separates the two readings of this event, Ortega's and ours. The clue to the reason for our puzzlement lies in the casual, enigmatic remark, already recorded, to the effect that his own generation's philosophy "would have to be called psychology if placed in the perspective of 1870." But what is *their* philosophy? We have been told that it has to do with "the idea of life." And what is the perspective of 1870? No such generation is mentioned in the entire essay. What is there about an 1870 perspective in philosophy that would require that the ideas of Ortega's generation be classed with those of Dilthey and Brentano and rejected as psychological? The beginning of an answer lies in the date 1870 itself.

It was the year when the *"zurück auf Kant"* movement crystallized, at least for the Marburg School, and Hermann Cohen appeared on the scene. Although Zeller, Lange, Drobisch, and Otto Liebmann in Germany, and Cournot and Renouvier in France, reawakened interest in critical philosophy, it was the dispute between Fischer and Trendelenburg that placed Kantian philosophy at the center of the stage. Yet the debate itself—a measure of the Anglo-French influence mentioned by Ortega—was cast in empirical terms, revolving as it did around whether or not the *a priori* forms were innate and subjective, and whether what was at issue, in Kant, was not a species of psychological idealism.[12]

To this debate Cohen, only recently come down from university,

[12] Alice Stériad, *L'Interpretation de la doctrine de Kant par L'École de Marburg* (Paris: V. Giard et Bière, 1913), p. 11.

contributed the article "Zur Controverse zwischen Trendelenburg und Kuno Fischer," published in *Zeitschrift für Voelkerpsychologie und Sprachwissenschaft* (VII, 239–96). The following year the appearance of Cohen's revolutionary *Kants Theorie der Erfahrung* (Berlin, 1871) confirmed what most had surmised from his article of the previous year— that Cohen had a new and seemingly definitive solution to the question of *a priori* forms. It was equally clear that he was a powerful philosophical mind in his own right. This was just as well for his task was a formidable one—he would have to defend Kant not only from his severest critics such as Hegel, but from his own supporters, specifically from Kant's two most important lines of descent. The first was the metaphysics of the subject developed by Fichte; the second was the anthropological interpretation of the *a priori*, against which Husserl himself would react with a parallel charge of "psychologism." It was against this latter group, well represented in the past by such an important figure as Helmholtz, that Cohen directed his considerable exegetical powers. Taken together, these two groups of "friendly" adversaries defined the philosophical, if not the political, parameters of the Marburg School; for the Marburg "return to Kant" involved a *de*-psychologizing of Kant's transcendental method, in order to avoid the two extremes of "anthropological empiricism" and "speculative metaphysics."[13] Nevertheless, the philosophers of Marburg obviously could not restrict their activities to a rejection of the extremes of "positivism" and "psychologism," since both these views were descendants of the skepticism and dogmatism with which Kant himself had had to deal. All this Ortega implies with the date 1870.

In order to understand the power wielded by the Marburg School in Germany after 1890, a power that attracted Cassirer in 1896 and Ortega in 1906, one has to appreciate the particular genius that had been apparent in Cohen from the first. His seminal article on the Fischer-Trendelenburg debate in 1870 contained a preview of the twofold strategy that the Neo-Kantian School of Marburg would follow. Cohen's strategy, clear in his book of the following year, consisted in a brilliant redefinition of Kant's place in the history of philosophy. Kant's remark

[13] Dussort, *L'École de Marbourg*, pp. 135, 136.

about English empiricism having awakened him from his dogmatic slumbers had itself led to his consideration in the sensationist tradition of Locke, Berkeley, and Hume. This view of Kant was strong in the sixties in Germany, despite Kant's obvious kinship with Descartes and Leibniz, due to his rationalistic solution to the problem Hume had posed.[14] Cohen's method was to shift the ground under his adversaries' feet by heeding not what Kant thought he was doing but the "truth" of what he had done. The task, as Ortega later said, was to understand an author better than he had understood himself. In Kant's case this meant a relocation of allegiances; that is, of the two irreconcilable elements, rationalism and empiricism, in his own philosophy.

There was no problem with Kant's rationalist vein. Cohen aligned Kant anew with Leibniz and Descartes and traced a direct line all the way back to Plato—the *a priori* became the methódological culmination of Descartes' "Cogito" and Leibniz's "Intellectus ipse." But with the empiricist strain in Kant, the Marburg School worked a more radical relocation. Cohen demonstrated that as a philosophy of experience empiricism was not Bacon and his English successors, *tout court*. Hobbes and Locke were not empiricists because of their responsiveness to Descartes and contemporary science but because of their sensationist underpinnings. Rather, Berkeley and Hume were deemed the true representatives of English empiricism, since they rejected the criteria of positive science in favor of sensation and common sense in their philosophy: This redefinition of empiricism as sensationism made room for Kepler and Galileo, two figures that Marburg felt the historians of philosophy had unjustly neglected. These two Renaissance men were the acknowledged founders of modern science, but the merit of having systematized their findings and made them "philosophical" had always remained with Bacon. Now Natorp asserted that while Bacon had popularized science, it was Kepler and Galileo who had both created modern science conceptually and recognized the methodological importance of the new concepts they were introducing. Galileo, then, was really the creator of the new empirical method. Thus, Galileo's empiricism was

---

[14] Stériad, *Doctrine de Kant*, pp. 12, 15. I follow throughout this historical description Stériad's excellent account.

not primarily based on the observation of nature, on induction without a rational basis; rather, for him "experience" was a "hypothesis," and only secondarily did it entail sensual verification. Truth, the goal of all scientific investigation, was not given by way of the senses; instead each intellect knew it directly. This was the Marburg School's view of the problem of "experience" in Kant. No matter what initial stimulus Kant had derived from Hume and the sensationists, his own empiricism, both as mathematical and philosophical value, had its true origins in the tradition founded by Plato and renewed by Kepler and Galileo, both philosophers and scientists, in the Renaissance. Once Kant had been put in this new context the contradictions disappeared. His rationalism and his empiricism were joined in the scientific concept of experience that Newton had bequeathed him. With this much secure, oppositions such as reason and sensation, form and matter, ceased their antagonism and became relative to the higher methodological concept of "experience," now knowledge. And since the only knowledge was scientific and the question "How are synthetic *a priori* judgments possible?" applied only to scientific judgments and not those of "naïve consciousness," not only were Hegel and Fichte outflanked, but the original meaning of the *a priori* was made clear; that is, "son sens platonicien de méthode analytique qui, dans la Renaissance, est ressuscitée sous forme d'hypothèse et devient, en langage kantien: *la méthode transcendentale.*" [15] In this way Cohen and Natorp separated Kant from English empiricism and cut the ground neatly away from under their German opponents' feet. If for Kant analysis of consciousness had meant analysis of objective consciousness and not of a subjective process, if the *a priori* was no ultimate psychological "simple," but an ultimate logical foundation, then Kant had little to do with English empiricism. Kant, it is true, in the preface to the second edition of the *Critique of Pure Reason*, had allowed for two discrete and equally justifiable ways of studying knowledge. Therefore, it was perfectly correct for English philosophy to follow a psychological path; what must be avoided at all costs was the intromission of this approach in the field of theory of knowledge, or any attempt to interpret Kant from such a point of view.

[15] Stériad, p. 19.

As we have seen, this was the state of affairs when Cohen's article appeared in 1870, and the one which his *Kants Theorie der Erfahrung* was designed to correct. The *a priori* as method became Marburg's device, scientific knowledge became the prototype for all cognition, and epistemology an analysis of the logical foundations of the exact sciences. *Die logischen Grundlagen der exakten Wissenschaften* was the title of a book published by Paul Natorp in 1910, and Cohen's last work, *Aesthetik des reinen Gefühls* (1912), was the exact counterpart of his *Logik der reinen Erkenntnis* (1902). Not only had the Marburg philosophers rewritten the history of philosophy so that all great figures from Plato forward were either arrayed behind them or declared out-of-bounds, they also moved forward *systematically* like a philosophical praetorian guard behind the three *Critiques*. Cohen called his work a system, which of course never meant closure at Marburg, but "ce trait fondamental de la philosophie d'être architectonique, de comporter un ordre strict de problèmes, à l'intérieur d'une même problématique d'ensemble, la problématique transcendentale."[16] In third place came Esthetics, after Ethics. And, since all judgments aimed at truth, and Logic dealt with this problem "directly," it was first, with Philosophical Psychology being assigned the problem of unifying the three kinds of judgment as well as that of the unity of culture. Logic, of course, was understood not as Formal or Modern, but as Transcendental, Logic, that is, the systematic examination of all the presuppositions of scientific truth.[17]

In brief, the Marburg School offered a formidable and united front against which almost no one could stand. Not until after the Great War of 1914, when Marburg's "rationalistic optimism" had received, together with the rest of the world, such a stunning blow, did the movements in philosophy with which we are more familiar—the "life" philosophies, the revival of Romantic philosophy, the mysticism of Heidegger—become possible.[18] Between 1890 and 1914, the philosophical citadel at Marburg seemed impregnable, and other original philosophers were cowed by it to an extent difficult to imagine. Hans Vaihinger, for

[16] Dussort, *L'École de Marbourg*, p. 138.   [17] Dussort, pp. 138, 139.
[18] Dussort, p. 139.

example, is said to have kept the completed manuscript of his *Philosophy of As If* (1911) in his desk for years while he wrote an orthodox, line-by-line commentary on Kant; and Cassirer was first directed to Marburg by a remark that Simmel made during one of his lectures on Kant at the University of Berlin. This extraordinary "philosopher of life" allowed that "undoubtedly the best books of Kant are written by Hermann Cohen; but I must confess that I do not understand them."[19] Because he was the kind of student he was, this remark decided the course of Cassirer's life. He went out and ordered all Cohen's books, and then set himself to study Kant and Cohen, Plato, Descartes, Leibniz, mathematics, mechanics, and biology for two solid years before he felt ready to put in an appearance at Marburg. Not only did Cassirer become Cohen's most distinguished disciple, responsible in his own right for a new turn in Marburg philosophy after the Great War, but so powerful was Cohen's influence, so total was the Marburg Neo-Kantian conception of philosophy itself, that Cassirer never moved beyond the confines of its philosophy of culture *Weltanschauung;* not even when confronted with the work on aphasia of Adheman Gelb and Kurt Goldstein at the Frankfurt Neurological Institute, research that made possible Maurice Merleau-Ponty's "radical anthropology."

Since the prestige of the Marburg School was, if anything, greater between 1907 and 1911 when Ortega and his contemporaries studied with Cohen and Natorp, their disaffection is all the more impressive. None of them knew then exactly what to put in its place, but they were all certain they could not be Neo-Kantians. What Cohen and Natorp had made Descartes and Plato "say" was not to be tolerated; it might be correct, but in a larger and, to them, more important sense, it was untrue. Thus when Ortega and his generation parted company with Marburg, besides their desire to be systematic, they took little doctrine with them. But that they ultimately managed to subsume Plato, Descartes, German Romantic idealism, and Neo-Kantian critical philosophy under the single rubric of idealism and reject it is perhaps the highest tribute they could pay their Neo-Kantian teachers. Thus, the especially deep knowl-

[19] Cited by Dimitry Gawronsky, "Ernst Cassirer: His Life and His Works," in *Ernst Cassirer,* ed. Schilpp, p. 6.

edge of the history of philosophy they acquired at Marburg was the first major resource they took with them. And the movement known as phenomenology became a second, equally powerful, one. Here are Ortega's own words:

There was, then, no alternative but to pull for an imaginary coastline. A safe arrival was unlikely. Nevertheless, fortune had given us a prodigious instrument: phenomenology. That group of young men had never been, strictly speaking, Neo-Kantians. Nor did they entirely place themselves in the hands of phenomenology. Our desire to be systematic kept us from doing so. Phenomenology, by its very consistency, is incapable of a systematic form or shape. Its inestimable value lies in the "delicate structure" of fleshy tissues it can add to the architecture of a system. This is why phenomenology was never a philosophy for us; instead it was . . . a stroke of good fortune. (*Prólogo*, p. 58)

If we attempt to weigh the relative value of what I have called the two powerful resources of Ortega's generation as they turned their backs on Marburg, it is virtually impossible to rank one above the other—especially once we understand the extent of their strength. Ortega, it is true, tends to play both Neo-Kantian philosophy and phenomenology down, but we must remember that he wrote his "Preface for Germans" in 1934, long after he had begun to promise disciples his own magnum opus, called, variously, *The Rise of Historical Reason* and *On Vital Reason*. Perhaps the surest way of dealing with the relative value for them of the two philosophies is to notice especially Ortega's reference to the idea of systematic philosophy. After our survey of the Neo-Kantian School of Marburg, the precise meaning of this term is somewhat clearer. "Systematic" meant the formal articulation of a series of problem areas—as in the three Kantian critiques—in terms of one unifying problematic, the transcendental method. Therefore we must assume that in the perspective of 1911, phenomenology, despite Husserl's own claims, and whatever the subsequent claims of his disciples and followers, did not meet this criterion of a system. Notice Ortega's reasoning: he and his contemporaries were never Neo-Kantians because that philosophy lacked conviction, veracity; and they were never wholehearted phenomenologists either, but for a different reason: their desire for a "system" kept them from being so; and lacking a "systematic form," phenomenology was not even, in their eyes, a philosophy. Still, in the light of what we know today about phenomenology, there seems to be an inconsistency in what Ortega says. For, as we shall soon observe, phenomenology and Neo-Kantian philosophy were not as far apart as one might think. In fact, one could even say, since phenomenology planned to deal with the contents as well as the forms of experience, that it was even more systematic than the Kantian philosophy of Marburg. In addition, there was the similarity between Husserl's description of Intentionality in the *Logical Investigations* (1900–01) and Natorp's earlier description of *Bewusstsein* in his *Einleitung* of 1888.[20] At any rate, Ortega's systematic-asystematic distinction cannot be based on an absence or presence of formal method, for in 1911 Husserl was not only announcing phenomenology's method, but also declaring phenomenology to be the first truly scientific philosophy, the first "philosophy from the ground up" (*Philosophie von unten*).[21] Rather, in Ortega's (Neo-Kantian) view, phenomenology fell short as a philosophy because it was *only* a methodology, a new and, it is true, more refined instrument, but only that; an additional tool for the ongoing work of descriptive psychology. Thus, from the vantage point of 1911 what phenomenology really needed to make it systematical was a fundamental problematic, a principle or "hypothesis" like the transcendental method or the "idea of Life as the fundamental reality" that Ortega would soon discover; without, as he would later say, *positive* intimations from anyone . . . ," but "directed to it by the problems then confronting philosophy" (*Prólogo*, pp. 65–66). That this was (and remained) for Ortega the missing ingredient in phenomenology is confirmed—as we can now see—by the following important words from his *The Idea of Principle in Leibniz:* "for a systematic phenomenological thinking to be possible, it is necessary to start from a phenomenon that *is itself* systematic. This systematic phenomenon is human life and one must start with its intuition and analysis" (VIII, 273). But despite phenomenology's failure as a system and as a philosophy, Ortega still considered it a "prodigious instrument"; and what this means we may infer from the above quotation.

[20] Dussort, *L'École de Marbourg*, p. 143.

[21] Edmund Husserl, "Philosophy as Rigorous Science," in *Phenomenology and the Crisis of Philosophy*, trans. with an introd. by Quentin Lauer (New York: Harper and Row, 1965), p. 122, n. 60.

But it does not explain why he should call phenomenology a "prodigious instrument" *before* he has discovered that "idea of Life as the fundamental reality" which will allow him to meet his own Marburg criterion for what is systematic. Of what use to Ortega could phenomenology have been in 1911? It could certainly not add any "delicate structure of fleshy tissues" to the architecture of a system that did not yet exist.

So that we must wonder again if we have quite understood what Ortega means by phenomenology. In view of the long programmatic statement quoted at the beginning of this study, there can be no irony in Ortega's calling phenomenology a prodigious instrument with reference to the year 1911; and this in spite of the fact that the whole fourth section of the "Preface" deals in detail with what Ortega considers the capital error of Husserlian phenomenology, the idea of pure consciousness itself. In addition, there is the remark in *The Idea of Principle in Leibniz* that follows the long footnote in which Ortega gives a second version of his critique of Husserl. There, after outlining the objections he put to Dr. Fink, he says: "In this way I abandoned phenomenology (*la Fenomenología*) at the very moment of tasting it" (VIII, 273). Because the three-page long footnote begins: "Since 1914 (see my *Meditaciones del Quijote, Obras Completas,* Vol. I) the basis of all my thought has been the contemplation of the phenomenon of "human life," and because *Meditations* was probably written (or rewritten) during the first half of 1914, and because Husserl's *Ideas* I appeared in the first *Jahrbuch für Philosophie und phänomenologische Forschung* in the spring of 1913, the term "phenomenology" (here with a capital P) must generally refer to what we think of today as *Husserlian* phenomenology, that is, to the post-*Ideas* Transcendental Phenomenology at whose "introduction" Husserl labored until his death in 1936. At the same time this Transcendental Phenomenology can in no way, ever, have been considered a prodigious instrument by Ortega; before 1913 it did not exist, and afterward, as he says, he rejected it the moment it came into his hands, that is, in the late spring of 1913. And this means that the phenomenology he considered such a prodigious instrument, apparently as early as 1911, must have been either the pre-*Ideas* phenomenology of Husserl, or a version of it more likely to have attracted a young Spaniard

Philosophy As Rigorous Science

bent on opening a breach in idealism. What *did* Ortega mean by a phenomenology of 1911?

Even if Ortega had never before heard of phenomenology in the new sense, it seems unlikely that Husserl's article "Philosophy as Rigorous Science," appearing in the first volume, third number, of *Logos: Zeitschrift für Philosophie der Kultur* in the spring of 1911, would have escaped his notice. Once he had read that article, which in good measure anticipated the transcendental turn of Husserl's phenomenology, he would also have heard of Stumpf and Lipps, those two "rare psychologists," who "with others of their kind," had seen the absurdity of an experimental psychology not based on "the analysis of consciousness itself." He would also be aware that these men (together with Husserl) were following Brentano's "truly epoch-making impulse," in continuing the "thorough analytical and descriptive investigation of intentional experiences" begun by the latter. It is more than likely, however, that Ortega had been aware of Husserl's work for several years, or at least since his work in General Psychology with Paul Natorp in 1907. For there had been a curious rapprochement between Husserl and the Marburg School, although Husserl was not at first aware of it. While both worked separately to destroy the "psychologism" of Sigwart, Husserl's own teacher, Brentano, had been unsympathetic to Kant. In fact Brentano felt that Kant had made "tragic errors" and as Husserl later wrote to Natorp, he, in his turn, could make no headway with Kant until 1910. Yet at the turn of the century when Husserl's first volume of *Logical Investigations* appeared, Natorp, as we saw, gave it "the earliest and strongest recognition it received at the time (*Kantstudien*, VI, 270 ff.)."[22] This interest on Natorp's part was due to the fact that he had voiced his own criticism of psychologism thirteen years earlier in "Ueber objektive and subjektive Begründung der Erkenntnis," where he had stressed the incompatibility of psychological investigation and theory of science.[23] And although Natorp's "this-worldly" view of logic was radically different from Husserl's, he made bold to predict that

[22] Herbert Spiegelberg, *The Phenomenological Movement: A Historical Introduction* (The Hague: Martinus Nijhoff, 1960), I, 110, n. 2.

[23] René Schérer, *La Phénoménologie des "Recherches logique" de Husserl* (Paris: Presses Universitaires de France, 1967), p. 13.

"Husserl's attempt to give his pure logic philosophical foundations would eventually lead him into the path of Kantian epistemology with its emphasis on spontaneity and construction"; a prediction that was seemingly fulfilled by the transcendental turn of Husserl's phenomenology in the *Ideas* of 1913.[24] Clearly, Ortega would have heard of Husserl from Natorp or Cohen. What is certain is that Husserl's article in *Logos*, a new and very carefully edited journal, would certainly have been much commented upon at Marburg; inevitably so, since Husserl had challenged the readers of *Logos* to show that any significant revolution in philosophy, any future philosophical "system," was possible, except under the aegis of "phenomenology." But then Husserl went on to separate phenomenology from psychology in such a confused way as to leave everyone supposing that phenomenology was still descriptive psychology. Husserl wrote:

With this (phenomenology) we meet a science of whose extraordinary extent our contemporaries have as yet no concept; a science, it is true, of consciousness that is still not psychology; a phenomenology of consciousness as opposed to a natural science about consciousness. But since there will be no question here of an accidental equivocation, it is to be expected beforehand that phenomenology and psychology must stand in close relationship to each other, since both are concerned with consciousness, even though in a different way, according to a different "orientation." This we may express by saying that psychology is concerned with "empirical consciousness," with consciousness from the empirical point of view, as an empirical being in the ensemble of nature, whereas phenomenology is concerned with "pure consciousness," *i.e.*, consciousness from the phenomenological point of view. If this is correct, the result would then be—without taking away from the truth that psychology is not nor can be any more philosophy than the physical sciences of nature can—that for essential reasons psychology must be more closely related to philosophy (*i.e.*, through the medium of phenomenology) and must in its destiny remain most intimately bound up with philosophy.[25]

From the vantage point of over half a century, this passage offers no problems, but to Husserl's contemporaries in 1911 it must have sounded very like Brentano's "descriptive" or "phenomenological" psychology. Especially since Brentano, in whose *Psychology from an Em-*

[24] Spiegelberg, *Phenomenological Movement*, I, 110–11, no. 2.
[25] Husserl, "Rigorous Science," in *Phenomenology*, pp. 91–92.

pirical Standpoint the distinction between descriptive or phenomenological and genetic or explanatory psychology was already implicit, had long ago spoken of his own psychology as "the very foundation of all the other sciences and their 'crowning pinnacle'." To make the parallel more exact—and more confusing—the preparatory work done by Brentano in 1874 had been for the sole purpose of delineating the proper subject matter of psychology; nor was there anything parochial in this; his descriptive or phenomenological psychology would also provide "the starting point of all scientific endeavors, including philosophy."[26] But if it was not easy to be certain that phenomenology was no longer descriptive psychology (as Husserl himself had described it in the *Logical Investigations*), the distinction between psychology and philosophy was no more finely drawn.

As for the term "phenomenology," in 1910–11 Husserl was only beginning to establish an exclusive right to the designation. Even Brentano's *Psychology*, first published in 1874, began with the words: "Experience alone is my teacher. But I share with others the conviction that a certain ideal intuition (*'ideale Anschauung'*) can well be combined with such a standpoint." In fact, Stumpf, Meinong, and Husserl had all been pupils of Brentano. At any rate, Stumpf adopted the rubric of "phenomenology" in 1906, and Husserl felt Meinong's *Gegenstandstheorie* (1904) was an "unacknowledged loan" from the general theory of objects (*allgemeine Gegenstandstheorie*) he had advocated in at least two sections of his *Logical Investigations* of 1901. Therefore, the more closely one scrutinized phenomenology, the more it seemed to combine a firm rejection of "psychologism" with a fascination for "phenomena without reality status."[27] Meinong, who received an earlier and more sympathetic hearing in England than Husserl—Russell published three articles on his work in *Mind* in 1904—seemed especially to have caught the spirit of the times. It was his achievement to have shown, as J. N. Findlay says, that if the real world was bountiful, the realm of (ideal) objects was practically boundless.[28]

[26] Rancurello, *Study of Franz Brentano*, pp. 37, 29.

[27] Cited in Spiegelberg, *Phenomenological Movement*, I, 35, 99, 100.

[28] J. N. Findlay, *Meinong's Theory of Objects and Values*, 2nd ed. (Oxford: Clarendon Press, 1963), pp. 42–43.

Philosophy As Rigorous Science

We have seen that although Ortega's generation at Marburg had no positive reasons for knowing that idealism was no longer *the* truth, they did profess to have *negative* reasons for objecting to idealism (*Prólogo*, p. 57). And while there is little tangible evidence as to what the latter were in Ortega's case, the essays he wrote in his last year in Marburg give some indication of why phenomenology or descriptive psychology would have caught and held his attention. For in addition to his dissatisfaction with idealism, Ortega had assumed the burden, in 1909 and 1910, of describing a Spanish esthetics, by which he meant, literally, a Spanish way of perceiving things. But his pursuit of this goal was impossible if he followed Cohen's Neo-Kantian esthetics to its outer limit. This is clearly seen in Ortega's 1911 essay, "Esthetics of 'Dwarf Gregorio, Wine-Skin Seller,' " where it becomes obvious that Ortega's own "esthetic" characterization of Spaniards as "impressionists," based in part on Worringer, is potentially more useful and productive of more specific insights than Cohen's esthetics. The trouble with the esthetics of Marburg, as Ortega saw, was that it was not fine enough to describe a *Spanish* esthetic. This is probably why in an effort to follow Cohen, Ortega was forced to conclude the Zuloaga essay with this far from satisfactory observation: "in the end we realize that the painting is above and beyond both (the figure and the landscape), in their relationship, in their unity, in what was not painted, in an infinitude of different men inhabiting different countries" (I, 544). Certainly Ortega's own (antithetical) 1911 characterization of the Spanish esthetic in "Art of This World and the Next," where he terms it one of "aggression and defiance towards all that is suprasensible, and an affirmation *malgré tout* of all things small, fleeting, or disavowed . . . ," (I, 200) was much more satisfying. Therefore, a movement like the new phenomenology, which had collapsed Kant's phenomena-noumena distinction and promised direct access to the things themselves, must have seemed singularly attractive. In distinct contrast to critical philosophy, it held out the promise of a closer attention to the world without any diminution of reality. In fact, given his notion of Mediterranean Man, the centerpiece of which was the Spaniards' marked antipathy to all ideality, Ortega must have welcomed phenomenology as both a proto-"esthetic" and as the "First Philosophy" he had returned to Germany to discover.

Philosophy As Rigorous Science

In stressing not just the "real," and the "ideal," but the correlation between them as well, the proto-phenomenology of Brentano's early work and of Husserl's *Logical Investigations* also seemed to promise a happier union between the philosopher and the orator than any Oretega had been able to find. This makes it almost certain that the primary focus of Ortega's interest shifted, in this crucial year of 1911, from the work of Natorp and Cohen, to that of Brentano, Husserl, Max Scheler, and the phenomenological movement as a whole.

There are scant indications as to how Ortega proceeded to acquaint himself more thoroughly with phenomenology, once the *Logos* article appeared in 1911. Almost certainly, as we have seen, he knew of Husserl's *Logical Investigations* before then. As for Brentano's work, as we noted, Ortega questioned Cohen about him in Marburg in 1911, a whole year before he began to "seriously study phenomenology," in 1912. This means, and it is important, that Ortega probably read Brentano before the appearance of Husserl's *Ideas*. At least his questioning of Cohen suggests that by 1911 Ortega could well have been familiar with Brentano's *Psychology* as published in 1874, or else in the new, second edition, *Von der Klassifikation der psychischen Phänomene*, which had just appeared in 1911, as well as with his seminal *Von der mannigfachen Bedeutung des Seienden nach Aristoteles* (1862), and his *Vom Ursprung sittlicher Erkenntnis* (1889). At least, in partial confirmation of Ortega's early encounter with phenomenology, in his essay "Castilian Landscapes" of 1911, there appears something that sounds very much like a diachronic version of Brentano's and Husserl's originary insight about the evidential superiority of "inner perception" and "ideal intuition":

The value we place on many present realities is not owed the realities themselves; if we concern ourselves with them it is because they exist, there before us, affronting us or serving us. It is their existence, not the things themselves, that has value. On the other hand, what interests us about what *was*, but is no longer present, is its very own inner quality. Therefore, when things enter this realm of the past they are stripped of their utilitarian shell, of any vestige of hierarchy based on the services they rendered when they existed, and thus completely naked, they begin to live with their own quintessential force. (II, 13)

A second, closer look, however, reveals a different source for this passage, yet one still very much within the young phenomenological movement. Ortega's emphasis in this passage is precisely not on an ideal or phenomenological intuition *tout court*. Rather than seize on the phenomenological *method* of Husserl, Brentano, or even Scheler, here Ortega seems interested especially in the anti-utilitarian (anti-Kantian) message of so many of Scheler's early essays. In fact, the incontestable source of these remarks of Ortega's is Scheler's 1911 essay, "Über Selbsttäuschungen," later collected with the title "Die Idole der Selbsterkenntnis." In this fundamental essay Scheler made available to Ortega, in the guise of a critique of unmediated self-knowledge, the ground for a rejection of the transcendental turn of phenomenology itself, and a first glimpse at a vitalistic philosophical anthropology, beyond both Realism and Idealism, that would be no more than implicit in Scheler's own thought for many years to come. Indeed, it would seem that although he returned to Marburg, it was in phenomenology that Ortega found the science and the method he had gone there to seek.

ORTEGA AND TRANSCENDENTAL PHENOMENOLOGY, 1912–1914

---

*Perception, on the other hand, has no need of any problematic
notion of its objects whatsoever; rather, it is itself an originally
assertoric notion—is, in other words, an* immediate *cognition.*

We must now scrutinize this factual *character of cognition. Once
one is clear in one's mind about it, one will see a problem not in
the possibility of cognition but rather in the possibility of*
error . . .[1]

BECAUSE the past has such authority in philosophy, it is difficult to
conceive of Ortega's encounter with phenomenology as at all separate from his experience of Husserl. This is especially true since the
canonization of Husserl by French and American phenomenologists,
most of whom tend to see him as the all but solitary founder of their
movement. This is why we are well advised to begin our examination of
Ortega's encounter with phenomenology by listening to an outsider's
view, offered in 1940 by the Marxist critic Theodor Adorno. The latter's
dialectical notion of Husserl's work is that "the very abstraction which
the contrast of the real and the ideal implies is derivative to such a
degree that we are not entitled to regard this abstraction as a basic principle which could be attributed to the nature of being itself. Whoever
tries to reduce the world to either the factual or the essence, comes in
some way or other into the position of Münchhausen, who tried to drag
himself out of the swamp by his own pigtail. One has to concede that
Husserl, in his Münchhausen attempts to dispense with the factual altogether, while still treating the ideal as something given, as only the

---

[1] Leonard Nelson, "The Impossibility of the 'Theory of Knowledge' " [1912],
in *Socratic Method and Critical Philosophy: Selected Essays*, trans. Thomas K.
Brown III (New Haven: Yale University Press, 1949), p. 192.

fact can be given, was faced with insurmountable difficulties."[2] Even if erroneous or intentionally misstated, Adorno's view has the salutary effect of preparing us to see how, already in revolt against the Neo-Kantians at Marburg, Ortega might have been equally unenthusiastic about what Paul Ricœur has called Husserl's "methodological idealism." Moreover, since the Spanish philosopher's interest in Husserl roughly coincided with a crucial change in the latter's phenomenology, it is all the more understandable that Ortega should see the Husserl of 1913 as an epiphenomenon of the idealism he himself was trying to overcome. For if in 1900–01, in the two parts of his *Logical Investigations*, Husserl's descriptive psychology or phenomenology had been concerned with a pure consciousness that contained no absolute ego or subject, in the *Ideas* of 1913 Husserl introduced the notion of a "consciousness that is always someone's because it contains an ego." So that here, in 1913, in addition to what had already been described as the intuition of essences—achieved by what was now termed an "eidetic reduction"—Husserl also proposed a second reduction—this time an "egological" one—"which reduces the world to the transcendental [non-empirical, or "pure"] ego and its intentional acts." In the *Logical Investigations*, Husserl had based his claim that phenomenology was scientific on the fact that it dealt with "pure" and not with individual consciousness. But now, just when Ortega's interest had been quickened by a reading of Brentano and Scheler, Husserl was maintaining that phenomenology's truths were still not contingent even though it dealt with individual consciousness.[3] Thus, with the introduction of a transcendental subject, Husserl seemed to have betrayed—in a Kantian direction—what had previously been the most promising feature of phenomenology, namely, the world-relatedness implicit in Brentano's notion of intentionality. Of course, at the same time, because Husserl could now be construed as having erased what was a relatively clear distinction between the phenomenology of pure consciousness and what he referred to as "phenomenological psychology" or "reflection on one's own psychological phe-

[2] Theodor W. Adorno, "Husserl and the Problem of Idealism," *Journal of Philosophy*, 37, (January 4, 1940), 11.

[3] Richard Schmitt, *Martin Heidegger: On Being Human: An Introduction to "Sein und Zeit"* (New York: Random House, 1969), pp. 114, 115.

nomena," certain later philosophers—among them, J.-P. Sartre, M. Merleau-Ponty, and E. Levinas—could still turn to good account much in the *Ideas* of 1913 that otherwise they would have been obliged to reject out of hand. But in doing so, Sartre and other existential phenomenologists were following unwittingly in the footsteps of Max Scheler and José Ortega y Gasset, in the practice of what we may provisionally call, with Scheler, "pure psychology." For Ortega, and to a lesser extent Scheler, were quick to distance themselves from the transcendental idealism made explicit in the phenomenology of Husserl's *Ideas.* In fact, by considering together Ortega's sympathy for Scheler and his antipathy towards Husserl, we can now complete our elucidation of Ortega's seemingly contradictory remarks on phenomenology in "Preface for Germans." For if, in the last chapter, we were able to explain why, as a disciple of Neo-Kantians, Ortega had found phenomenology to be less than a systematic philosophy, we can now, in the course of the present chapter, also show in what respect and to what extent Ortega still found phenomenology to be a "prodigious instrument."

Today the phenomenological movement is so vast, touching so many philosophers—from Martínez Bonati of Chile to Tran Duc Thao of Viet Nam—and with so involuted a history, that it is difficult to recall how in 1901 Husserl merely appropriated a name already in the air. Carl Stumpf, for example, was an extremely early practitioner of phenomenology, and Max Scheler also claimed to have worked out the basic phenomenological conceptions he would use before reading anything by Husserl.[4] But it was of course Husserl's teacher, Franz Brentano, who had first used the word descriptively in lectures and had anticipated Husserl in attempting to yoke together empiricism and "a certain ideal intuition (*'ideale Anschauung'*)" as early as the first edition of his *Psychology from an Empirical Standpoint.*[5] In addition, Husserl both followed Brentano in his desire to make philosophy scientific and duly acknowledged modifying the latter's notion of intentionality. Therefore, the prevailing view, and the one espoused by the move-

[4] David R. Lachterman, "Translator's Introduction," in Max Scheler, *Selected Philosophical Essays* (Evanston, Ill.: Northwestern University Press, 1973), p. xix, n. 14.

[5] Spiegelberg, *Phenomenological Movement,* I, 35.

ment's historian, Spiegelberg, is that phenomenology has developed in a continuous wave from Brentano to Husserl, from Husserl to Heidegger, and from Heidegger to Sartre and Merleau-Ponty. Indeed, there is much to recommend this as the correct diachronic view of the phenomenological movement. Especially when phenomenology's coherence can be shown to lie, not in subscription to an *already* established method, as Spiegelberg holds, but rather in an ongoing attempt "to develop an empirical but non-inductive, non-experimental method for philosophy."[6] And naturally, even according to this more catholic principle of coherence, Husserl is still unquestionably the central figure. But what any such generalizing account of phenomenology plays down is a dialectic within the movement itself between fundamental ontology and the thematization of experience. It is to Husserl himself that phenomenology owes this legacy, which in his work amounts to two life-long and contradictory aims. On the one hand, against Kant, Husserl was determined to create a phenomenological methodology that would escape phenomenalism in any form and gain access, in immediate experience, "to the things themselves," and at the same time, in seeming deference to Kant, Husserl also meant to produce a total rationalization of experience. One has only to look to discover a Husserl for whom consciousness is "pure," impersonal, and constitutive of the world-as-meaning, or if one's preferences lie elsewhere, there is equally the Husserl for whom consciousness is a life-experiencing-the-world (*welter-fahrendes Leben*). These two opposing selves, as James Edie remarks, run through all Husserl's writings and give rise "to the conflicting idealistic and existential interpretations of his thought."[7]

But for near contemporaries of Husserl, like Scheler and Ortega, without benefit of this longer diachronic view, what seemed to happen with the appearance of *Ideas* was a species of self-betrayal. It was not simply that in 1913 Husserl made explicit a phenomenological method he had already employed throughout the *Logical Investigations* of

[6] Richard Schmitt, "In Search of Phenomenology," *Review of Metaphysics*, 15 (September 1961–June 1962), 453.

[7] James M. Edie, "Transcendental Phenomenology and Existentialism," in Joseph J. Kockelmans (ed.), *Phenomenology: The Philosophy of Edmund Husserl and Its Interpretation* (Garden City, N.Y.: Doubleday, 1967), p. 242.

1900–01. This explicitation had already been hinted at in the *Logos* article of 1911, "Philosophy as a Rigorous Science." It was rather that in the *Ideas*, in addition to introducing the "general thesis of the natural attitude," the eidetic and transcendental reductions, the *epoche* and the pure Ego, in short, in making explicit his general theory of the reduction, Husserl also linked this theory to his "idealism of absolute consciousness." As Scheler later wrote: "The reduction is totally independent of the epistemological antithesis idealism-realism . . . What remains after the deactualization of the world is indeed the 'ideal' world of essence, but not something that can be automatically considered merely immanent to consciousness. Husserl's assertion that 'immanent essence' precedes 'transcendent essence' and that therefore the essential laws of the 'consciousness' of something must also be laws of the objects of consciousness (the form which Kant's Copernican revolution acquires in Husserl), in no way follows from the procedure of the reduction. It is an epistemological standpoint which comes from elsewhere and follows from the well-known principle, first expressed by Descartes, that every given is originally immanent to consciousness. We have already rejected this principle. Moreover we shall show that the origin of reflection or the being of consciousness (*Bewusstseins*) is bound up by an essential law with the prior ecstatic having and enduring (*ekstatische Haben und Erleiden*), the experience of resistance. This experience furnishes the factor of reality."[8] But it was not only that Husserl's new "ontological conviction" seemed to betray the spirit of the *Logical Investigations*, it was even inconsistent with what Husserl had said elsewhere in the *Ideas*. As J. N. Findlay observes, it not only made nonsense of the Cartesian doubt he had been practicing, and violated "the phenomenological suspense he had elsewhere recommended," but it must also have carried slight weight with philosophers—such as Scheler and Ortega—who, in the wake of Kant's own Refutation of Idealism, "can make no sense of a conscious life without permanent, independent objects in space with which consciousness can be busied, which objects must be actual and not merely logically conceived, and which must ac-

[8] Max Scheler, "Idealism and Realism," in *Selected Philosophical Essays*, p. 317.

tually control, and be actually felt to control, the constitution of natural objects by consciousness."[9] Stated this way, Findlay's extrapolation from Kant simply reiterates Scheler's argument against Husserl in "Idealism and Realism" (1927), that is, if Husserl could say in Section 49 of *Ideas*, that: "The whole spatio-temporal world, in which human being and human ego have their subordinate individual reality, has by its very sense merely an intentional being, one that enjoys the merely secondary, relative sense of a being *for* a consciousness," Scheler could respond in his "Idealism and Realism" that "the particular form of being which consciousness or reflexive being has, though on the one hand contemporaneous with the experience of reality, actually is its consequence, and not its foundation." Of course for Scheler the crux of the matter was what he called the experience of reality. Husserl was unfortunately so eager to pass through the entrance gate to phenomenology, that is, to perform the phenomenological reductions, that he had not even paused to examine phenomenologically his general thesis of the natural attitude. Instead he had simply asserted a faith in the existence of the natural world without deriving it phenomenologically. To Scheler this seemed more serious than the fact that Husserl had violated his own reduction to make a second metaphysical assertion about the contingency of the natural world. This was because for Scheler, Husserl's reduction itself was a mere "thought procedure," a childish withholding of an existential judgment that changed nothing, whereas what was really needed was "a techné, a process of inner action through which certain functions, which are continually being carried on in the natural attitude, are in fact put out of operation."[10] As these harsh words show, Scheler still pretended to see Husserl as primarily concerned with an "all-too-simple 'logical' method," whereas Scheler himself, we are meant to infer, had long since delved deeper into the "factor of reality," beneath the judgmental level, with its Kantian overtones, to the ante-predicative level. But whether real or feigned, Scheler's sar-

---

[9]J. N. Findlay, "Phenomenology and the Meaning of Realism," in *Phenomenology and Philosophical Understanding*, ed. Edo Pivčević (Cambridge: Cambridge University Press, 1975), p. 157.

[10]Scheler, "Idealism and Realism," *Selected Philosophical Essays*, pp. 317, 316.

casm vis-à-vis Husserl—in, be it noticed, the year Heidegger published *Sein und Zeit*—gives us an exact measure of the distance that must have separated his work from Husserl's as early as 1911. For Scheler's notions of "striving" and "resistance," which together are basic to his concept of the Person in the second part of his *Ethics*, published in 1916, are not only already suggested in the first part, in 1913, but are even implicit in as early an essay as "On Self-Deceptions" of 1911. Or, to put the matter somewhat differently, if Scheler could be disparaging about the direction of Husserl's phenomenology after the *Ideas* of 1913, it was simply because as early as 1911 he had been engaged in formulating a theory of the body that made both Husserl's persistent "logicism" and his newly stated "ontological conviction" seem a remnant of the past.

In fact, however, even in such late works as the *Crisis* lectures of 1935 or the posthumous *Experience and Judgment*, there is scant acknowledgment on Husserl's part that his work had been bypassed— either by Heidegger or by Scheler. But to Ortega, who had been a reader of Max Scheler's work since 1911, and who was therefore in a better position than most to compare the first part of Scheler's *Ethics* and Husserl's *Ideas* when they appeared in the first volume of the *Jahrbuch für Philosophie und phänomenologische Forschung* in 1913, it was obvious that Husserl, no less than Ortega's Marburg teachers—perhaps even under their influence—had in an important sense turned "zurück auf Kant." This does not mean that it was only Ortega's reading of Scheler—who was, after all, an enthusiastic phénomenologist—nor even his first-hand experience of Neo-Kantian philosophy at Marburg, that made Husserl's *Ideas* seem retrograde. For there were at least two other circumstances that helped predispose Ortega not to follow blindly in the direction Husserl was heading. On the one hand, in philosophy, there was Franz Brentano's reversal of his position on the fundamental question of *entia irrealia*, and, on the other, there was the related thrust of contemporary, that is, pre-World War I, para-phenomenological experimental psychology, which in 1904 or 1905 was already moving, in Würzburg and in Göttingen, in a proto-Gestaltist direction. In other words, as regards psychology, Scheler and Ortega already had available to them before the First World War substantially the same kinds of empirical research that Merleau-Ponty drew on in the forties and fifties. At this time a brief examination of these two revolutions in contemporary thought will add depth and perspective to the genetic account we already have of the phenomenological movement proper. It is even likely that without these two accompanying movements in philosophy and psychology, Ortega would never have broken with Husserl at all.

Whatever Ortega's predisposition to favor genetic over descriptive or phenomenological psychology, as a student at Marburg he was acutely aware of the need for categorical or *a priori* judgments; and so the problem, once he abandoned the 1908 position of "Descartes and the Transcendental Method," was to discover a way of thinking that guaranteed apodicticity. But Brentano had first held that it was the judgments of descriptive, not genetic, psychology that were self-evident, and this forced Ortega to look more closely at what Brentano had to say on the subject of categorical judgments. In this regard, Anton Marty and Ortega seem the only original philosophers who paid careful attention to both the early and the late Brentano. Chiefly known today as the proto-phenomenologist whose distinction between physical and mental phenomena made possible Husserl's "mathematization of logic," Brentano seems shortly after to have become the first Ordinary Language philosopher as well. In his *Psychology from an Empirical Standpoint,* in speaking of the classification of mental phenomena as either presentations, judgments, or feelings of love or hate, Brentano had triggered what became an extraordinary proliferation of *entia irrealia* by Meinong in his essay "Theory of Objects," first published in 1904. But soon enough Brentano began to have second thoughts. He recalled Kant's point to the effect that "in an existential proposition, i e., in a proposition of the form 'A exists,' existence 'is not a real predicate, i. e., a concept of something which can be added to the concept of a thing.' 'It is,' he says, 'only the positing of a thing or of certain determinations, as existing in themselves.' " But instead of concluding, with Kant, that an existential proposition was a species of synthetic proposition, Brentano saw it was not a categorical proposition at all. And so by the time he published the shorter *Klassifikation* version of his *Psychology* in 1911 he had concluded that "The reducibility of categorical propositions, indeed the reducibility of all propositions which express a judgement, to existential propositions is therefore indubitable."[11] As Brentano later told A. Kastil, the "erroneous doctrine of *entia irrealia*" had come about because (a) following Aristotle, he had thought that the "is" of "A is" was not attributive, but merely synsemantic; (b) this led to the view, apparently confirmed by St. Thomas' contention that created things are composed of *essentia* and *existentia*, that "the word 'is' has the same function . . . in 'A thing is', and in 'An impossibility is' . . ." since in both cases it is merely synsemantic and not attributive. But as he later realized, this had not been Aristotle's view at all. Instead, he suggested:

If Aristotle holds that "is" in "There is the impossibility of a round square" pertains to being in the sense of the true, he does *not* hold this of the "is" in "Socrates is." In the latter case, it indicates the affirmation or acknowledgement of Socrates; but in the former it says that whoever asserts that the thing is impossible thinks correctly. Hence Aristotle says that this being in the sense of the true is to be found only in our mind. What is accepted or affirmed is not the impossibility of a round square, but, at most, *the person who denies or rejects a round square and who does so with evidence.* I am aware of myself as someone who rejects correctly (The one who denies is himself something positive: Leibniz). [Italics mine.][12]

In short, Brentano realized that "consideration of these contents and states of affairs involves the analysis of abbreviated linguistic fictions," and nothing more.[13] The preceding reported conversation gives a perfect idea of the kind of reversal that Brentano made possible for philosophers after 1911. Instead of intentionally inexistent objects for consciousness (early Brentano, Husserl, and Meinong), instead of "contents of consciousness" (Wundt), or "categorical judgments" (Kant), we have a person who denies or affirms x with evidence (late Brentano, Marty).

[11] Franz Brentano, *Psychology from an Empirical Standpoint*, ed. Oskar Kraus; trans. Antos C. Rancurello, D. B. Terrell, and Linda L. McAlister (London: Routledge and Kegan Paul, 1973), pp. 211, 218.

[12] Franz Brentano, "On the Origin of the Erroneous Doctrine of *Entia Irrealia*," in *The True and the Evident*, ed. Oskar Kraus; trans. Roderick M. Chisholm, Ilse Politzer, and Kurt R. Fischer (London: Routledge and Kegan Paul, 1966), pp. 141–42. (What precedes the quotation is paraphrase of the same appendix.)

[13] Oskar Kraus, "Introduction to the 1924 Edition," in Brentano, *Psychology*, p. 388.

This of course meant, as Ortega would later say in "Preface for Germans," that for the philosopher the only true "given," was everything that he left behind: "The philosophical enterprise is both inseparable from what was there before it began and limited dialectically to it; it has its truth in a pre-philosophical realm."[14] In this way Brentano's remarkable step backward, anticipated in *The Origin of our Knowledge of Right and Wrong* (1889), and clearly announced in the *Klassifikation* of 1911 and 1925, made it possible for Ortega to later say of Husserl that

In *fact* the man convinced that what there is is pure ideality, "pure *Erlebnis*," *is a real man who must deal with a world beyond himself* [italics mine], one made up, independently, of an enormous thing *called* "consciousness," or else of many smaller things *called* "noemas," "Meanings," etc. And these are no more and no less things, inter-subjectivities, *things to be dealt with, willingly or not*, than the stones against which his body stumbles. (Prólogo, VIII, 50)

The above passage seems a very clear echo of the passage quoted from Brentano; for Brentano, too, by 1911, there were only real objects for consciousness; but then this meant that only language itself could be the true locus of essences, since its very nature was to abstract from the factual existence of objects.[15] Of course this reversal by Brentano placed Husserl, together with Meinong, in the curious position of being the most quixotic of philosophers.

We shall be in an even better position to comprehend the significance of Ortega's philosophical achievement, if we next locate his palace revolution within the larger context of the revolution in psychology. It was this latter revolution that gave both Scheler and Ortega their particular advantage. This next excursus is useful for two reasons. First, because the new paradigm in psychology put both Scheler and Ortega on the right path, and second, because together the revolutions in psychology and philosophy revived the Kantian paradigm in a new and unexpected form. We have already noticed Ortega's feeling of kinship with the "psychologistic" generation of Brentano, Dilthey, and Wundt, because of their shared view of "whole" perception as a synthesis that

[14] Ortega, "Prólogo," *Obras Completas*, VIII, 53.

[15] André de Muralt, *L'Idée de la phénoménologie* (Paris: Gallimard, 1958), pp. 124–25.

operates as a fact; this "psychologism" is now our passkey to the new paradigm that began to gain ascendancy in philosophy and psychology around 1911.

In nineteenth-century psychology, modeled as it was on the physical sciences, sense perception was approached and understood in terms of simple cause (stimulus) and effect (sensation). This 1 : 1 correlation was christened the *constancy hypothesis* and its eventual demise marked the beginning of a new era in psychology. As Aron Gurwitsch describes it:

If the same neural element (for example, a circumscribed region of the retina) is repeatedly stimulated in the same manner, the same sensation will arise each time. Sensations differ from one another as the respective stimulations differ. What determines the nature and intensity of sensory data are the stimuli and nothing else; however—those stimuli are *local stimuli. Excitation produced in one neural element does not in any way whatever depend upon what happens in other elements, even the most proximate ones.* [Italics, Gurwitsch.][16]

And this view of a static constancy of response for a given stimulus stood for a whole view of mind as essentially a passive synthesizer of scientifically observable and discrete, objective stimuli. Therefore, when C. von Ehrenfels came forward with what he called Gestalt-qualities, he was proposing the key to what would develop into a new paradigm and replace the old sensationist one and its *und-Verbindung* view of complexes of sensations. Von Ehrenfels noticed that in hearing a musical phrase we perceive something that is neither the sum of the individual notes nor the sum of their relations but a curious fusion that we usually call "melody," and it was to this he applied his term *Gestalt-qualität.* In his view, this "Gestalt-quality arises when the elementary facts on which it is founded are present in consciousness; it comes ready-made from the outside and imposes itself without any mental effort being required to produce it." As soon became apparent, what von Ehrenfels had in fact discovered were sensory facts not caused by stimuli.[17] In fact, as experiments demonstrated, the new kind of sensory data could even be made to work against "pure" stimuli. For example,

[16] Aron Gurwitsch, "Some Aspects and Developments of Gestalt Psychology," in *Studies in Phenomenology and Psychology* (Evanston, Ill.: Northwestern University Press, 1966), pp. 4–5.

[17] Gurwitsch, pp. 6, 7.

in a strict sensationist or elementist view, the shape of everything in a room would constantly change as the subject moved among the chairs to the table to take his seat. Yet no normal subject ever faces such a bewildering chaos. Instead, the room and its furnishings remain fixed as he moves. The room is always a room, the same room; and the subject's orientation is "instinctive"; it is never the result of higher acts of intellection (of any "judgments" in the philosophical sense) based on prior knowledge of the room. In point of fact, to a normal subject, a room always exhibits what later Gestaltists called "form constancy,"[18] as well as color constancy and size constancy; and so ordinary experience, when thematized, amounted to a de facto contradiction of the *constancy hypothesis*, and spoke for a substitution of a holistic view of perception for the older atomistic one. This was the significance of Wertheimer's epochal study of visual perception of movement, and of W. Köhler's earliest research in 1912 and 1913, that is, of the earliest members of the Gestalt movement proper.

But as Merleau-Ponty notes, although the Gestaltists' experiments with human and animal perception were fascinating, the conclusions they managed to draw were of little moment. Thus, in *The Structure of Behavior*, Merleau-Ponty indicts Koffka by quoting the following from the latter's *Princples of Gestalt Psychology*. "I admit that in our *ultimate* explanations, we can have but *one* universe of discourse and that it must be the one about which physics has taught us so much."[19] Merleau-Ponty's point is that where Köhler and Koffka saw forms, they should have seen structures and total processes; their discovery of *Gestalten* should have made them realize that the true significance of their discovery lay in a metaphysical direction. That is, as Merleau-Ponty felt, their forms should have meant an end to both epistemological and metaphysical dualism.[20]

Thus, at the most profound level, the revolution in psychology sig-

[18] David Katz, *Gestalt Psychology: Its Nature and Significance*, trans. Robert Tyson (New York: Ronald Press, 1950), p. 10.

[19] Cited in Maurice Merleau-Ponty, *The Structure of Behavior*, trans. Alden L. Fisher (Boston: Beacon Press, 1963), p. 133.

[20] John F. Bannan, *The Philosophy of Merleau-Ponty* (New York: Harcourt, Brace & World, 1967), pp. 42–43.

nalled a shift from supposedly scientifically measurable "facts" of perception to a phenomenology of perception; that is, from a markedly Kantian study of the scientific possibility of perception to perception as a function of the lived body's orientation in space. The difference was as radical as the difference, for a child too young to read, between a pictureless text and a book of pop-up illustrations in color. Instead of mind and matter and their supposedly causal relationship, the revolution in psychology made inevitable the eventual thematization—that is, the full entry into philosophy—of what Merleau-Ponty would call the *corps phenomenal*.

Of course, at the time of Ortega's encounter with Husserlian phenomenology, in 1912 or 1913, the first indications of this new philosophical anthropology of embodiedness were only just beginning to appear in Max Scheler's essays. And Ortega certainly took cognizance of them, as one would have expected a self-styled "Mediterranean man" to have done. But what especially captured and held his attention in these essays was that here, in Scheler's phenomenologically-derived descriptions of human existence as a dialectic of "striving" and "resistance," was clearly what amounted to a fundamental ontology of which Scheler himself seemed all but unaware. Thus, before we turn to the specifics of Ortega's own exposition and critique of Husserl's transcendental phenomenology, we ought to pause to examine this implicit ontological "quotient" in Scheler's thought, as well as his resulting explicit critique of Husserl's easy ways with the *notion* of the "world of the natural attitude." By examining first these facets of Scheler's work we will be able to sort out just what Ortega learned from Scheler and what he discovered on his own. This last is fundamental if we are to explain what Ortega felt he himself had done that was preemptive of discoveries announced by Heidegger in 1927.

Certainly Ortega never meant that he had preempted the analysis by Heidegger of *Dasein* in terms of temporality, for in fact he scarcely mentions it. Rather, his explicit claim in *The Idea of Principle in Leibniz* is that he had already executed a more profound reexamination of the question of Being than Heidegger had done in *Sein und Zeit*. Although Aristotle in his *Metaphysics* and Brentano in his short book on the multiple meanings of Being in Aristotle both spoke of the diverse meanings of "Being," and although Heidegger, in contrast, had insisted that his guiding concern throughout had been the one, unitary determination of "Being" underlying its multiple meanings,[21] Ortega taxes the Heidegger of 1927 with neglecting the major question about Being for a scholastic enumeration of the being of beings, including *Dasein*, and, therefore, with barely distinguishing himself from Aristotle and Brentano. Even assuming the importance of such distinctions, what Heidegger should have done, and what Ortega claims he did do beginning with "Hegel's Philosophy of History and Historiology" and "Supplement to Kant," was to inquire instead "what Being means when we use the word in the question 'what *is* something?', that is, before we know what kind of thing, what being, we are asking about."[22] And at this point in the text, the very one in *The Idea of Principle in Leibniz* from which our study set out, Ortega refers his readers first to Cohen's *Logik der reinen Erkenntnis* of 1902 and then to the notion of "human life" as fundamental to all his own philosophy beginning with *Meditations on Quixote* in 1914. He does this so that his readers will understand the abyss that separates his reference to a *question* of Being from Heidegger's. Until now, however, we have not been in a position to understand Ortega's intentions. Until this point in our account it has been too great a leap from Ortega's notion of "human life" to the sense in which "Being" is a question distinct from the sense in which there is a question about Being (Heidegger). But now our scrutiny of Scheler's critique of Husserl will serve to bridge this gap, especially if we begin with the "virtual" ontological "quotient" that underlies it at every point.

While his phenomenological researches proved to be an inexhaustible mine for Ortega and others, Scheler himself saw phenomenology as an artistic discipline, primarily concerned with its own peculiar facts; unlike Husserl and, to a lesser extent, Ortega, Scheler had no interest in providing the fundament for any non-phenomenological experience, whether scientific or philosophical.[23] And although his descriptions of

[21] David R. Lachterman, "Translator's Introduction," in Scheler, *Essays*, pp. xxiii–xxiv.

[22] *Obras Completas*, VIII, 273.

[23] David R. Lachterman, "Translator's Introduction," p. xxii.

his version of the phenomenological method make it sound like an "amateur pursuit" that anyone could engage in,[24] because he was, in the end, a "pure" or phenomenological psychologist, the ontological significance of many passages from his early essays seems to have escaped him; here is an example from the essay originally published in 1911 as "On Self-Deceptions":

In every act of external perception the existence of the physical, of "nature," is immediately evident. Any further question can only concern the level of *existential relativity* of the object within this appearance which we grasp in thought; that is, the question concerns the degree and type of its dependence on the properties of the being who comprehends it (e.g., general and individual, normal and abnormal, properties). This is often summarily called "the question of the reality of the external world." However, the external world is not a previously assumed reality "beyond consciousness" (as the obscure expression has it); rather, the further question of what is "real" in that world and in what sense it is real must be based on the evidentially given existence of the external world as a "phenomenon." We need no "lawful conjunction" of the contents of several acts, no special "ordering," to lead us to something "physical." Rather, "nature" is given to us as an indeterminate *whole* in every act of external perception; it provides the background against which the sensory contents of the present moment stand out more sharply. It is not the case that the contents of different sense-functions are first given to us in separate little parcels—for example, red, hard, sour, loud—which must first be "bound together" by an additional activity of conjunction and ordering; instead, it is immediately this same material unity which we touch *and* see when we touch and see a red hard surface, for example. Even the existence of the matter or the unity of the thing in the sphere of external perception is self-evidently given to us in every act of external perception. The only thing that might involve hypothesis or interpretation is the question of inner constitution (continuous or discrete) or the problem of what properties we ascribe to its ultimate elements in the present state of science.[25]

Moreover, because of his desire to put ethics on a non-formal yet a priori basis, Scheler was forced to describe our being-in-the-world as first and foremost a volitional-affective, rather than a theoretical-judg-

---

[24] The expression "amateur pursuit" is used by Peter Heath in "The Idea of a Phenomenological Ethics," *Phenomenology and Philosophical Understanding*, p. 165.

[25] Scheler, *Selected Philosophical Essays*, pp. 36–37.

mental, experience. In natural intuition, as he wrote, there was always a "crypto-mechanism" of programmatic concerns operating continually in each person's commerce with the world, and which was constitutive of each "world" in the sense made explicit by Husserl in the expression "operative intentionality." Borrowing an idea from J. von Uexküll, Scheler held that a being's environment (*Umwelt*) was an "intentional" selection (in both senses) and not merely the pragmatic adaptation *to* a milieu as Kant held. As Scheler explains in Part I of his *Ethics*: "A living being already provides a 'plan' for possible goods through its own kind of drive-constellation, a plan that does not rely on a living being's experiences in a milieu, but that corresponds to its bodily organization."[26] Furthermore, and this was the keystone of his argument against Kant, it was simply wrong to identify the a priori only with thought, with rationalism: "For it is our *whole* spiritual life—and not simply objective thinking in the sense of cognition of being—that possesses 'pure' acts and laws of acts which are, according to their nature and contents, *independent* of human organization. The *emotive* elements of spirit, such as feeling, preferring, loving, hating, and *willing*, also possess original a priori contents which are not borrowed from 'thinking,' and which ethics must show to be independent of logic. There is an a priori *ordre du cœur*, or *logique du cœur*, as Blaise Pascal aptly calls it."[27] Although Scheler's "emotive apriorism" seems self-contradictory, as an ethics it had nevertheless the tremendous virtue of first centering formal philosophy's attention on the auxiliary nature of reason, as the mere a posteriori explication of our peculiar condition of already being in and knowing the world. This fundamental point of Scheler's was not lost on Ortega, just as it probably did not escape Heidegger's notice either. But Scheler's penetration of the problem of embodiedness went even deeper than the notion of the "umwelt" or "life-world." That is, if we take "*Lebenswelt*" to refer not only to the anthropocentric world of "common sense" but to some features of the scientific world as well as of the

[26] Max Scheler, *Formalism in Ethics and Non-Formal Ethics of Values: A New Attempt toward the Foundation of an Ethical Personalism*, trans. Manfred S. Frings and Roger L. Funk (Evanston, Ill.: Northwestern University Press, 1973), p. 158.

[27] Scheler, *Formalism*, p. 63.

pre-objective world of original experience,[28] it must be acknowledged that Scheler's descriptions are remarkably complete, for he not only speaks in terms of a pre-theoretical, pre-judgmental, practical being-in-the-world, but delves deeper to an essentially pre-objective world experience in which, unless an obstacle arises to thwart our task, we "float" in an instinctive world. In other words, beneath or rather, this side of the world present-at-hand, the world of *Vorhandenheit*, Scheler actually glimpsed and partially thematized the world not of things, but of "facilities" and "obstacles," of pre-things, of *pragmata*. Here is Scheler speaking in "The Idols of Self-Knowledge":

The "world" is here actually, not in the perverted, epistemological sense of a *soi-disant* "idealistic philosophy" given to him as his "idea." This is true not only of the domain of representation but also of the activity of the will. *Normal* willing looks directly to the realization of the willed content, for example, leaving the room. Any willing of the requisite means, like "crossing to the door," "lowering the latch," the execution of the various movements, etc., is subordinated to the content of this goal and takes place, so far as there are no particular obstacles, almost by automatic impulse. If the willing meets with an obstacle, that is, if the willed content does not realize itself according to expectation, then a phenomenon of resistance is "given."[29]

Of course, the very thrust of Scheler's argument against Kant was to establish *"a realm of non-formal values which is independent of all experience* and any *success in deeds"* [italics in original],[30] and this led him to see a two-storied world of thing-qualities and value-qualities with an appropriate kind of intuitive apprehension for each. So that Scheler stopped short of what might have been, in anticipation of Heidegger, an ontological description of these "facilities" as *Zuhandenheit*. Nevertheless, his extremely fine descriptions of being-in-the-world stress the intuitive, utilitarian orientation of our perceptual life, its *"practical, biological focus"* [italics in original], which he felt had led to such a detrimental obscuring of phenomenal being, and a consequent spiritual

[28] H. L. Dreyfus and S. J. Todes, "The Three Worlds of Merleau-Ponty," *Philosophy and Phenomenological Research*, 22 (June 1962), 565.

[29] Scheler, *Selected Philosophical Essays*, p. 56. The source of Ortega's notion of "Being"?

[30] Scheler, *Formalism*, pp. 158–59.

closure. Thus, in a reference to Simmel, Scheler spoke of how the "society of money tends to empty values of their qualities as thoroughly as the mechanistic view of nature 'dequalifies' intuitive sense-qualities." And he continues:

The "commodity character" of things, which does not rest on an intrinsic property of these things but only in their exchangeability with a view to increasing wealth, becomes, as it were, a *substance* to which other qualities, the aesthetic, for example, are first attributed. And this is not merely an accidental analogy, as some have thought; both facts have *the same* root. Both phenomena follow the same law, that all phenomenal contents of the world as a whole (felt-values as well as perceived contents) tend to become *bare symbols for*, and *means for distinguishing among*, those contents upon which the *most elementary, most general, and most forceful drives* of an animal are directed. In *both cases* the artificial forms of the society of money and the mechanistic view of nature only make absolute tendencies which already inhere in man's natural behavior and which diminish the concrete qualitative fullness of the world.[31]

Not only does this critical passage contain *in nuce* Ortega's whole anti-utilitarian program of socio-political reform for Spain, exactly in the form in which it began to appear after 1913, it also shows precisely how Scheler enabled Ortega to bridge the gap between a Neo-Kantian essay in esthetics like "Adam in Paradise" (1910) and his own, more personal diagnosis of Spanish art as it appears in the Worringer-influenced essays of 1911 such as "Three Paintings about Wine" and "Art of This World and the Next." But even more important for our immediate purpose, in this description of the "practical, biological focus" of human life, we have the very ground, the very philosophical grounds, for Scheler's harsh criticism of Husserl's transcendental phenomenology, a criticism which, however, he allowed to remain implicit until the incomplete essay, "Idealism and Realism" of 1927.

Not unexpectedly, in view of what we have seen to be his major concern together with ethics, that is, a philosophical anthropology, Scheler's criticism of Husserl's *Ideas* is directed against the latter's apparently careful, but in the end summary, description of the "general thesis of the natural attitude." In the late essay "Idealism and Realism," Scheler complains that epistemology thus far, in the hands of the Neo-Kantians

[31] Scheler, *Selected Philosophical Essays*, p. 75.

and others has been exclusively concerned with the question: "under what conditions does the reality of an object subsist (*besteht*) and under what conditions can one ascribe reality to an object?" What ought to be decisive for the "technique of essential insight"—Husserl's "phenomenological reduction"—are rather "the questions concerning the factor of reality itself and the acts that furnish it." And this is so because, as Scheler explains, "if the factor of reality must be nullified (*aufgehoben*) in order that genuine essence may come to light, if a 'deactualization' of the world must be carried out as the condition of its decomposition into essences (*Verwesentlichung*), then it must above all be clear what the moment of reality itself is and in what acts it is given. It is this factor we must strip off in the reduction and it is just those acts and modes of behavior which first furnish this factor and make real being accessible which we must suspend."[32] Husserl has never discussed this question, Scheler says, but has limited himself to the "false declaration" that real being is the same as " 'having a place in time.' " Although Husserl has "posed this basic problem of theoretical philosophy in a profound and original way," he has not been clear about its resolution. It is not enough, says Scheler, to eliminate or suspend the mere positing of reality. Husserl, in spite of his insistence on presuppositionlessness, has been caught in an unexamined positing, for he had spoken, after all, of the general *thesis* of the natural attitude. This is clearly Scheler's bone of contention with Husserl, and this is why he insists that the latter has not confronted the real issue, why he says: "It is a matter here not of suppressing existential judgment, but of stripping away the factor of reality itself which fulfills the meaning of the predicate in the existential judgment. Or, it is a question of eliminating the acts furnishing this factor. Merely to suppress existential judgment is child's play. It is quite another thing to set aside the factor of reality itself by putting out of operation those (involuntary) functions which furnish it. To accomplish this requires very different techniques."[33] But it was left to Ortega, not to Scheler, to conclude, as much against Scheler himself as against Husserl, that, in the light of Scheler's careful analysis of the factor of

---

[32] Scheler, *Selected Philosophical Essays*, p. 315.
[33] Scheler, *Selected Philosophical Essays*, pp. 315–16.

reality, there were no "different techniques" such that could put the acts which produced it out of play.

If we turn now to the several essays on phenomenology written by Ortega in the years 1912 to 1914, it is relatively easy to see him antici-pating the substance of the critique implicit in Scheler's early essays. Because Ortega was primarily concerned to overthrow all philosophy of consciousness, because he had been reading, as Heidegger did for the first time in 1907, Brentano on Aristotle's discriminations of "Being," and finally because his concerns led him to see the ontological implica-tions in both Scheler's early essays and Husserl's *Ideas* of 1913, Ortega and not Scheler was the first European philosopher to break publicly with transcendental phenomenology, or at least refuse to entertain it. This is not to suggest that, in the essays on phenomenology we have from the period 1912 to 1914, Ortega delivers himself of as pointed a critique of Husserl as Sartre did in 1937 in "The Transcendence of the Ego." But not because Ortega's disagreement with Husserl was any less profound. On the contrary, while Sartre was in substantial agreement with the phenomenological method as presented in *Ideas*, at least as an inestimable tool for a phenomenological psychology, he merely ques-tions whether Husserl's pure consciousness could really be presided over by a transcendental ego. Ortega's reaction to the *Ideas* was more radical. In fact, it seems to have provoked him to assimilate Husserl as ontol-ogist to the idealist tradition of Descartes and Kant, as a kind of epigonic philosopher of consciousness, bent on reducing—like Kant—all ques-tions of the nature of objects to questions of the nature of thought's ac-tivities. While he was perfectly prepared to accept as correct a version of Scheler's "emotive apriorism" and his phenomenological descriptions of the acts that produced the factor of reality, Ortega saw with great clarity the catachresis involved in Husserl's step from the mere "bracketing" of the natural world in order to achieve the phenomenological standpoint, to "the metaphysical assertion" of the very being of the natural world "as consisting simply in its constitution by consciousness,"[34] and he was no more inclined to accept the one than the other. Nevertheless, be-cause of his reading of Scheler, Ortega now saw that to relinquish tran-

---

[34] J. N. Findlay, in *Phenomenology and Philosophical Understanding*, p. 155.

scendental phenomenology was not to remain in the natural attitude, for beneath it was an environing world of involuntarily pre-selected "facilities" and "obstacles," that Ortega would first call "individual, spontaneous life," and then simply, "my life." Of course, since it was in essence temporal and, hence, historical, it could only be narrated, never "bracketed," nor "reduced."

To examine Ortega's essays on phenomenology from this period, that is, "Sensation, Construction, and Intuition," a paper delivered in 1913 but perhaps dating from 1912, "On the Concept of Sensation," and above all the curious preface for a friend's book of poems, "Essay in Esthetics by Way of a Preface," is to follow the gradual enunciation of a complete skepticism about the viability of Husserl's transcendental phenomenology. In the first essay, "Sensation, Construction, and Intuition," there is reflected what might have been Ortega's initial interest in the "Pure Logic" Husserl announced in *Logical Investigations*. And if Ortega approached Husserl's work because of the latter's manifesto in *Logos* in 1911, his attention can only have been drawn there by the latter's claim that phenomenology could realize, as the Neo-Kantians could not, the Cartesian dream of a "*Sciencie universelle.*" Instead of psychology founding philosophy (Brentano), Husserl explained, in the "Introduction" to Volume II of the *Investigations*, that philosophy (phenomenology) would be the science of theory from which all other natural and human sciences would derive their claims to validity; not only that, but phenomenology would have its own method, its own subject matter, be "logically consistent, and provide certainty of ground." In large measure, this was the claim made more obliquely by Kant, but with the important difference that in Husserl's definition of science the idea of founding was linked essentially to the important—as we have seen—principle of "freedom from presuppositions (*Voraussetzungslosigkeit*)."[35] And since by the time Ortega read Husserl he must have come to see Marburg's re-writing of philosophy from Parmenides to Kant as *itself* an enormous hypothesis, at first he may have welcomed what promised to be a new and more scientific beginning in

[35] B. H. Son, *Science and Person: A Study of the Idea of "Philosophy as Rigorous Science" in Kant and Husserl*, Bijdragen Tot De Filosofie, No. 2 (Assen: Van Gorcum, 1972), pp. 62–63, 73.

Husserlian phenomenology. But only at first. By the time he came to write "Sensation, Construction, and Intuition," he had digested, as a superior kind of phenomenological psychology, all of Scheler's works to date. Because of this, and because Ortega seems to have viewed himself, in the line of Brentano, Wundt, Dilthey, and Scheler, as a psychologically-oriented philosopher, he was also interested to see how Husserl's new phenomenology would advance his own cause, namely, that of discovering a subject matter peculiar to philosophy in order to mark it off clearly from all the other sciences. But a careful reading of the essay "Sensation, Construction, and Intuition," in which Ortega examines the epistemologies of radical empiricism (Mach and Ziehen), critical philosophy (Cohen and Natorp), and phenomenology (Husserl), shows that the conditions laid down for the possibility of cognitive knowledge are such as to make it questionable if even the phenomenology of Husserl's *Ideas* will meet them. If one holds strictly to what is *given*—Ortega italicizes the word three times in a short essay—labors without any presuppositions at all, without any positings, the radical empiricsts are left with none of their associationist "elements," and the critical idealists are deprived of their "scientific consciousness." Both are equally metaphysical positings, and only Husserl's intuition seems an acceptable candidate—thus far. Still, Ortega will not commit himself. As he says, in concluding the essay: "The discussions provoked by this new principle of intuition of Husserl's are both varied and profound. Its very novelty means it is too soon to see its limits and its constitution. I am content to broach the theme with you so that it may serve as subject matter for discussions at our future meetings."[36] In fact, as becomes clear in the next two essays, and as Scheler's work clearly suggested, the theory or problem of cognitive knowledge was insoluble. As Ortega had stated the requirements in "Sensation, Construction, and Intuition," it was a matter of finding "a cognitive function that by virtue of its own character, without any external guarantees and without mediation, will secure the status of truth for its contents. This exemplary function will then serve as a benchmark to which the derived knowledge can then be referred in each case, as to a criterion."[37] Clearly, of the three, only Hus-

[36] Ortega, *Apuntes*, p. 117.   [37] Ortega, *Apuntes*, p. 102.

serl's ideal intuition or ideation was such a cognitive function, yet when Ortega passed from an understanding of this intuition as described in *Logical Investigations* to its complete explication in *Ideas*, he saw that Husserl's instrumental phenomenological reduction would not meet the latter's own criterion of presuppositionlessness.

"On the Concept of Sensation" and "Essay in Esthetics by way of a Preface" make this and much more abundantly clear; yet in both essays Ortega's criticism of Husserl is oblique, for the latter's phenomenology never directly engages his attention. This is especially clear in "On the Concept of Sensation." As Spiegelberg remarks: "that this rather specialized study in descriptive psychology (Heinrich Hoffmann's *"Über den Empfindungsbegriff"*) by one of the less known members of the Göttingen Circle, which referred to Husserl only in passing, should have been singled out for such special attention is still in need of an explanation."[38] And yet three of the five installments in which this review-article was published deal exclusively with Husserlian phenomenology. What in fact *was* Ortega's primary interest in this long review? At first blush it seems to be contained in these words: "Mr. Hoffmann is a disciple of Edmund Husserl, a professor at Göttingen. This explains the principle thrust of his work." Instead, however, the following sentences show where Ortega's interests really lie, for he continues: "The ever-increasing influence of phenomenology on psychology has caused a fundamental and salutory division of the latter into a descriptive and genetic part." And, again, at the end of the first installment, Ortega summarizes, saying: "The doctoral thesis we refer to is a welcome product of a certain very new movement that has its center in Göttingen. And it will be useful to expound and discuss its method and conclusions, taking as the subject of an extended commentary *a whole group of recent works conceived in the same or nearly the same spirit*" [italics mine]. "A certain very new movement" will pass, but it is curious indeed to speak of Husserl's "conclusions" in reference to the *Ideas;* and "a whole group of works" must certainly bring us up short, for if Husserl has just published his *Ideas* and for the first time said what *his* phenomenology is all about, how can there already be "a whole group of (kin-

[38] Spiegelberg, *The Phenomenological Movement*, II, 612–13.

dred) works?" It can only be that Ortega is less interested in the *Ideas*, to which he does refer, than in something close to it, no less basic, and even more congenial. And this is indeed the case. Apropos of Hoffmann's discussion of Wundt's view of primary and transitional colors, Ortega remarks: "This shows that the subject is still in doubt. How much this is so would be clearer if there were time to mention the splendid work of Jaensch and Hatz [sic], both of whom have heavily influenced Hoffmann, even though he only mentions the latter."[39] Much more is going on here than meets the eye, for the "Hatz" referred to is really David Katz, whose *Die Erscheinungsweisen der Farben und ihre Beeinflussung durch die individuelle Erfahrung*, translated into English from the second edition as *The World of Color*, and not Husserl's *Ideas* is the perfect example of what Ortega really means by "a certain very new movement that has its center in Göttingen." Thus, the main subject of the review is not Husserl's phenomenology in *Ideas*, nor even precisely Hoffmann's work, but the Göttingen school of phenomenological or eidetic psychologists trained there by Köhler's predecessor, G. E. Müller. Of these, Erich R. Jaensch (1883–1940), David Katz (1884–1953), and the Dane, Edgar Rubin, published a series of monographs between 1909 and 1915 that according to E. G. Boring anticipated Wertheimer's supposed founding of Gestalt psychology in 1912. One of these monographs was Katz's epoch-making phenomenological study of color, and it is to works such as these that Ortega was obviously drawn. The work by Katz, and the work on eidetic imagery by Jaensch, were the latest contributions of what Boring calls the Austrian School of Act Psychology, a geographically homogeneous collection of philosopher-psychologists including Brentano, Meinong, Stumpf (by adoption), Lipps, Ehrenfels, Cornelius, Witasek and Benussi, Katz, Jaensch and Rubin. All of them to a degree, and Katz and Jaensch unquestionably, anticipated the concerted attack by Wertheimer, Köhler, and Koffka on psychology as "elementism, sensationism and associationism, (as) *sinnlose Und-Verbindungen.*"[40] Since, therefore, in "On the Concept of Sensation," Ortega uses information specifically taken from

[39] Ortega, *Apuntes*, p. 78.
[40] Boring, *Experimental Psychology*, pp. 604, 595.

Ortega and Transcendental Phenomenology

Katz's monograph on color, and since his final remarks in the review deal with the phenomenology of whole perception, that is, with variations between the perceived size of objects in space and the size of their corresponding retinal images, a topic also consequent with Jaensch's interests in 1911, there can be no doubt that Hoffmann is no stand-in for Husserlian phenomenology, as Spiegelberg supposes, but for the phenomenological or eidetic psychology of Katz and Jaensch. Especially since the latter's work on eidetic imagery, together with that of Külpe and the Würzburg school, is the source for that apodictic proof that Ortega, out of deference to his readers, chose to omit from *Meditations on Quixote*. Indeed the phenomenology that Ortega describes in the review, with several references to the *Ideas*, is specifically contrasted with what Ortega calls explanatory psychology and, if anything, Hoffmann's work seems too close to Husserl. Or rather Ortega in this essay seems to want to push Husserl in the direction not just of phenomenological or eidetic psychology, as Kockelmans and Merleau-Ponty were later to do, but of the phenomenology that the latter evolved on the basis of papers from the Husserl archives. Ortega has chosen Hoffmann's monograph not because he is interested in the absolute certainty that transcendental phenomenology will seek in going *beyond* whole visual perception; what interests Ortega is what psychologists have to say about what lies *this* side of perception, that is, about what the simplest acts that "ground" perception itself are. For, if a judgment is possible because of what Brentano calls "presentations," what are the "presentations" themselves founded on? Since in 1913 Ortega sees perception as an original assertoric notion, he answers as follows: "To resolve this difficulty and to arrive at the essence of these simplest acts which ground the complex edifice of our integral consciousness, it is necessary, then, to subject the most important presentative act—perception—to a detailed analysis."[41] Incredibly, Ortega's underlying interest in this book review of 1913 is what Husserl reportedly termed "operative intentionality" (*fungierende Intentionalität*), precisely that which underlies the structure of the *Le-*

[41]"Sobre el concepto de sensación," *Apuntes*, p. 81. By "perception" Ortega of course means not just visual perception, for he later complains (p. 93) that "In fact, this larger purpose is abandoned in favor of a more modest one. Hoffmann only pursues what one of the senses—sight—contributes to perception."

benswelt.[42] Ortega's interest is no longer in phenomenology as a possible general theory of truth to found the sciences: instead he even gives signs here of being more interested in explanatory or genetic psychology than in the descriptive variety, for at one point he says: "Naturally there is a place for a special phenomenology of human consciousness; this is perhaps what interests us most of all—but how is it possible without a general phenomenology?" In fact, then, Ortega's interests, following those of Brentano, are first holistic and ultimately genetic, for he shows special interest as a psychologist in explaining how "the ideal body of mechanics, the 'consciousness of' mechanics, came to inhabit the body of an Englishman on a specific date."[43] Thus the fact that Ortega is headed in 1913 in a direction whose very existence Husserl could scarcely acknowledge until the late "teleological-historical" essays such as "The Origin of Geometry,"[44] suggests that Ortega had grounds for rejecting both the phenomenology revealed in the *Ideas* and the descriptive phenomenology of the "consciousness of," or eidetic phenomenology, as practiced by Katz and Jaensch. Moreover, although it is only a passing remark, those grounds certainly have to do with Husserl's second "egological" reduction, for like Lothar Eley, Derrida, and others, Ortega feels it is logically inconsistent to circumscribe pure consciousness with a limiting term like "human." And this would mean, against Husserl's own criterion of presuppositionlessness, that "consciousness of," or "pure consciousness," was simply a hypothesis, no more and no less than that of Kant and Cohen, or Plato and Descartes as interpreted by the Neo-Kantians of Marburg. Husserl's effort was only the most recent example in the history of philosophy of idealism's continuing attempt to achieve a Platonic security, for this was how Ortega had come to view Cohen's astute assimilation—as hypothesis and foundation—of the Platonic Idea to the Kantian *a priori*.[45] However, what is not so eas-

---

[42] Spiegelberg, *Phenomenological Movement*, I, 161.

[43] Ortega, "Sobre el concepto de sensación," *Apuntes*, pp. 88, 93.

[44] See David Carr's Introduction to Edmund Husserl, *The Crisis of European Science and Transcendental Phenomenology: An Introduction to Phenomenological Philosophy*, trans. with an introd. by David Carr (Evanston, Ill.: Northwestern University Press, 1970), pp. iv, vii.

[45] Stériad, *Doctrine de Kant*, p. 31.

ily seen in "On the Concept of Sensation" is what "hypothesis" Ortega would put in its place, or rather, what "central problematic." Nor is it overly clear in this essay how Ortega made his way from phenomenological psychology to the idea of "life" as the "final court of appeals" he had been seeking.

Not until his "Essay in Esthetics by Way of a Preface," written the same year as *Meditations on Quixote*, does it become clear that Ortega's "systematic principle" ("un fenómeno que sea *él por sí* sistema") fell into his lap, as it were, as a consequence of his diverse interests in ontology (Aristotle, Brentano), epistemology (Cohen, Natorp, Mach, Ziehen, Husserl), ethics (Kant, Brentano, Scheler), phenomenology of perception (Külpe, Katz, Jaensch, Scheler), and philosophical anthropology (Kant, Scheler, von Uexküll).

The "Essay in Esthetics" has heretofore usually been approached as simply an essay in esthetics. Only Julián Marías has made a specific philosophical claim for it not tied to esthetics.[46] It is his contention that the "Essay in Esthetics" represents Ortega's first overcoming of phenomenology. But in this, Marías is merely repeating what Ortega says by implication in several places; most notably in "Preface for Germans" and in *The Idea of Principle in Leibniz*, his last work. But the claim itself, whether on Marías's or Ortega's lips, is a little surprising to contemporary ears. It seems to be another exaggerated posture, like Ortega's related dismissal of Heidegger, the ontologist, in 1928, and his ridicule of French existentialism in *Man and People*.

Of course it is not Ortega's aim in this essay to offer an explicit critique of Husserlian phenomenology, but instead to state a philosophical position at the essay's entrance with which to undermine the Expression Theory of Art. But this means that the major thrust of Ortega's argument is to rebut the "Modern" idea of subjectivity. And this is the ploy that engages him with Husserl. Yet the essay itself begins with significant references to Kant, to utilitarianism, and to ethics, that reveal the sources of Ortega's anti-idealist weapons. Clearly he is drawing on the first part of Scheler's *Ethics*. And with these arms he mounts the following attack: if as Scheler had written in "On Self-Deception," "an act

[46] Julián Marías, "La primera superación orteguiana de la fenomenología," *La escuela de Madrid* (Buenos Aires: Emece Editores, 1959), 257–64.

can *never* become the object of any sort of perception; it can never turn into an object at all, never become an 'entity' (*Dasein*),"[47] then even Husserl's own very sophisticated version of *Selbstbewusstsein*, his transcendental reduction, is self-contradictory. Clearly, if, as Ortega writes, the "I" is pure act, pure performance ("lo ejecutivo"), then it can never be anything except an object *for* consciousness, something to be looked back upon, an object, moreover, set inviolably in the past. But this further meant, as Scheler would recognize in 1927, that "*the particular being which consciousness or reflexive being* (itself) has, though on the one hand contemporaneous with the experience of reality, *actually is its consequence, and not its foundation*" [italics mine].[48] Or, as Ortega himself later wrote, that not only pure consciousness (Husserl), but very consciousness, in the sense of *Selbstbewusstsein* (Descartes, Kant, Husserl), was merely a hypothesis and in no way the *primary* form of relation between the so-called "subject" and so-called "objects." That primary form of relation was instead what Ortega called *ejecutividad* in the "Essay on Esthetics." Husserl had indeed erred in not examining the *thesis* of the natural attitude. If he had done so, if he had returned to Aristotle's *De anima*, he might have discovered that his view of the natural attitude, of man's primary relation with things, was based on an unexamined notion of vision as a purely "esthetic" and "noetic" relation to things, and that, since for Aristotle both of these "faculties" were static ones, they were therefore linked to what Saint Thomas translated as *potentia apetitiva*: in short, that man's primary relation to the world was really "pragmatic." In other words, as Scheler had intimated and as Ortega had seen clearly—with Brentano's and Aristotle's help—the relationship to so-called "objects" was not primarily one of *aísthetón* nor of *noetón*, but *praktón*, as Aristotle had said; in fact, "things" were not even primarily things, but *prágmata*, facilities and obstacles, precisely because the basis of "life" was its *potentia apetitiva*.[49] And this was why

[47] Scheler, *Selected Philosophical Essays*, p. 26.

[48] Scheler, *Selected Philosophical Essays*, p. 317.

[49] See Danilo Cruz Vélez' *Filosofía sin supuestos: De Husserl a Heidegger* (Buenos Aires: Editorial Sudamericana, 1970), pp. 259–85, for an extremely illuminating account of Heidegger's "overcoming" of Husserl in this same respect. I have simply replaced Heidegger with Ortega in Cruz Vélez' version in my reconstruction of what must have been the steps that carried Ortega beyond Scheler and Husserl in 1914.

Ortega and Transcendental Phenomenology

Ortega later felt he could suggest that by the time he wrote *Meditations on Quixote* in 1914 he was in possession of Heidegger's "non-thematic circumspective absorption in references and assignments constitutive for the readiness-to-hand of a totality of equipment (Being-in-the-world)," and most of what that entailed for his own version of the question of Being. Especially since, as Heidegger seems to admit in *Sein und Zeit*, he himself was only developing an ontology based on this same Greek notion of *prágma*.[50] Therefore, we must allow that to the extent described above, in the discovery of the new "ontological" category or region of "human life," Ortega's *Meditations on Quixote* was indeed preemptive of Heidegger's notion of Being-in-the-world, and, therefore, that when Ortega says "Since 1914 (see my *Meditations on Quixote*, in *Complete Works*, I), the intuition of the phenomenon 'human life' has been the foundation of all my work," the claim is entirely justified.[51] Of course, now, however, with "Knowing" become a

[50] See Cruz Vélez, p. 277, for this suggestion. The passage to which he refers the reader is found in Martin Heidegger, *Being And Time*, trans. John Macquarrie and Edward Robinson (New York: Harper and Row, 1962), pp. 96–97, and reads: "The Greeks had an appropriate term for 'Things': *prágmata*—that is to say, that which one has to do with in one's concernful dealings (*prâxis*). But ontologically, the specifically 'pragmatic' character of the *prágmata* is just what the Greeks left in obscurity; they thought of these 'proximally' as 'mere Things'."

[51] Against this claim, based as it is on the notion of *ejecutividad*, Ciriaco Morón Arroyo has objected (*El sistema de Ortega y Gasset*, pp. 212–16, and 367–68.) that in the "Essay in Esthetics," Ortega also writes: "There is nothing we can make an object of cognition, nothing that can exist for us unless it becomes an image, a concept, an idea—unless, that is, it stops being what it is in order to become instead a shadow or outline of itself. With one thing only are we on intimate terms: our Person (*individuo*), our life, but when this inwardness of ours becomes an image it too ceases to be inwardness. . . . But true inwardness, or anything in the act of executing itself (*ejecutándose*), stands at an equal distance from our image of the external and our image of the internal." C. Morón Arroyo's point is that if our Person is as inaccessible as all that, then the *ejecutividad* with which it is synonymous cannot possibly already be, in 1914, "human life," Ortega's "radical (root) reality," since the latter is, by definition, absolute *transparency* and presence. My reply, as this chapter shows, is that Ortega, like Heidegger, already saw in 1913 or 1914 that the problem of knowledge as traditionally framed had indeed been superceded. While antepredicative knowledge was consubstantial with "life," no *cognitive* knowledge, in the old sense, *was* possible because (Heidegger, *Being and Time*, p. 90.): "in

86

Ortega and Transcendental Phenomenology

"kind of Being which belongs to Being-in-the-world" and the problem
of knowledge as such thus "nullified" (Heidegger), the problem for Ortega, and later for Heidegger as well, became not one of how cognition
was possible but of how errors of cognition were possible, that is to say,
the problem became one of authenticity.[52]

Knowing, Dasein achieves a new *status of Being (Seinsstand)* toward a world
which has already been discovered in Dasein itself. This new possibility of
Being can develop itself autonomously; it can become a task to be accomplished, and as scientific knowledge it can take over the guidance for Being-
in-the-world. But a *'commercium'* of the subject with a world does not get
created for the first time by knowing, nor does it *arise* from some way in which
the world acts upon a subject. Knowing is a mode of Dasein founded upon
Being-in-the-world." And Being-in-the-world, "vida espontánea," *ejecutividad*,
human life, are so obvious in what they signify that perhaps Ortega came even
closer to suggesting what he meant with the expression "absolute present." Of
course, an example clears up the matter at once. "My life" in the Ortegean
sense is simply what is "bracketed" when I am reading a novel, nothing more
and nothing less.

[52] Martin Heidegger, *Being and Time*, p. 88.

5

TOWARD A MUNDANE PHENOMENOLOGY: THE LIFE-WORLD, THE REDUCTION

Perception is precisely that kind of act in which there can be no question of setting the act itself apart from the end to which it is directed. Perception and the percept necessarily have the same existential modality, since perception is inseparable from the consciousness which it has, or rather is, of reaching the thing itself. Any contention that the perception is indubitable, whereas the thing perceived is not, must be ruled out.

M. Merleau Ponty, *Phenomenology of Perception*

HEN Merleau-Ponty writes that "Phenomenology is accessible only through a phenomenological method," what he must mean is that to most of its adherents the experience of phenomenology was not so much one of happening on a brand-new philosophy, as it was one of discovering what they had always been looking for.[1] However typical in this regard, Ortega's accession to phenomenology still involved a somewhat serpentine maneuver. Starting out as an unconvinced Neo-Kantian with a will-to-science, he became so enthralled with the descriptive psychology of Husserl's *Logical Investigations* and the philosophical anthropology of the early Scheler that he balked at the seeming reversal in Husserl's *Ideas* of 1913. His consequent reaction was strong enough to make him the first existential phenomenologist. If Husserlian phenomenology was taking so transcendental a turn, then Ortega would repudi-

[1]M. Merleau-Ponty, *Phenomenology of Perception*, trans. Colin Smith (New York: Humanities Press, 1967), p. viii.

ate phenomenology. But, paradoxically, he instead discovered its future direction. By using the Neo-Kantian requirement of a systematic approach as a foundation and the new ontological thesis he extracted from Scheler and the *Ideas* as a first story, he constructed a mundane phenomenology he was pleased to call Vital or Historical Reason.

If, heretofore, it has seemed an exaggeration to claim that Ortega is a phenomenologist, or if his own implicit claim to have discovered new notions of Thinking and Being has seemed in excess of truth, it is simply because invariably these claims have been advanced and examined without regard for their historical context or their textual history. Too often critics have remarked on Ortega's explicit rejection of phenomenology, without noting that what disturbed him were rather those very metaphysical assertions in the *Ideas* that, as we saw in the last chapter, have since troubled J. N. Findlay and a host of others. Nor is it fair to fault Ortega for "misunderstanding" the Husserl of the *Ideas;* on the contrary, as the direction of his mundane phenomenology shows, Ortega seems to have understood the implications of the *Ideas* better than most. For Ortega did indeed anticipate the turn toward historicity in Husserl's later work. In his posthumous *Experience and Judgment* and the Crisis lectures of 1935, and in contrast to the *Logical Investigations* and the *Ideas*, Husserl finally tried to face down the contradictions of his twin aims for phenomenology: on the one hand, to achieve a transcendental philosophy and, on the other, to trace to its source in spontaneous life the horizonal ground against which figural meanings displayed themselves. But certainly no reader of Husserl's *Ideas* in 1913, unless he was also able to attend the latter's lectures from 1905 to 1911 on the phenomenology of inner time-consciousness, could possibly have foreseen this direction of Husserl's later work.[2] And since Ortega, as we have seen, was in no such position, having divided his time between Marburg and Madrid, his prescient development of the early Husserl can only have been managed through clever extrapolations of

---

[2] Husserl's *Phenomenology of Inner Time-Consciousness*, ed. Heidegger, and the former's *Cartesian Meditations* (Sec. 15), seem to escape, in "anticipating," the criticism Ortega levelled at the *Ideas*. For a succinct account of the first of these important works see J. N. Findlay, "Phenomenology and the Meaning of Realism," *Phenomenology and Philosophical Understanding*, pp. 151–52.

his own. This development and these extrapolations, together with his Neo-Kantian criterion of a central problematic, explain how Ortega came to be an existential phenomenologist *avant la lettre*. Of course, in view of Ortega's aversion to the term "existentialist," it seems preferable to call him a *mundane* phenomenologist and to explain just what this means. Once this has been done, and the full extent of Ortega's conversion has been determined, it should be a small matter then to detail the specifics of Ortega's twin notions of a life-world (the substance of his ontological thesis), and the enabling phenomenological reduction. But first we must state the parameters of Ortega's mundane phenomenology.

It will not have escaped the reader's attention that Scheler and Ortega, in the use they made of proto-Gestaltist psychology, largely anticipated many of Merleau-Ponty's characteristic insights. It should thus be no surprise to find that in every particular Ortega's *mundane* phenomenology meets the criteria for phenomenology set down in the "Preface" of Merleau-Ponty's *Phenomenology of Perception*. As a simple introduction the merest listing of coincidences should suffice. To begin with, Ortega's first rejection of sensationism, elementism, and constructionism accord perfectly with Husserl's return to the "things themselves." Ortega, and later Husserl, are at one with Merleau-Ponty in their rejection of all scientific prejudices; all three agreed that "first comes the lived-world, of which scientific schematization is an abstract." Second, instead of the apodicticity of Augustine's or Descartes's "inner man," for all three there is "a subject destined to be in the world," one whose only "truth" is his perspective. Again, on the question of the phenomenological reduction, Merleau-Ponty, Ortega, and the later Husserl, are in essential agreement; the reduction's ultimate lesson is "the impossibility of a complete reduction." For as even Husserl was forced to recognize (in *Experience and Judgment*), its "radical reflection amounts to a consciousness of its own dependence on an unreflective life which is its initial situation." Two further points bear out the remarkable similarity. In speaking of the notion of "essences" Merleau-Ponty gives what amounts to a concise formulation of Ortega's very thesis in *Meditations* when he writes: "The need to proceed by way of essences does not mean that philosophy takes them as its object, but, on the contrary, that our existence is too tightly held in the world to be able to know itself as such at the moment of its involvement, and that it requires the field of ideality in order to become acquainted with and to prevail over its facticity." Not only that, but for Husserl, Ortega, and Merleau-Ponty, the Hegelian notion also pertains that the only "separated essences are those of language." And finally, all three philosophers agree in distinguishing an "intentionality of act," that is, of judgments, from a more fundamental "operative intentionality (*fungierende Intentionalität*), . . . which produces the natural and antepredicative unity of the world and of our life, being apparent in our desires, our evaluations and in the landscape we see."[3]

Certainly no reader familiar with Ortega's essays can fail to be struck by the parallels, and when we add to this the notorious fact that from 1913 on Ortega was the foremost promoter of phenomenology in Spain and Latin America, it seems inconceivable that he should ever have been considered anything but a thorough-going phenomenologist after 1914. The family resemblance between Merleau-Ponty's description of operative intentionality and what García Morente called Ortega's Perspectivism is too strong to be easily missed.

Perhaps the easiest way to show how Ortega's new notion of the life-world came into existence together with his new ontology of pure or absolute presence is by examining Ortega's catalyzing experience of Husserl's *Ideas*. Of course, any version of this story that neglected further reference to Scheler's *Ethics* would be incomplete. But let us begin, as we must, with the famous Section 42 of Husserl's *Ideas* in which he lays down the fundamental distinction between "Consciousness and Reality." Husserl's words are:

It is not an accidental caprice of the Thing nor an accident of "our human constitution" that "our" perception can reach things themselves only and merely through their perspective modifications. On the contrary, it is evident, and it follows from the essential nature of spatial thinghood . . . that Being of this species can, in principle, be given in perceptions only by way of perspective manifestations; and it follows likewise from the essential nature of *cogitationes*, of experiences in general, that they exclude these perspectival shadings; or, otherwise stated, when referring to that which has being in this region, anything of the nature of "appearing," or self-revealing through perspective variations,

[3] M. Merleau-Ponty, *Phenomenology*, pp. ix, xi, xiv–xv, xviii.

has simply no meaning. Where there is no Being in space, it is senseless to speak of seeing from different standpoints with a changing orientation, and under different aspects thereby opened up, or through varying appearances and perspective shadings; on the other hand, it is an essential necessity to be apprehended as such with apodeictic insight that spatial Being in general can be perceived by an Ego actual or possible only when presented in the way described. It can "appear" only with a certain "orientation" which necessarily carries with it, sketched out in advance, the system of arrangements which makes fresh orientations possible, each of which corresponds again to a certain "way of appearing," which we perhaps express as a being presented from this or that "aspect," and so forth.[4]

Quite clearly, Ortega's doctrine of Perspectivism took its departure from the fundamental notion of "perceptual adumbration," first outlined by Husserl in the *Logical Investigations* and again here in the *Ideas* of 1913. But because in *Ideas* Husserl also used the above distinction to establish the indubitability of immanent, and the dubitability of transcendent, perception, in an incredible catachresis of the formerly quite innocent "bracketing" of the world of the natural attitude, Ortega was moved to question root and branch the whole enterprise of phenomenology. And, with Scheler's help, he found its weakest point in the "suspension" or *epoche* itself as described in Sections 31 and 32 of the *Ideas*. For Husserl, after describing the world of the "natural attitude" with a degree of phenomenological rigor that seemed insufficient to Scheler, went on to refer repeatedly to the *epoche* as though it were merely the suppression of an existential judgment. Whereas, both Scheler and Ortega maintained, to be effective the *epoche* would instead have to make "the factor of reality, and not only the judgment of reality about it,"[5] disappear. At the same time, if the factor of reality itself could be bracketed, the result would be the paradoxical defeat of phenomenology. For if, as David Carr writes, "the natural attitude is really the subject matter of phenomenology, it must be relived at the same time it is being overthrown-discovered."[6] And, of course, to escape the

[4] Edmund Husserl, *Ideas: General Introduction to Pure Phenomenology*, trans. W. R. Boyce Gibson (London: Collier-Macmillan, 1969), pp. 121–22.

[5] Max Scheler, "Idealism and Realism," *Selected Philosophical Essays*, p. 316.

[6] David Carr, *Phenomenology and the Problem of History: A Study of Husserl's Transcendental Philosophy* (Evanston, Ill.: Northwestern University Press, 1974), p. 116.

paradox, Husserl was forced to resort to his "splitting of the self" that Ortega felt he had easily faulted in "Essay in Esthetics by way of a Preface" on temporal and logical grounds. In other words, he rejected the transcendental reduction because he would not accept the idea that consciousness could simultaneously "mean" the world and transcend itself. On the other hand, the phenomenological notion of intentionality, which guaranteed the transcendence of the world in relation to consciousness, seemed to Ortega a definitive "refutation of idealism." Especially did this seem so because he viewed intentionality on the model of visual perception, precisely that one mode of consciousness that "maintains its transcendental irreducibility . . . [and] stubbornly resists the Husserlian method." [7] Thus, from Husserl's own notions of "perspective variation" and "perspected variables" Ortega went on to make an original "metaphysical assertion" of his own that García Morente popularized as Perspectivism. In fact the doctrine of Perspectivism in the *Meditations* subsumes three discrete but related notions, and, as a species of notation or umbrella concept, was never meant to be more than an occasional formulation. First, there is its ontological meaning, that is, reality is neither matter nor spirit but a striving-resistance coordinate termed "individual life." Second, Perspectivism means, noematically, that real things are aspectually perceived, that perception is "one-sided"; and third, Perspectivism means, noetically, that things are perceived *as* this or that. Thus: (1) reality itself is perspectival; (2) I see things perspectivally, that is, partially; and (3) I "take up" (I am) a perspective.

It is ironic that Ortega should react so strongly to the Kantian turn in Husserl's transcendental phenomenology, but it compounds the irony that he should reject the central metaphysical thesis of the *Ideas* in favor of a notion similar to the operative intentionality that Husserl would later describe in *Ideas* II. But now that we have seen how Ortega's Perspectivism derives in part from his very contestation of the *Ideas* and observed, in the last chapter, the importance for Ortega of Scheler's holistic phenomenology of perception, how can we still agree to characterize Ortega's mundane phenomenology as original? How can we explain his extreme claims for his own early work?

In the Buenos Aires lectures of 1916, in which Ortega treated his list-

[7] David M. Levin, "Husserl's Notion of Self-Evidence," *Phenomenology and Philosophical Understanding*, p. 59, n. 5.

Toward a Mundane Phenomenology

eners to an account of the latest trends in philosophy, his presentation centers on what he calls "the new science of 'meanings.' " This science, he says, has at last provided philosophy with a definite answer to the relativism, positivism, biologism, and psychologism of the nineteenth century. "Meanings" or ideas—he avoids the term "essences"—are ideal objects that provide the apriotic certainty that is the fundament of philosophy. His rendering here sounds like a popularization of Husserl's *First Investigation*, which deals with theory of meaning. And yet, in what seems a significant departure or extension of what is available in the *Logical Investigations*, Ortega goes on to describe a species of eidetic psychology that is, he reports, the centerpiece of the "current philosophy of life." Moreover, the central, revolutionary thesis of this new life philosophy, one that can only be stated metaphorically, is that:

Consciousness, far from being a relationship of container and contents, with an identity of subject and object—is a relationship of exclusion. The subject and the object are heterogeneous; no two more different things are imaginable. The object and I are face to face, each outside the other, yet inseparably joined. The metaphor corresponding to this third interpretation—in addition to the first, the wax tablet, and the second, the glass and its contents—might well be one of those pairs of divinities so common to Mediterranean mythology, like Castor and Pollux, that were called *De consentes* and *De complices*, the linked gods destined to be born and die together. In this wise the richness of the world is doubled. We escape the eternal monotony of the self, where everything seemed contained within, and now objects appear before us in all their boundless variety.[8]

Of course, in the Buenos Aires lectures Ortega does not claim to be talking about an original philosophy of his own, and perhaps this is just as well.[9] The "new science of meanings" sounds very much like the

[8]"El curso de Don José Ortega y Gasset (1916)," *Anales de la Institución Cultural Española*, I (1912–20), 176.

[9]"El curso," p. 153. Before leaving Spain for Argentina, in the company of his father, Ortega Munilla, and Eduardo Marquina, Ortega was reported in the daily *España* to have announced his intentions: "I will give a course on the most current problems in philosophy. I expect to offer a panorama of the situation of philosophical investigations just as they were when the war interrupted them. I will try to give my impressions of the fruitful renovation overtaking philosophy. I will point out in this cycle of lectures that for philosophy the year 1899 marks off the past from the present." Clearly, this last remark is a preference to the publication date of Husserl's *Logical Investigations*.

phenomenology of the *Logical Investigations,* and the "current philosophy of life," in which Ortega shows such a proprietary interest, bears distinct traces of Scheler's hand. If this is so, what grounds can there be for Ortega's later claims that by 1914 he was already in possession of an original philosophy of his own?

Curiously enough, the answer to this question is made easier, not harder, to fathom by the fact that Ortega's criteria for what constituted a philosophy were—and remained—essentially Neo-Kantian. That meant, above all, as we observed in chapter 3, that philosophy must be systematically organized around a basic problematic, as it was with the "transcendental problematic" of the Neo-Kantians. Thus, on the one hand, Ortega could fault the Husserlian phenomenology of his day for its protestations of ontological neutrality, and, on the other, could claim originality in 1914 because he discovered a new notion of Being implicit in Scheler's non-formal grounding of ethics. In short, because he consciously did for ontology what Scheler had done for ethics, Ortega felt he had earned the right to consider himself an original philosopher. Moreover, like Sartre, Ortega took his departure from Husserl's notion of intentionality in the *Logical Investigations.* In fact, in an essay of 1939 Sartre speaks in precisely those terms used by Ortega in the 1916 lecture cited above. Sartre reveals the same need to resort to metaphor and he draws—with Heidegger's help, of course—nearly the same ontological conclusions. Sartre writes:

Contre la philosophie digestive de l'empirio-criticisme, du néo-kantisme, contre tout "psychologisme," Husserl ne se lasse pas d'affirmer qu'on ne peut pas dissoudre les choses dans la conscience. . . . La conscience et le monde sont donnés d'un même coup: extérieur par essence à la conscience, le monde est, par essence, relatif à elle. C'est que Husserl voit dans la conscience un fait irréductible qu'aucune image physique ne peut rendre. Sauf, peut-être, l'image rapide et obscure de l'éclatement. . . . "Toute conscience est conscience *de* quelque chose." Il n'en faut pas plus pour mettre un terme à la philosophie douillette de l'immanence . . . La philosophie de la transcendence nous jette sur la grand' route, au milieu des menaces, sous une aveuglante lumière. Être, dit Heidegger, c'est être-dans-le-monde. Comprenez cet "être-dans" au sens de mouvement. Être, c'est éclater dans le monde, c'est partir d'un néant de monde et de conscience pour soudain s'éclater-conscience-dans-le-monde.[10]

[10] Jean-Paul Sartre, "Une Idée fondamentale de la phénoménologie de Husserl: L'intentionnalité," *Situations,* I, 32–33.

Toward a Mundane Phenomenology

Although here Sartre is casting about for a middle ground of his own between Husserl and Heidegger—Hegel and Solger are nowhere in view—and although he finally found it in a phenomenological ontology, Ortega's own third metaphor of the *De consentes* or *De complices* places him closer in 1916 to the Merleau-Ponty of *The Structure of Behavior* and *Phenomenology of Perception* than to Sartre, that is, not just beyond Husserl's notion of "pure consciousness," but beyond ontology itself. It was this point that Ortega had in mind when he wrote the long footnote in *The Idea of Principle in Leibniz* with which our study began. That footnote started as a rejection of Husserl's transcendental reduction and of his notion of pure consciousness, but concluded with a statement of Ortega's new "ontology" that really signals the "end" of ontology. Here, again, are the last words of that footnote:

A description that attended strictly to phenomena—I said then (1914)—would state in a phenomenon of consciousness like perception we discover the *coexistence of myself and something*, and that, therefore, this coexistence is not ideality or intentionality, but very reality. So that in the "fact" of perception what we have is: on the one hand, myself, "being-to" the thing perceived, and, on the other, the thing "being-to" me; that is to say there *is* no phenomenon such as "consciousness-of . . . ." as a general form of the mind. Instead, there is the reality that I am, opening out on, and undergoing, the reality that my surroundings are; and the supposed description of the phenomenon "consciousness" becomes a description of the phenomenon "real human life" as the coexistence of myself and the things around me, or my circumstances. *The result, therefore, is that there is not this consciousness as phenomenon and consciousness is a hypothesis, the very one we inherited from Descartes.* (VIII, 274–75, n.)

Of course, a fairly cogent argument could be, and has been, advanced alleging that this quote from *The Idea of Principle* is the result of post-1927, Heideggerian hindsight, and that in 1916 or before, Ortega "believed" in "consciousness" as much and as fervently as did Scheler and Husserl. Fortunately, there is a way of reading Ortega's "Essay in Esthetics by way of a Preface" that will produce a definitive rebuttal of this allegation and salvage, once and for all, Ortega's claim to have been, as early as 1914, an original philosopher and an original ontologist. This reading will also provide, as a corollary, a clarification of Ortega's remark about the interrelationship of those two other philosophical Dioscuri, Being and Thinking.

Toward a Mundane Phenomenology

Unlike "Sensation, Construction, and Intuition," or "On the Concepts of Sensation," "An Essay in Esthetics by way of a Preface," contains unequivocal evidence that, unlike Husserl and Scheler, Ortega had escaped the prison of consciousness by 1914 and had, moreover, evolved a new hypothesis of "human life" to put in its place. It was not Ortega's aim in "An Essay" either to lodge a direct complaint against Husserlian phenomenology, or much less to outline his own new ontology; instead, he merely prepared a philosophical position from which to attack the Expression Theory of Art. His wish was to rebut the "Modern" (Cartesian) idea of subjectivity in order to show that the artist can have no direct, *unmediated cognitive* knowledge of his own or any subjectivity. All reflection, he seems to be saying, even the phenomenological-transcendental reduction of Husserl, grasps only what *was*, never what *is*. Clearly, if, as he says in "An Essay," the "I" is the "executant," it can never be anything but transparent action, and hence, at best, and only later, an Other *for* itself. And so Section Two of the essay concludes: "Now we see why we cannot assume a utilitarian posture with respect to the "I": simply because we cannot place ourselves before it, because a state of perfect interpenetration with anything is indivisible, because it is everything viewed from the inside (*en cuanto intimidad*)" (VI, 252). This seems clear enough; and it suggests the same critique of Husserl that Sartre made some years later. But the curious point for our present purposes is that while Julián Marías adduces this notion of "executivity" as evidence of Ortega's "overcoming" of Husserlian phenomenology,[11] it is this same notion—or rather its illustration —that would cause him to throw up his hands and declare the essay confused and immature. The reason for this consternation would be that Ortega, in the paragraph before the one quoted above, delivers himself of the following "poetic" asseveration:

"I" means, then, not this person as distinct from another, nor, even less, people as distinct from things, but rather all things—men, things, situations—inasmuch as they are occurring, being, executing themselves. Each of us is "I" according to this, not for belonging to a privileged zoological species equipped with a project-making apparatus called consciousness, but more sim-

[11] See his "La primera superación orteguiana de la fenomenología," *La escuela de Madrid*, pp. 257–64.

ply because he *is* something. This red leather box that I have before me is not an "I" because it is only an image I have, and an image is exactly not what is imaged. Image, concept, etc., are always *image, concept of . . .* , and that *of which* they are an image is the real being. There is the same difference between a pain that someone tells me about and a pain that I feel as there is between the red that I see and the being-red of this red leather box. *Being red* is for it what hurting is for me. Just as there is an I-John Doe, there is also an I-red, an I-water, and an I-star. Everything, from a point of view within itself, is an "I." (VI, 252)

Now, in the ordinary way, there is much in this quote that seems to make no sense at all. Especially does it make no sense *not* to make obvious generic distinctions, and strong ones, between a red leather box, John Doe, and a star. But in addition, there is not only the expected central thesis of the essay that I can grasp an image only of my own "I"; there is also the confounding notion that, in the same way, I only "have" images of everything I see, or rather, "see." For on the following page Ortega says: "The thing I see appear on the horizon, resting momentarily on the lengthened clouds of dawn like a gold amphora, is not the sun but an image of the sun; in the same way, the 'I' that I seem to have so close at hand is only an image of my 'I' " (VI, 253).

Thus the fundamental problem with "An Essay" involves two inseparable, peculiarly complementary notions, that of "executivity," and something suggesting Husserl's "persepectival adumbrations," although significantly the notion of "executivity" is given prominence here. Now we could accept "executivity" as a synonym for "viewed from inside" (*intimidad*) and for "our individuality, our life" (*nuestro individuo, nuestra vida*), but scarcely as a characteristic, and a constitutive one, of everything that exists. And so, without having quite understood the relation between this notion of "executivity" and "our life," "our individuality," we must depart from "An Essay" and look elsewhere for a solution to this conundrum. In a very real sense this defeat is a bitter one, because "An Essay in Esthetics" represents a diminutive version of *Meditations on Quixote*, similar in structure and in what it seems almost to say. In fact, it may even be viewed as a replication of *Meditations on Quixote* if we take its terms "*image, concept of . . .*" as equivalents of Culture and the Concept in the major work, and "executivity" as a stand-in for "spontaneous and immediate life" (*vida espontánea e inmediata*). But still the disregard of genera is unacceptable. This is why we must turn to other Ortegean texts in the hope of clarifying the perplexing notion of "executivity" in his early essays.

In this connection there is an apposite passage from *Man and People*, in which Ortega ridicules the French existentialists. Although the word "executivity" does not put in an appearance, the idea itself is there, now in the guise of "my life." This passage is also welcome because, while it bears a family resemblance to the earlier passage quoted from "An Essay," the confusing disregard of genera is no longer in evidence. In *Man and People* we read:

A certain terminological arbitrariness that approaches the intolerable has for several years now permitted the use of the words "exist" and "existence" with an abstruse and uncontrolled meaning that is the very opposite of the one this millenary word really bears and signifies. Today certain people would like so to designate the being of man, but man, who is always an "I"—the "I" each one is—,is the only "thing" that does not exist, but instead *lives* or *is* in the act of living. It is precisely all the other things that are not man, not "I," which *exist*, because they appear, surge, leap up, resist me, affirm themselves within the medium that is my life. (VII, 101)

Here we have the distinction, palpably easier to follow, between man and all else: man "lives" while all other things "exist," exactly as Ortega says in his pessimistic, Cervantean conclusions to *Meditations*. Thus the existentialists stand accused of the very same "terminological arbitrariness" for which, as we recall, Heidegger was taken to task in *The Idea of Principle in Leibniz*. For in this latter work, and in the very pages from which our study set out, Ortega held that Heidegger had substituted the term "existence" (*Dasein*) for the more natural term "life" (*vida*). Of course, the natural response to Ortega at this point is to remind him that it is just as arbitrary to call Whatever-it-is, "life," as it is to call it *Dasein*, or existence. But if we respond in this way it is a sure sign we have not understood where Ortega is heading. What, for example, lies behind his reference to the meaning the millenary word "existence" really has? And if Ortega is not just carping, in what sense is it proper to say man lives but things exist?

In order to clarify this point, we must turn briefly to *Some Lessons in Metaphysics*. The prospect is promising since a subsection of Lesson IV

is called "Parenthesis on the Semantics of Existence: Executive Being."
Ortega has been explaining the meaning of each element in the phrase
"I am in the room." And he has saved the verb "to be" (*estar*) for last.
What, he asks, does this insignificant word mean? and he answers: "my
being in the room is a matter of my existing in what is not myself;
therefore, it is in existing outside of myself, in foreign territory . . ."[12]
In contrast to my being in a heterogeneous element, Ortega says, things
exist in a homogeneous one. The table is a material object existing in
space; I, that is, my life, is neither a material object nor does it take
place in a material space. But this distinction remains opaque until Ortega makes a further one. We distinguish between the being of centaurs
and the being of horses by saying of the first that "they are," and of the
second that they "exist" or that "they really are." The reason Ortega appeals to this distinction is that he wants to illustrate a difference between
"the something that exists and the existence of that something." As he
explains:

The centaur and the horse each has its essence, the one neither more nor less
than the other. But the centaur does not make its essence effective, it is not effectively what it is; the centaur is ineffectively itself—it does not exist. The essence is not executed (*se queda sin ejecución*). Well then, in its primary and
strict sense, the existence of something means the execution or achievement of
that something. (*Unas lecciones*, pp. 90–91)

Existir, therefore, is to execute or "put into effect" an essence, which
the horse does but the centaur cannot do. But everything, a red box, or
John Doe, that (really) *is*, can and does execute its essence. As Ortega
says:

If we say that the whiteness of this wall exists, we mean to say that the essence
of this whiteness is executed, actualized; we would say that the white whitens,
that it makes its whiteness effective. On the other hand, the whiteness of Leda's
swan does not effect its whiteness, does not achieve execution. (*Unas lecciones*,
p. 91)

Both these passages are of inestimable value in answering the question posed initially. Now we can see why Ortega accuses the French ex-

[12]Ortega, *Unas lecciones de metafísica* (Madrid: Alianza Editorial, 1966),
p. 87.

Toward a Mundane Phenomenology

istentialists of arbitrariness, and Heidegger of a catachresis of Being, and see, as well, the justice of his accusations. To say that "existence" is characteristic of man has meaning only in contrast to its syncategorematic pair, essence. But man, unlike all else, has no essence to execute. Thus Ortega has a clear and evident reason for putting "life" or "to live" in place of "exist." This, like *"ejecutividad,"* is the natural way to express the "execution" of *our* "essence." We *live.* But Ortega's appeal to semantic naturalness is not an appeal to Ordinary Language. Far from it. He is alluding, and this is why the word "executivity" (*ejecutividad*) is given pride of place, to the Aristotelian term for existence from the *Metaphysics, "energeía ón."* Here are Ortega's words from *Some Lessons in Metaphysics:* "Instead of using our word 'existence,' Aristotle said 'put to work, operative'—*energeía ón*—, and the Scholastics translated the term saying, 'put in force,' being in act or actuality" (p. 91). The term *ejecutividad* is not only the translation of a German term which Scheler used, but a translation of Aristotle. It derives from the potency-act determination of *ousia* (substantiality). Perhaps Ortega decided he could do no better, in the wake of Brentano's post-1911 questioning of phenomenology's underpinnings, than return to the wellsprings of metaphysics in Aristotle himself.

In perusing *Some Lessons in Metaphysics* we have gone a long way toward explaining the "poetic" passage in "An Essay in Esthetics." Now we understand Ortega's disregard for genera, his lumping together of red boxes, stars, and ourselves as having been done under the aegis of Aristotle. But to fully comprehend the extent of Ortega's escape from the prison of consciousness, instead of returning to "An Essay," we must double back and look more closely at the place in *The Idea of Principle in Leibniz* where Ortega denounces Heidegger's catachresis of the word Being. In doing so we close a circle opened in the first chapter of our study, for the long footnote on Husserl, with which we commenced, was attached, as the reader will recall, to Ortega's discussion of Being in Heidegger *and* Aristotle.

In essence, Ortega's criticism of Heidegger is that he has not, in 1927, reexamined the idea of Being from the ground up. Instead, he went no deeper than the Scholastics, who in fact had less of Aristotle to work from than Heidegger. As for specifics, Ortega taxes Heidegger with

Toward a Mundane Phenomenology

having accepted "the popular opinion that the Greeks did not understand Being in any way other than as 'that which is,' as that which man finds before him." But to assert this about the Greeks is neither correct nor completely honest, in Ortega's view. Of course, he writes:

The Greek conception of Being . . . has a static aspect which derives not so much from being oriented according as the objects are there before him and appear to him as aspects or "spectacles," but because of the fixity or "crystallization" that concepts impose on them. The concept, in effect, is immutable (identical with itself); it does not vary, exert itself, or *live*. It is what it already is and nothing more. But Being to the Greeks, although marked by that fixity and paralysis imposed on it by the concept—and whose projection on the plane of "outward existence," τό ἐχτός, it is—really consists, if I may use the expression, in putting its essence in force, in executing it (*estarla ejecutando*). This aspect of Being, as opposed to its static side, is authoritatively formulated in the Aristotelian idea of Being *as* actuality: ἐνεργεία ὄν (*energeía ón*) the operative Ens. "Be-ing" is the more primordial and authentic operation. "Be-ing a horse" is not only presenting man with the visible form "horse" but *being it from within*, making or supporting its "horseness" in the ontological realm; in short, be-ing a horse is "horsing," as be-ing a flower is "flowering" and be-ing a color is "coloring." Being, in Aristotle, has the valence of an active verb. One cannot mark off, then, the peculiar being of man by saying he is an Ens whose Being consists in his own being "being in jeopardy," in his own existence being problematic for him; because this also happens to the animal and to the plant, although in very different ways in each of the three—plant, animal, and man. (VIII, 278)

Here we seem to have returned to our point of departure in "An Essay in Esthetics." This passage offers us the Aristotelian reason for Ortega's disregard of generic distinctions there. But we also have, perfectly delineated, a static view of being, from without, which corresponds to the "*image, concept of . . .*" of "An Essay" and the Concept of *Meditations*, as a superposition on its dynamic correlate, being-from-within, which perfectly matches the "executivity" of "An Essay" and the "spontaneous life" of *Meditations*. Now no conundrums remain in "An Essay" at all. But what is it that we have uncovered? Have we merely explained an essay in Poetics, and discovered Ortega to have been a continuer of Aristotle in this respect alone? Or have we penetrated to the center of Ortega's underlying philosophical discovery?

Clearly, the latter is the case. The discovery of Ortega's central doctrine or thesis here, present both in "An Essay" of 1914 and, as we shall see, in *Meditations* as well, and central, moreover, *in everything he wrote thereafter*, means that much more than an overcoming of Husserl's idealistic notion of consciousness has taken place. It means that in 1914, in "An Essay" and in *Meditations on Quixote*, Ortega staked out a claim to something quite close to what Husserl would later call the "life-world." And he did this, not with Dilthey's help, nor Heidegger's, but thanks to a careful reading of Scheler, Husserl, Brentano, and Aristotle. To conclude this meta-metaphysical part of the chapter, some further remarks on Ortega's Aristotelian connection are in order, and then we can turn at last to Ortega's approach to the question of the phenomenological reduction.

There is a footnote to the long passage quoted from *The Idea of Principle in Leibniz* in which Ortega refers to his Preface to the Spanish translation of Bréhier's *History of Philosophy*, and in connection with this Preface we find the most telling remarks on Aristotle in Ortega's works. These remarks amount to commentary on a passage from Aristotle's *De Anima*, written during Ortega's exile in Portugal, when he had only Aristotle's text and a commentary by "old Zeller" at hand. And a footnote to this Preface contains the closest thing we have to an acknowledgement of Ortega's filiation to Aristotle.

In the section from the Preface to Bréhier's *History* to which this second footnote is appended, Ortega has dealt with the major thrust of Aristotle's philosophy, namely, his frontal assault on the problem that had perplexed Greek philosophy until his day: the question of movement or change. Ortega says in this regard: "The *previous* idea and, for that reason, the basic idea that Greeks had of Being was that it was an imperturbable stillness. Being for them was the identity of the thing with itself, 'being what it was' for ever and ever, absolute ontological repose" (VI, 409). But Aristotle responded by proposing an ontology of change. And Aristotle did this, explained what he called "movement *sensu stricto*" in *Metaphysics*, Book IX, 1048, b. 33, by supposing, in the case of something white that turned black, that "the thing that is now effectively or actually white is also, and at this time, potentially black" (VI, 410). In other words, as Ortega comments, change would consist in "the passage from what something is potentially to being that effectively, fully or perfectly (*entelequia*), to being it in 'act' or operatively (*energeía*)" (VI, 410). And the reality "change" would then be "a peculiar mode of being that unites the opposing characteristics of potentiality and actuality: it is potential in act or actually" (VI, 411).

Fortunately for Ortega, Aristotle noticed another, different kind of change in addition to "movement *sensu stricto.*" In movement *sensu stricto* the change and its *telos* were different: getting thin was not the same as always being thin; being cured was not the same as being well. Also, stasis ruled again when white had turned to black. Yet with Aristotle's second kind of change none of this applied; the reality of man thinking, "theorizing," meditating, for example, was altogether different. Here, Ortega noted, "as with all change, there was passage, transit, but here there was also the paradoxical condition that thinking was not passage to *another* thing but, on the contrary, an increment, a march, an advance or 'progress toward itself' " (VI, 412). And it was to this movement which was its own *telos* that Aristotle applied his term *act—energeía.* It was this change that for Aristotle was "Being in the plenitude of its meaning."

Obviously, this is only a brief account of Ortega's commentary on Aristotle; but without at least this much the footnote to the Bréhier Preface would be unintelligible. Notice especially how the following words of Ortega might equally refer to what was most enigmatic in "An Essay in Esthetics." This final footnote begins with the importance of Aristotle's conceptualization of the movement of "thinking":

He felt he was seeing Being from within. The Being of things may seem static. The changes and movements of bodies seem to end in stability. But in the reality "thinking," "Being" is not something static, not a quiet figure, but Being making itself, a continual self-creation; in sum, the word "Being" acquires the value of an active verb, of executivity, of making effective. This man, born on the rim of Hellas, substituted a dynamic concept for the static one of the pure Greeks. No longer will Being be exemplified by a geometrical figure that is pure aspect or spectacle; "Being" will henceforth be a thing's effort to sustain itself in existence. . . . The other examples Aristotle adduces in addition to thinking are seeing, being happy, loving, living. These too are movements with their "ending" in themselves. They all belong to the human realm and are "envisioned from within." . . . The notion of an energetic Being triumphs over the notion of static Being. (VI, 415, n.l)

Still, says Ortega, Aristotle could only *glimpse* this energetic Being; he could not "inhabit it and even less use it as the basis for his whole system" (VI, 415–16, n.). But, of course, what Aristotle could not do, Ortega, the "Neo-Aristotelian," could and did do. And he did it, as "An Essay" proves, before or while he wrote *Meditations*.

At last we have an answer to why Ortega considers Being and Thinking Dioscuri and why he suggests that the discovery of a new notion of thinking leads to a new conception of Being, and, of course, why "executivity" has such a prominent place in "An Essay in Esthetics." It was because of his conceptualization of the movement of thinking that Aristotle arrived at the new notion of dynamic Being or *energeía ón*, just as, Ortega felt, as a result of his own superpositivistic or phenomenological scrutiny of Husserl's version of *Selbstbewusstsein*, he himself had discovered a new notion of Being as striving-resistance or "human life." Of course, in "An Essay," Ortega does not yet speak of "my life" as an "absolute (ontological) event," as he does in "Preface for Germans," but rather of "our individuality" (or "Person"), "our life," and especially of "executivity." But if here Ortega seems to overextend the notion of "executivity," that is, to ignore important distinctions between the ontological subject and other objects in the world, as Heidegger accused Husserl of doing, this catachresis is perfectly justified in what is, understandably, a polemical essay against all idealism. Ortega derides the notion of "a privileged zoological species equipped with a project-making apparatus called consciousness" in order to underline his contention that our *primary* relationship with the world is not one of *aistheton* or *noeton* but of *prakton*, and that this relationship can only be seized in a "logicization" as "*image, concept of*. . . ." The problem is that Ortega's absolutism on this point raises the question of whether he in fact can already have in mind in "An Essay" his later ontological category, "my life," or whether, since he also refers to it as "inwardness" in 1914 he is not referring to some psychological category.[13] But our discovery that Ortega's notion of executivity derives from Aristotle's *energeía ón* seems conclusive proof that in 1914 Ortega is speaking in ontological terms, as Aristotle does in his *Psychology*. What is more, there is additional proof

[13] See C. Morón Arroyo, *El sistema de Ortega*, pp. 80–81.

that executivity and "my life" bear more than a family resemblance to each other. It has been argued, for instance, that executivity and "my life" or "life as the fundamental reality" cannot be related topics since Ortega's main thesis in "An Essay"—that there is no unmediated self-knowledge—contradicts his later, repeated characterization of "life" and "my life" as "immediate" and eminently "transparent," as indeed it would have to be as the "medium" in which all else we encounter appears. But to maintain this is to misconstrue both Ortega's central argument in "An Essay" and his later use of the word "transparent" as we have seen. When Ortega speaks in "An Essay" of the impossibility of self-knowledge he specifically has in mind the unmediated self-knowledge implied in Descartes's concept of the *cogito* and throughout the idealist tradition down to Husserl in the *Ideas*. But this argument is refuted by reference to what Sartre calls the pre-reflexive *cogito*. In "An Essay" Ortega could not say "There is the same difference between a pain that someone tells me about and a pain that I feel . . ." if he had meant there was no kind of self-awareness at all. Ortega never suggests we do not know when we are in pain, or even when we are "seeing the sun." Therefore, even in "An Essay" executivity or our own individuality, our life, is accompanied by a constitutive pre-reflexive *cogito*. And, indeed, this is precisely the meaning of the later "transparency" of our life. As Ortega told Frédéric Lefèvre in 1929:

Notre vie a toujours ce caractère essentiel d'être transparent à elle-même.

Le sujet assiste toujours à sa vie. Il "voit" sa vie, il "sait" sa vie. Une douleur de dents que je ne sais n'est pas une douleur. Eh bien, c'est la dimension essentielle du *cogito*, de la pensée cartésienne, d'exister pour elle-même, ce qu'un Allemand appellerait sa réflexivité.

Mais ce qui demeure vraiment curieux c'est que, de la richesse qui est enfermée dans le *cogito* on n'ait jamais fait emploi. On a conservé seulement la pure abstraction de la pensée qui se connait elle-même mais lorsqu'on voit que toute notre vie se connait elle-même, se sait, on découvre que la donnée est bien plus riche. D'abord notre vie n'est pas seulement le sujet qui vit: vivre, c'est s'occuper des choses du monde. . . .

Il suffit de nous mettre d'accord avec nous-mêmes, de traduire en concept purement descriptif le contenu de notre vie immédiate pour trouver un point de départ assez riche, rien, vous le voyez, qu'*en faisant subir au 'cogito' cartésien une dilation* . . .

Cette présence, cette nécessité parfois terrible qu'a toute vie et tout morceau de notre vie de se "savoir" elle-même n'a rien encore d'intellectuel mais toute intellection, toute connaissance n'est qu'une spécialisation et dans une certaine mesure une limitation de ce *savoir élémentaire*. [Italics in original.][14]

Clearly, what Ortega calls *savoir élémentaire* has the same epistemological status as Sartre's pre-reflexive *cogito* and is an even closer approximation of Husserl's "operative" or "founding" intentionality.[15] But although it clearly antedates both conceptions, Ortega's Paris interview did take place two years after Heidegger had published his own analysis of *Dasein* in *Sein und Zeit*. Is there any *more* direct evidence than we have seen that Ortega had formulated a mundane or existential phenomenology before that date? Had Ortega, before 1927, done no more than criticize Husserl's transcendental reduction and put forward a new ontological notion,[16] in "On the Concept of Sensation," "Essay in Esthetics" and *Meditations on Quixote*? That is, did he not also speak, well before 1927, of both a life-world, as we have suggested, *and* a phenomenological reduction of his own? A definitive answer to these questions still stands between us and a correct reading of *Meditations on Quixote*. For while it is abundantly clear that what Ortega has described in the previous essays as "executivity" and "our life," has much in common with Husserl's conception of the *Lebenswelt*, we cannot really say that we have heard Ortega make any clear reference to a phenomenological reduction of his own.

The reason is that thus far we have seen Ortega engage phenomenology only in a descriptive and surreptitious way—in "Sensation, Construction, and Intuition," "On the Concept of Sensation," and "An Essay in Esthetics." What we need is a more specific formulation of a mundane phenomenology, incorporating Ortega's new ontological notion of "executivity" or "life" as fundamental reality, and his notion of a reduction, into a concrete phenomenological program. But this is precisely the kind of program Ortega announced with the publication of

[14]Frédéric Lefèvre, "Une Heure avec José Ortega y Gasset, philosophe espagnol," *Les Nouvelles Litteraires*, No. 339 (April 13, 1929), p. 8.

[15]M. Merleau-Ponty, *Phenomenology of Perception*, p. xviii.

[16]In addition to the implied criticism of "An Essay in Esthetics" see also "On the Concept of Sensation," where Ortega refers to phenomenology as idealism (*O. C.*, I, 255–56).

Toward a Mundane Phenomenology

The Spectator, Vol. i, in 1916. In the Preface ("Truth and Perspective") to what proved to be the first of eight volumes that appeared between 1916 and 1934, Ortega first explained the urgent need for such a program, as well as its substance and its objectives. The subject of the need for this program is introduced at the outset because one of the future subscribers to *The Spectator* had remarked that he was sorry *The Spectator* would only *be* a spectator and not an actor. Here is the substance of Ortega's response:

My distant friend need not worry, ... : life in Spain forces us all into political action, whether we will it or no. The immediate future, a time of social restlessness, will do so with even greater brusqueness. *This is precisely why I must set aside a part of myself that is contemplative.* And what is happening to me, happens to everyone. These last fifty years, within Spain and without, politics—that is, the subordination of theory to utility—has ruled the human spirit. The most extreme expression of this fact is found in a pragmatic philosophy that finds the essence of truth, which is supremely theoretical, in the *practical*, in the useful. So that thought has seen itself reduced to looking for the best means to particular ends, without consideration for the latter. That is politics: utilitarian thinking.

. . . . . .

Of all the lessons life has taught me, the hardest, the most disquieting, the most disturbing, has been the conviction that truthful men are the rarest species on earth. . . . Like Ibn-Batuta, I took up the pilgrim's staff and travelled the world over in search of the saints of This World, men of serene and speculative spirit who receive the pure reflection of the being of things. And I found so few, so very few, that I was dismayed.

. . . . . .

Therefore, one must reaffirm his obligation to truth, his right to truth.

In *The Book of Estates* Don Juan Manuel writes: "*All the Estates of the world are limited to three: one is called the defenders, another the prayer-sayers, and the last, the laborers.*" I'm sorry, Prince Juan Manuel; so constituted the world would be incomplete! I demand a place for the estate called the spectators. Their name has a famous geneology: Plato discovered it. In his *Republic* he reserves a special mission for those he calls τιλοθεχμόνες—*friends of seeing*. These are the speculative ones, and at their head stand the philosophers, the theoreticians—, which means the contemplative ones.

Consequently, *The Spectator* has as its first intention: to build a redoubt against politics for myself and those who share my desire for pure vision, for theory.

The writer, in order to channel his efforts, needs a public, as a liqueur the

Toward a Mundane Phenomenology

glass in which it is poured. For this reason *The Spectator* is a cordial appeal to a public of *friends of seeing,* of readers interested in things apart from their consequences . . .

This does not mean, of course, that Ortega holds theory or philosophy as such to be the supreme value:

I am far from meaning such a thing. I don't assert that theoretical activity is supreme; that we ought to philosophize first and live afterward. Rather, I say the opposite. I only claim that, from time to time, the clear eye of theory should gaze down on spontaneous life, and that then, the theoretical activity be undertaken in all purity and with high seriousness (*"con toda tragedia"*).

It has been necessary to stress the difference between contemplation and life—life, with its political articulation of interests, desires, and accommodations—. Because *The Spectator* has a second intention: it speculates, it looks—but what it wants to see is life flowing before it.

. . . . . .

Truth, the real, the universe, life—however you choose to call it—, divides into innumerable facets, into countless sides, each one facing some one person. If the latter manages to be faithful to his point of view, if he fights off the eternal temptation to exchange his own retina for an imaginary one, what he sees will be a real aspect of the world.

And vice versa: each man has a mission of truth. Where his eye is, there is no other: no eye but mine sees what I see of reality. We are all unexpendable, necessary. . . .

Reality, then, is given in individual perspectives. Something in the background for one person, is in the foreground for someone else. A landscape composes its sizes and distances according to our retina, and our heart metes out the grace notes. To the visual and the intellectual perspectives the valuative perspective adds a rich complexity. Instead of arguing, let us integrate our seeing in a generous spiritual collaboration, and, as distinct creeks flow together in a bold river, let us constitute the torrent of the real.

The luminous surge of existence rushes by us: let us intercept its forward movement with the sensitive prism of our personality, and on the other side, on paper, in a book, a rainbow will appear. This is the only way to rid theory of its tone in gray minor.

And, finally, in the same 1916 volume, but in a later essay, we find this closing apostrophe to the "friends of seeing":

Poets, thinkers, politicians, you who aspire to originality, to ever new worlds! Don't attempt to create things, because this might be an objection against your work. A created thing is never more than a fiction. Things are not created, but invented, in the best old acceptation of the word: they are found. And the new things, the undiscovered mines, are not to be found somewhere off beyond, but this side of, the already known and consecrated, nearer to inwardness and the domestic, nearer your very centers, filling the humblest hours of your lives with a rich vein. (II, 15–20, 28)

Clearly, then, Ortega's mundane phenomenology is a program and a method for discovering—in John O'Neil's phrase—"the project toward the world that we are."

Naturally, the closest discipline to this examination is what Ortega referred to in his 1916 Buenos Aires lectures as (phenomenological) psychology. Here, in a somewhat more technical vein than in *The Spectator*, Ortega spoke of the kind of "spiritual exercises" the "friends of seeing" would have to submit themselves to. Since what he called the biological "principle of vital utility" is continually forcing us to engage our attention in material objects, we are normally disinclined to notice the essential structures, the ideas or schemata with which we appropriate aspects of the world. And yet these "ideas" are an infinite resource of apodictic knowledge. As Ortega explained in Buenos Aires: "The spontaneous life of consciousness, when we reflect on it and live in the reflexive attitude, offers us an infinite number of 'objects' that are indubitable. This obvious point is the foundation of philosophy. We must start out, not from things, but from our ideal states themselves, in which we can have absolute faith."[17]

Nevertheless, he continued, because they are so close to us, and because of a constitutional prejudice in favor of the real, it requires a special *tessitura* to perceive these dispositional schemata in ourselves:

Philosophical "objects" are essentially spiritual or mental ones; we use them constantly, but only the philosopher has the habit, the *tessitura*, of making them the objects of his mental vision the way the grammarian does with words. In the realm of real things nothing is closer to us than psychic objects, those realities which constitute our person, and nevertheless, in the realm of immediate knowledge nothing is so far removed. ("El curso," p. 171).

Clearly this is the same cognitive dilemma referred to in "An Essay in Esthetics" which led to the apparent division of Being into "executivity" and "image or concept of." As Ortega stated it in 1916 in Buenos Aires:

[17]"El curso de José Ortega y Gasset (1916)," p. 169.

Toward a Mundane Phenomenology

Of all that we have before us, we only see at each instant what is of immediate concern for our life. The animate creature is all action; his perception is geared to intervene in reality. On the other hand, theory and contemplation are an essay, an effort, the desire, to grasp things without deforming them, preserving them in all their purity and integrity so as to reproduce them as they are in themselves. The most genuine characteristic of thinking is to reflect things as they really are.[18]

In fact, as we see here, in a manner similar to the Husserlian bracketing of the being or non-being of its "object," the Ortegean reduction as *"theoria"* attempts to sever all our utilitarian entailments with practical, "biological" life. Therefore, the philosopher and the authentic man are generous and ascetic in attitude; instead of taking their ideas of things for the things themselves, that is, the reduced, merely symbolic schematizations for the things themselves, they know that the world is infinitely more variegated and bountiful than any possible conceptualization or "idea" of it. Thus, to Ortega's way of thinking, there is a close kinship among the philosopher, the authentic man, and the artist; all three, indeed, are mundane phenomenologists. Instead of reducing the "concrete qualitative fullness of the world" to "bare symbols for . . . the most elementary, most general, and most forceful drives" of biological life, they allow life to well up before them in all its unconditioned richness. And they are able to do this because they have learned to turn away from practical, external action and to discover in their hearts, beneath the socially determined layers of personality, beneath the already institutionalized schemata, new and original forms of expression and existence. Thus a reduction, not unlike Husserl's "philosophical" or historical reduction, is in order. Not only because we are always *already* caught up in "life," since life is a *potentia apetetiva*, a having-to-do with *pragma*, but, additionally, and no less importantly, because "life" too must be salvaged from a similar subordination to the false value of utility: life, especially, must be rediscovered as a value in its own right. Of course, Ortega's own notion of "life" has none of the religious overtones found in Scheler. Life in Ortega's essays is only discontinuous, spontaneous, *human* life; precisely that life-as-value that he proposes to salvage in *Meditations on Quixote, The Theme of Our Time,* and in *The*

[18]"El curso," pp. 163–64. See also Section Nine of *The Dehumanization of Art*, for a complete description of Ortega's reduction.

Toward a Mundane Phenomenology

Dehumanization of Art. If this fundamental point has been misunderstood by students of Ortega, it is because, like Husserl's, Ortega's methodological proposal is paradoxical. At one and the same time he urges both a distancing from life in contemplation (*theoria*) and the apotheosis of life as a supreme value.

While not exactly given to speaking in parables, because he took the role of philosopher *in partibus infidelium* seriously, Ortega did, now and then, resort to an especially telling illustrative example. And of all these, the most graphic, the most revealing, deals precisely with this paradoxical overthrow-discovery of the project toward the world that each of us is. In varying contexts, and significantly, for the first time in "An Essay in Esthetics" of 1914, Ortega speaks of gazing through a windowpane at a garden or landscape. In the most complete version of this image, from a 1919 Madrid lecture, published as "The Perception of the Other" in 1929, we read:

When we look through a windowpane, our gaze, and with it our attention, pierces the glass without pausing there and becomes attached to the surfaces of the objects that make up the landscape: like a tentacle of the mind our glance pats the blue flank of a distant mountain, slips down its sides, crosses the floor of the valley and spends its fine thrust in the cotton clouds that float on the horizon. Doing this requires no effort at all on our part: we only have to give free rein to our attention, letting it direct our gaze. But if instead we want to see the window glass itself and not the landscape, we become aware of the extraordinary effort required to keep our gaze focused on the transparent surface of the glass. Accustomed to having the windowpane be the passage and medium through which we see everything else, it takes a good deal of work to make it the end object of our seeing. (VI, 154–55)

Now, although as used here, the image of the glass illustrates, not the ideal objects of esthetics, but a point of (philosophical) psychology, in both instances the illustrative image has the weight of a methodological parable. Since, as Ortega writes in the same essay, life is a constant having-to-do with things around us, since man's fundamental task is to dominate his circumstances, because we are so caught up in this encounter we gaze right through the transparent, and hence to us invisible, medium of our spontaneous lives, overlook it completely as a separate value, and instead see objects set out as objective and independent entities. But, in fact—as Ortega hints in *Meditations on Quixote*—to so see objects is a scientific, philosophical, and cultural prejudice; they are objects only because we have made them so, and made them these objects rather than others, depending on our needs.[19] Therefore, what we must have is a method that will allow us to uproot ourselves from our objectivist stance so that we can focus on the very transparency itself, that is, on what is for Ortega the ultimate ontic-ontological medium: "My life." To do this, as he makes quite clear in the first two "Confessions of *The Spectator*" and in *Meditations on Quixote*, will be to place our individual and collective destinies once more in our own hands. For once we have managed to perceive "objects" as epiphanies in our lives we will find the extent to which their *meaning for us* is an individual and collective creation, or "interpretation" as Ortega prefers to say.

Clearly the profound change of attitude that Ortega demands here is closer to Husserl's *historical* than to his transcendental phenomenological reduction. But unlike Husserl, who had to labor against an initial idealistic *parti pris* of *Selbstbewusstsein*, as early as 1914 Ortega saw that a historical reduction was the only one possible. If there *were* unmediated self-*knowledge*, as the Cartesian tradition supposed, then Husserl's division of self into noetic and noematic "halves" to achieve his discovery-setting aside of the natural attitude would not be self-contradictory. But as Ortega makes clear, there is an older tradition beneath the reigning Eleatic one. As we have seen, he even finds it in Aristotle, and it certainly undercuts idealism's *Selbstbewusstsein*. This tradition holds that there is a fundamental and infrangible division between Being and Having. And Ortega, like Marcel and Merleau-Ponty, has simply unveiled—and this is the marrow of his philosophical thesis—this very real and insoluble cognitive "ambiguity" or dilemma. This is also the essence of his implicit critique of Husserl in "An Essay":

[19] As Ortega writes in a later essay, echoing *Meditations on Quixote*: "All seeing is, then, looking; all hearing, a listening, and, in general, our entire cognitive faculty is a luminous beam, a lantern that someone, behind, points at now one, now another quadrant of the universe, distributing here light and there shadow over the enormous and impassive surface of the cosmos. *We are not, therefore, ultimately mere cognition, since this depends on a prior and a deeper system of preferences existing in us*" [italics mine]. "Corazón y cabeza," (VI, 152). The essay originally appeared in *La Nación*, Buenos Aires, in July 1927.

Toward a Mundane Phenomenology

since being ("true being") is now defined as being-from-within or operative being (*ejecutividad*), we do not and cannot have true and immediate *knowledge* of any being(s). We can "be" or else we can "have," that
is, "Know," but only after the fact. Phenomenological reflection, like
any other kind of reflection, is as subject to time's strictures as music,
and is thus a proper subject for history, or at least biography.

This is the ultimate meaning of the Ortegean dictum that we must
always strive to view things, if we want to understand them, in *statu
nascendi*. And this is also why his Vital Reason was always, even from
the beginning, Historical Reason as well. This is nowhere more clearly
stated than at the end of Ortega's 1935 essay, "History as a System":

> Historical Reason, on the other hand, accepts nothing as a mere fact, but in-
> stead dissolves each fact back into the *fieri* from whence it comes: it *sees* how a
> fact comes to be a fact. It does not try to explain human phenomena by reduc-
> ing them to a repertoire of instincts and "faculties"—which would be, in effect,
> brute facts, like impact and attraction—, but instead it shows what man does
> with those instincts and faculties, and even explains how they—the instincts and
> faculties—came to be "facts," for they are nothing more, of course, than
> ideas—interpretations—that man has made at a certain juncture of his life (VI,
> 50).

As the reader conversant with Husserl's *Ideas* II or with Merleau-Ponty's
revision of the later Husserl will have realized, what the Ortegean reduction achieves is not only a suspension of philosophical theses
through their "discovery," but an "overcoming" of the scientific *natu-
ralism* that Merleau-Ponty saw as characteristic of Husserl's whole first
and major phase.[20]

[20] M. Merleau-Ponty, "The Philosopher and His Shadow," *Signs*, trans. with
an introd. by Richard C. McCleary (Evanston, Ill.: Northwestern University
Press, 1964), p. 163.

6

MEDITATIONS ON QUIXOTE
AS MUNDANE PHENOMENOLOGY

In the last analysis, phenomenology is neither a materialism nor a philosophy of mind. Its proper work is to unveil the pre-theoretical layer on which both of these idealizations find their relative justifications and are gone beyond.

M. Merleau-Ponty, "The Philosopher and His Shadow," *Signs*

I n what has gone before we have tried to suggest that, an unusual *tempo lento* in its explicit public revelation notwithstanding, Ortega's philosophy—his new ideas of Being and Thinking—were precipitated "all at once," and at a much earlier date than has commonly been allowed. This was possible because, when Ortega came to read Husserl's *Ideas* in 1913, he did so from the vantage point of the *Logical Investigations* and Schelerian phenomenological psychology. To show how this was possible, we have been obliged to unpack and expand in time an event that may have taken no time at all. This was done in the course of an examination of the essays written prior to, and contemporary with, the final rewriting of *Meditations*, which, with José Gaos, we place in the spring and early summer of 1914. Our purpose has been to imagine the discrete steps in a process of growth and thought, to show how—as Ortega himself seems to suggest—this process could have been quickened by a reading of Husserl, and, finally, to locate the "birth" of Ortega's "system" at a date prior to, or contemporaneous with, the writing of his first book. Our task for the rest of this study is to explicate the *Meditations* in such a way that they may be seen to support this, our principal contention.

One approach would be to point to isolated passages in the latter work and say that here Ortega was expounding his doctrine of human life and that there he was speaking of vital or historical reason. But this approach has at least two inconveniences. The first is that there *are* no isolated passages in the *Meditations*, and the second is that Ortega is simply not speaking of, that is to say, not expounding, either doctrine in the usual sense at any juncture of the book. And to suggest that he *is* doing so, is to transgress against the mode of being of the *Meditations* themselves. Yet to admit to these two inconveniences is to allow that we may not be able to use the *Meditations* to support our, or any other, contention about the birth date of Ortega's philosophy.

Fortunately there is another way in which the *Meditations* can be used as the capstone of our argument; one that is suggested by the two inconveniences mentioned above. For if there are no isolated passages, and if the exposition of Ortega's philosophical theses is not to be disentangled from the book's several parts, we ought to direct our inquiry instead to the question of the primary purpose of the book as a whole. Indeed, there exists the danger, if we only set out to find the philosophical bricks of which the work is constructed, of flattening it out, and of forcing to the surface what is meant to exist at a more profound level. If, then, we are to respect the work's manner of being, and to respect equally its silences and its utterances, we can only begin our examination by considering Ortega's purpose in writing the *Meditations*.

It was, of course, as Ortega says in the section "To the Reader," to encourage, by example, "experiments in a new Spain" (53).[1] Taking up again the abandoned project of the 1910 "salvations," Ortega meant his "meditations" to do for philosophy and culture what his speech "The Old and the New Politics," the League for Political Education, and the Republican Reform Party were to do in the political sphere. Thus the *Meditations* would examine and actualize the potential of a whole range of Spanish things, from *Don Quixote* to the bullfight in its classical, eighteenth-century form; and if Ortega began with the most important of Spanish cultural values, the *Quixote*, it was simply because he wanted to renew interest in a hierarchy of Spanish values that the nineteenth century had been unable to perceive. Yet Ortega's work was to be exemplary, and his purpose primarily a national, not a personal,

[1] José Ortega y Gasset, *Meditations on Quixote*, ed. Julián Marías, tr. Evelyn Rugg and Diego Marín (New York: Norton, 1961). Unless otherwise described, all references to *Meditations on Quixote* are to this edition.

achievement. As he said in 1908, in answer to a criticism by Maeztu, "I have no intention of making the national soul the fiefdom of a few university brahmans . . ."[2] His ostensive purpose, then, was to show Spaniards at large how to rediscover and re-assume the burden of their destiny as a nation among other European nations; and the way to promote this was not to expound a philosophy of vital reason as such, however exemplary that would have been, but to show, in an autobiographical and paradigmatic way, that Spain must begin by accepting "the heroic necessity of justifying its destiny and of throwing light on its mission in history" (103). Ortega would speak for Spain in his own voice, because fate, his circumstances, his vocation, decreed he should do so: just as fate had also decreed that the maximum circumstance (and value) confronting him should be the *Quixote*, and that he should have been born with a vocation for philosophy. This was simply his destiny and there could be no evasions.

Given Ortega's particular *tessitura* and the state of Cervantes studies in 1913, the first cultural "experiment" in a new Spain "would necessarily take the form of freeing the *Quixote* of all its nineteenth-century impedimenta, of the overlays of interpretation that kept it from assuming its rightful place as the primary touchstone of Spanish values." For, as Ortega made clear in "The Old and the New Politics," what passed in 1914 for the true tradition of Spain was a hindrance to, and a perversion of, "the Spain that could have been" (106). Cervantes was a "Spanish plenitude," and Spain could only discover herself by uncovering the selfhood of Cervantes. To ascertain "the Cervantean way of dealing with things" would be to come into possession of "a philosophy and an ethics, a science and a politics" (107).

Still, the reader new to *Meditations* may put the book down with the feeling that, while much has been promised, at most Ortega has given a perspicacious but incomplete study of the novel as genre. At first (and even second) reading, its reader may feel that too much has been undertaken, too little concluded. In his critical edition, Julián Marías gives a partial answer to these natural reservations.[3] The first section, "To The Reader," is a general introduction to the entire series of ten meditations

---

[2] Ortega, *Obras Completas*, i, 122.   [3] Ortega, *Meditations*, pp. 12–13.

Meditations As Mundane Phenomenology

as projected for the second time in 1914, and the second part, or "Preliminary Meditation," is both a methodological introduction to the ten meditations and a preface to the series of three meditations on the *Quixote*, while the elusive "Cervantean manner of dealing with things" would certainly have been the explicit subject of the second and perhaps the third of these meditations. But the fact that the Cervantean Meditations Two and Three were never written has had the unfortunate effect of making it difficult to see the extent to which "Cervantes' way of dealing with things" is already implicit in the three parts that constitute the only *Meditations on Quixote* we know. This, in turn, has made possible the current *over*-interpretation of that work and made impossible a clear understanding of all that the Cervantean perspective was to mean for Spain, not to mention all it meant for Ortega himself. Here, of course, Ortega's latter-day readers are at a disadvantage, while his more fortunate contemporaries could know perfectly well what he was about. At least, in the present instance, we have evidence that Ortega gave broad additional hints of what he was up to, as when he lectured on the subject of landscape as milieu in the Madrid Ateneo on April 9, 1915. On that occasion, with Antonio Machado, among others, in the audience, he was quite explicit about the Cervantean perspective or what Cervantes scholars have appropriated as the Perspectivism of the *Quixote*:

We may judge a man's actions absurd without perhaps realizing they are reactions to things before him that we do not see. To the common herd the gestures of the pure and heroic man always seem farcical; and that is because the commonalty does not find those delicate objects we call the noble, the dignified, the excellent, in its landscape. They are not equipped to perceive them. There are some people blind to what is noble just as there are others deaf to cannon fire.

There is, therefore, no other way to entirely understand our fellow man than by making an effort to reconstruct and divine his landscape, the world he engages and with which he carries on a living dialogue. And, conversely, we can only correctly see a landscape that is not ours by faithfully seeking out the eye that corresponds to it, the sole watchtower organically related to it.

This, gentlemen, is the Cervantean manner of dealing with things: to take each individual with his landscape, with what he sees, not with what we see—to take each landscape with its corresponding individual, with the one fully capable of seeing it. Thus Don Quixote, to end that endless conversation, says to

Meditations As Mundane Phenomenology

Sancho: "Very well, Sancho, what looks to you like a barber's basin, looks to me like Mambrino's helmet, and to someone else will look like a third thing."[4]

Of all that Ortega wrote immediately after *Meditations*, this comes closest to the center of what he began there and would have completed in the two successive and concluding *Meditations on Quixote*, "How Was Miguel de Cervantes Accustomed to View the World?" and "The Halcyonism of Cervantes." In the unwritten works he would have closed the circle, gradually thematizing or drawing forth his own Spanish philosophy, which was already given *in nuce* in the introductory section to the published *Meditations*. It is here that he breaks into the circle of language. Once that is done, we have the fundamental backward step of *Meditation One* which shows how Spain is different from Europe, and this gives the first principle and justification of the philosophy he would have "discovered" in Cervantes' style in Meditation Two, and finally possessed entire as Cervantes' "halcyonism" in his third and last meditation on the *Quixote*. But in the above passage we see only how Ortega would have gone on in Meditation Two. From the published "Preliminary Meditation" we learn in a general way how culture is originated and that the process is reversible, that it works both ways; but only at the end of the part entitled "First Meditation" do we begin to glimpse how, in particular, new areas of culture arise through an act of heroism—an act, paradoxically, of absolute limitation, in which the "hero" of the first "To The Reader" section ("the hero advances, impetuous and unswerving") is reversed, and now must attend *only* to himself, be authentically himself, and yet eschew all custom and habit. However, in *Meditations on Quixote* as published, this aspect of the tragic hero is primarily and simply a counter-motif for the final section about Darwin and the novel.

While it may seem strange to speak at such length of unwritten meditations, it is useful, even necessary, to do so, especially since so much has been said about the extent to which Ortega's writing, and none more so than the published *Meditations*, are "icebergs," that is, submerged presences. In the light of what we have said, however, they can

[4]Ortega, "Temas del Escorial," *Mapocho*, IV, No. 1 (1965), 8–9.

be seen to be icebergs only in the sense that Ortega knew what each of the three meditations on the *Quixote* was to contain when he dated the preface of Meditation One in July 1914. They are *not* icebergs in the sense of his having and yet not having a clear idea of what he was doing, what he had done, and what he would do next.

For this reason, while the Cervantean consideration of each man together with his landscape, as revealed in the 1915 Ateneo lecture, is both the key to the Cervantean "esthetic," his way of seeing the world, and the objective correlative of the aphorism that condenses Ortega's philosophy of vital or historical reason, its presence in *Meditations on Quixote* must not be confused with the purpose of this first meditation as a whole. That purpose, in addition to being one of grounding Ortega's philosophy in human life and national history, and in addition to giving a quick preview of his philosophy as thesis, method, and program, was to show by example what Spain must accept from Europe in order to achieve an integral selfhood, and then what Spain—as exemplified in the gift of Cervantes' novel—is in a position to offer Europe in exchange. But the main point of this meditation is that only if Spain first adopts a measure of phenomenological or non-Mediterranean ideality—that is, "distance"—will she be in a position to explain to herself and to Europe all that is philosophically profound in Cervantes' irony. And so in 1914 Ortega set out to achieve this twofold purpose. First, to add an upper story of ideality to the Spanish consciousness, and then to show how ideality is the necessary·complement of the Spaniard's own "impressionism." What becomes clear, of course, once the two parts are fitted together or more exactly, juxtaposed, is that they are immediately related to Being-from-without and Being-from-within in Aristotle, and to the notions of "image, concept of . . ." and "executivity" in the contemporary "Essay in Esthetics by Way of a Preface." However, in *Meditations on Quixote*, Ortega stresses the need for a return to a dialectical reintegration of the two terms and hence the later oxymoron, "vital reason." Of special concern in this meditation is a philosophical and Spanish-European convergence, although Spaniards must first be made aware that there *are* two terms to be combined. One might almost say that, far from expounding his philosophy of vital reason in the *Meditations*, what seems most urgent to Ortega is a "dismantling" of that philosophy so as to show Spaniards something of the prehistory of its parts.

Once this is understood we are in a position to say in what way the *Meditations* is a philosophical work. No philosophy, Ortega felt, deserved the name unless it could do what phenomenology, purporting to be the theory of theories, had not been able to do thus far. And that was to found itself, to illuminate a philosophical area large enough to encompass its own origination in the ante-predicative world of human life. This is why a full comprehension of *Meditations* requires that we view it as philosophical autobiography, "fictionalized" for the same dramatic reasons that Sartre's *Being and Nothingness* is in places fictionalized, but according to a different mode. By 1914 Ortega's philosophy of vital or historical reason had come into existence, but the exemplary task at hand was to show its continuity with a lived situation; to show, moreover, its paradigmatic character as a repeatable event, as Ortega's desire for an Aristotelian holism was a repetition, a distant echo, of a similar desire on the part of Cervantes; and in the process to suggest that, most important of all, the act of thematizing one's spontaneous life might, and must, be repeated again and again. If one wanted to reduce the major thrust of *Meditations on Quixote* to a sentence or two, one could say that Ortega urged on Spain a qualified acceptance of ideality, at least enough for Spaniards to be able to see the project toward the world that they were.[5] In point of fact, it mattered little if that phenomenological ideality was itself, as Ortega had Cervantes say, only a fiction.

In considering the *Meditations* we will no longer be concerned in a direct way with the origination of Ortega's new ideas of Being and Thinking. Naturally his new idea of Thinking, as a small island in a sea of life, is the method of *Meditations*, even though what is stressed here, no less than in *The Theme of Our Time*, is an integration. And, similarly, his new idea of Being, the doctrine of "Life as the fundamental reality" itself, need not detain us. A great deal has been written about the way this figures in the *Meditations* and, in fact, one could say that this particular element has been too much in view. So much so that its op-

[5] John O'Neill, *Perception, Expression, and History: The Social Phenomenology of Maurice Merleau-Ponty* (Evanston, Ill.: Northwestern University Press, 1970), p. 23.

posite number, which ought really to occupy the center of this Meditation, is almost lost sight of, or at least misunderstood. And by opposite
number I refer to the theory of the Concept or Idea, the form Ortega's
new notion of thinking takes here. Perhaps on this point more than on
any other, a complete understanding of the *Meditations* depends; thus,
in the present chapter it will receive all our attention. In many ways the
notion of the concept is the keystone of the *Meditations*, for without a
clear understanding of what he intends by this notion, the possibility
that by 1914 Ortega had evolved a philosophy of vital or historical
reason is difficult to conceive.

Much of the misunderstanding of Ortega's notion of the concept in
Meditations derives from the fact that he seems to be speaking of a static
entity. To such an extent is this the case that, in spite of the careful
preparation for its introduction with a description of the woods, it is not
altogether clear how the parts of his argument fit together. Instead, the
description of the woods seems to be no more than a way of suggesting
to the reader the relatedness of man and his circumstances. And this has
the effect of setting the notion of the concept off by itself. The result is
that it has seemed no more than an idea borrowed from Kant. Indeed, it
has this air about it, just as it has an equally Platonic ring. But we may
set these overtones aside and descend to a profounder level.

In view of Ortega's intention in *Meditations* to add a layer of ideality
to the Spanish consciousness, and because of his public sponsorship of
phenomenology in Spain, critics have suspected that, if not Kant, then
Husserl, Meinong, and the early Brentano, stand behind Ortega's notion of the concept. In fact, no one, familiar with Ortega's writings and
public lectures of the period right after he completed *Meditations*, and
familiar as well with the proliferation of superiora attendant upon the
birth of continental phenomenology, can have missed the echoes in Ortega's words. Therefore, it has always been supposed that this variety of
fervid idealism was present in *Meditations* too. Is it not a major part of
Ortega's argument there that Spain must rise above her spontaneity and
"fix" her impressions in a provisionally static system, that is, culture?
And is not culture in *Meditations*, according to Ortega, the concept
writ large? Stated this way, it seems that Ortega's notions of culture and
the concept are definitely within the idealist tradition. We must, there-

fore, examine anew what culture and the concept share, and in the process show how in *Meditations* these two notions retain few of their transcendental associations from the philosophies of Kant, Cohen, and Husserl. This is essential, since in order to qualify as mundane phenomenology Ortega's *Meditations* must steer a middle course between the Scylla of materialism and the Charybdis of philosophy of mind.

We can best begin our discussion by recalling that Ortega did adopt the phenomenological notion of intentionality, with its absolute distinction between imagining and the thing imagined, and then went on to focus, not primarily on the psychological "act" of imagining as Brentano did, nor primarily on the ideal objects and objectives intended as Husserl and Meinong had, but instead on all that was implicit in the peculiar relation of exclusion pertaining between the two poles. In fact, as we saw, in 1914 when Ortega rejected Husserl's notion of "pure consciousness" in favor of the primordiality of executivity (*ejecutividad*), derived from Scheler's and Aristotle's views, he had also to dismiss the disembodied ideal objects intended by pure consciousness. But while his revolution in ontology freed him from the prison of consciousness (Husserl) and of culture (Cohen), he was now faced with the challenge of developing an adjustment in the theory of knowledge. For while it was admirable to invite Spaniards to go out and generate "culture" on their own instead of borrowing it or living off the past, it would have been cavalier of Ortega neither to explain how this was to be done, nor to assure their protocultural concepts some truth status.

Since now, in the interests of authenticity, no point of view could be feigned, and reality would be *interpreted*, not invented, it followed that in the old sense, absolute and certain knowledge was no longer possible. This was clearly what led Ortega to make a virtue of necessity by saying that in any case absolute knowledge was only an abstraction and a falsification; and that, moreover, truths in the usual sense must be replaced by truth to one's own absolutely limited perspective on the world. Yet in fact a kind of absolute, although partial, truth was still conceivable under the new ontology. Concepts, and by implication, cultures, are still true with a *kind* of self-evidence, since each corresponded to one of the "faces or sides" of Ortega's *kosmos noetos*, his ante-predicative reality. But what Ortega has still to explain is how this partial, aspectual "truth," whether ultimately thematized as concept or culture, is in *origin* a *human* creation; something that can be said to have passed first, as in *Meditations*, through a human heart. And there is also the difficult question of how differences *in* experience, and hence different meanings *of* experience, can be said to arise at all. This was indeed the crux of the matter inasmuch as Ortega is urging Spaniards, and especially his contemporaries, to create *new* values and imagine *new* objectives in an effort to bring to light a new Spain.

Thus far, in preparing to read *Meditations on Quixote*, we have been reaffirming the consistency of its surface level of meaning; we have been treating things that lie, so to speak, in the public domain. In spite of the revolutionary nature of Ortega's thesis and program, and despite his elliptical style, we have so far touched only on what every reader must have already sensed is there. At this juncture, however, in order to learn more of the "how" of the *Meditations*, we must delve deeper. And here we break Ortega's injunction against forcing to the surface what he left in abeyance; but we do so as a last resort, to precipitate the reader the more quickly into a complete understanding of Ortega's first book.

Ortega spoke, as early as 1913, of an inborn or acquired mechanism of selection, of attentional and inattentional zones of consciousness, but without a clearer understanding of this point too much of *Meditations* remains obscure. For the idea of the concept, the idea of culture, and the whole discussion of "Germanic mists" and Spanish "impressionism" revolve around this very point. What is more, without a clear understanding here, the extent to which *Meditations* is science and philosophy, *episteme* and not *doxa*, or even the extent to which it is a serious contribution at all, and the keystone of Ortega's program for Spain, is not so much lost from view as never looked for. To all this it is incidental to add that we also miss the extent to which Ortega anticipated the anthropological cast of Merleau-Ponty's genetic phenomenology.

The best way to broach this curious subject is to recall Ortega's extraordinary diagnosis of the Spanish way of being in the world. Near the end of *Meditations* he warns, as a result of this diagnosis, and with an eye to a solution, that Spaniards are, because of their abject "impressionism," in danger of being transformed into "back doors on the highway through which a throng of objects come and go" (85). They are in danger, because of their innate lack of ideational powers, of never moving forward as a people, of not being able to build on what has gone before or to support what is to come. This is why Ortega calls Spain a "frontier culture." Yet if we keep in mind his diagnosis as it might pertain to individuals, it is astounding to realize that Ortega's description of Spaniards, as prime exemplars of the genus Mediterranean Man, is in every respect similar to that of the brain-injured subjects that Gelb and Goldstein reported on in their famous study on the amnesia of color names.[6]

Working within a narrow theoretical framework, these two psychologists were able to distinguish a "concrete" and a "categorial" attitude in subjects given the task of sorting color patches. The normal subjects, they found, were "not confined to abiding by the immediately given experiential features of perception," but were able to and did adopt an active attitude, a categorial one, and so imposed principles of classification on the perceptual data.[7] With brain-injured patients, on the other hand, just the opposite was true. They were unable to adopt the categorial attitude. Instead, when they matched colors they changed inexplicably from one criterion of selection to another, now sorting according to hue, now according to brightness. This was because

Every brain injury entails . . . a regression to the level of merely concrete behavior and attitude. Only that exists for the patient which offers itself in perceptual experience. Within the content of actual experience, there is no differentiation between the experiential features as to their relevancy and significance. . . . *The patients are somehow overwhelmed and overpowered by actual experience imposing itself upon them by a force of constraint from which they cannot emancipate themselves. Thus the patients are unable to conceive of eventual changes or modifications in the experiential content,* i.e., to conceive of the latter as possibly being different from what it actually is. [Italics mine.] (Gurwitsch, p. 367)

Since in his commentary it is Gurwitsch's purpose to show how the Gelb-Goldstein experiments confirm Husserl's delineation of categorial

[6] A. Gelb and K. Goldstein, "Über Farbennamenamnesie . . . ," *Psychologische Forschung*, VI (1924).

[7] Aron Gurwitsch, "Gelb-Goldstein's Concept of 'Concrete' and 'Categorial' Attitude and the Phenomenology of Ideation," in *Studies*, p. 366.

and sensuous equality or likeness, he translates their findings into Husserlian terms. Notice how he then seems to be speaking of the antidote of the concept that Ortega promotes in the *Meditations:*

To express it in Husserl's terminology, the normal person does not depend for his sorting upon sensuous equality or likeness but may, and does, group specimens according to the relation of equality in the categorial sense, which obtains between the specimens in question insofar and *only* insofar as the latter are considered as particularizations and actualizations of the *eidos* of redness. (Gurwitsch, p. 366)

In addition to showing how Husserl and the psychologists agree that ideation is a *sui generis* act, Gurwitsch suggests, on the basis of data provided by Gelb and Goldstein, that even the concrete attitude of normal and brain-injured persons must differ in kind. Since he wants the categorial attitude to be already implicit in the normal person's concrete attitude, he speaks of their ambiguity and plasticity of attitude, of how things are never mere data for normal people but "potential varieties of an invariant." Normal people, in short, can adopt a concrete attitude initially that allows for the possibility of eventual thematization.[8] This, too, implicitly echoes Ortega's prescription in the *Meditations.* But it was left to Merleau-Ponty's more penetrating theoretical use of these and similar Gelb-Goldstein materials to complete the circle by speaking in Ortegean terms. A philosopher of embodiedness, like Ortega, Merleau-Ponty built on Gabriel Marcel's and the Gestaltists' work to give an "existentialist" interpretation to the psychological data:

Before being thought or knowledge, categorial activity is a certain manner of relating oneself to the world and, correlatively, a style or a configuration of experience. Accordingly, . . . the disturbance of thinking which is discovered at the basis of amnesia . . . does not so much concern the judgment but rather the experiential milieu in which the judgment arises; it concerns less the spontaneity than the grasp of that spontaneity on the sensible world and our power of projecting any intention onto it. (Gurwitsch, p. 377)

Small wonder if this passage and all it suggests produces in readers of Ortega's *Meditations* a feeling of *déjà vu,* for the phenomenal field as "constituted" by the embodied individual is also the atomic fact behind

[8] Gurwitsch, *Studies,* pp. 379, 376.

Ortega's view of cultural differences. The difference in emphasis between Ortega and Merleau-Ponty can be explained as a difference between pre-World War I (and post-Marburgian) "culturalism" and post-World War II existentialist "atomism." What seems, however, beyond explaining is how Ortega could have preempted Merleau-Ponty's notion of the primacy of perception, before Sartre or Heidegger, before the Gestaltist movement in psychology, before the researches done by Gelb and Goldstein in the twenties, or even before it was quite clear to anyone outside Göttingen what Husserlian phenomenology was all about. How was it possible for Ortega to deliver himself of a scientifically founded, genetic account of racial differences in ideational ability in 1914? For Ortega's major theme in the *Meditations* is precisely this "grasp of [the Spaniard's] spontaneity on the sensible world and [his] power of projecting any intention onto it."[9] And the answer to this interesting problem is that while Husserl's view of external perception and Aristotle's notion of *aesthesis* prepared the way, Ortega's thinking received further confirmation from one of Scheler's sources, E. R. Jaensch, the Göttingen psychologist and colleague of David Katz. Although probably Stumpf's pupil, Schumann, working on perception from 1901 to 1904, was the first modern psychologist to consciously apply the phenomenological method, Jaensch and Katz followed close behind. Jaensch, especially, dealt with the kind of perceptual questions the Gestaltists would later concern themselves with, such as apparent size constancy, and the phenomenology of empty space.[10] Both Katz's and Jaensch's findings were published in Göttingen in 1911, and another colleague, Edgar Rubin, began to study figure and ground in visual perception in 1912. What primarily concerns us, however, is Jaensch's research on eidetic imagery, which, like Ostwald Külpe and the Würtzburg School's research into "pure" thought, seemed to Ortega like an updating of the Kantian categories.

Something of the sweep and importance that Jaensch claimed for his discoveries may be surmised from the full title of one of his books: *Eide-*

---

[9] Gurwitsch, *Studies*, p. 377.

[10] Edwin G. Boring, *Sensation and Perception in the History of Experimental Psychology* (New York: Appleton-Century, 1942), p. 249.

Meditations As Mundane Phenomenology

tic Imagery and Typological Methods of Investigation: Their Importance for the Psychology of Childhood, the Theory of Education, General Psychology, and the Psychophysiology of Human Personality.[11] Whereas Brentano had spoken only of a creative imagination, Jaensch felt that eidetic phenomena were of the utmost importance for the psychology of perception and conceptualization.[12] But an even more extraordinary coincidence is found in Brentano's notion of different levels of consciousness—an "implicit" and an "explicit" mode of presentation, for example—and Jaensch's view of the same topic. Here is Müller-Freienfels' account of Jaensch's position:

> In space perception as well as in thought and will there is not one form but an entire system of levels which are distributed among different individuals, but may also occur united in one individual and then work synergistically. Older, original levels of consciousness are preserved while newer, more differentiated ones are developed, so that even on a higher level of development the various means of solution, the older as well as the newer, can be alternatively used according to whether one or the other levels of consciousness is coordinated by corresponding mental "sets."[13]

In his investigations of schoolchildren, Jaensch found them to be more often "mnemonists" or "*eidetikers*" than adults were; it was also apparent that in extreme cases there was scarcely any difference in vividness and "objectivity" between an E. I. and an actual external perception. From this Jaensch concluded that in the maturation of children a kind of "iconic storage" took place.[14] Learning, development, the "efficacy of the past" was due to "the permanence of certain structures and forms of organization developed through the appropriate experiences in the past."[15] In short, Jaensch was suggesting the generation

[11] Eric R. Jaensch, *Eidetic Imagery . . .* , trans. from the 2nd ed. by Oscar Deser (New York: Harcourt, Brace, 1930).

[12] Rancurello, *Study of Franz Brentano*, p. 111.

[13] Richard Müller-Freienfels, *The Evolution of Modern Psychology*, trans. W. Béran Wolfe, M.D. (New Haven: Yale University Press, 1935), p. 128.

[14] The expression is taken from Ralph Norman Haber's "Where Are the Visions in Visual Perception?" in *Imagery: Current Cognitive Approaches*, ed. Sydney Joelson Segal (New York and London: Academic Press, 1971), p. 36.

[15] Gurwitsch, *Studies*, p. 388.

and retention of what Piaget calls "schemes." As Gurwitsch again explains:

> By virtue of its assimilating power, each of these "schemes" applies or at least tends to apply to whatever object is encountered. For that reason, Piaget considers these "schemes" as functional sensory-motor equivalents of concepts. However—and here we are following ideas which derive from Gestalt theory rather than from those of Piaget—reorganization and restructuring concern not only the psychic function (that function which is crystallized in "schemes") but also and above all the objective correlates of this function; namely, the objects, whether assimilated or still to be assimilated to "schemes." The objects become what the assimilating "schemes" make them to be—for example, "something for writing," "something to be handled in a certain way." . . . Its assimilation—whether actual or possible—to a certain "scheme" determines and defines the object as it figures in conscious life—that is, as it presents itself and therefore as that which it is from the phenomenal point of view. (pp. 388)

Jaensch realized that the philosophical and cultural implications of his work were fundamental. First, he saw "eidetics" as completing Helmholtz's theory of space perception by solving or rather "founding" the question of *a priori* categories. In speaking of Kant, Jaensch wrote:

> The theory of perception that is based on eidetic investigations shows that our inner world of ideas (*Vorstellungswelt*), an inner, *a priori* factor, is intimately concerned in the development of the perceptual world. Although in his work on Kant M. Heidegger does not mention the theory of perception and the epistemology based on eidetics, this latest and most penetrating interpretation of Kantian philosophy shows us that Kant was already aiming at these results of modern empirical and philosophical anthropology, and that some of its fundamental results have been pre-established by his profound intuition. For, from the way he describes it, the *Einbildungskraft* that he conceives as the basis of our form of spatial perception, is the same as the eidetic faculty; and when he describes it as the common root of "the two branches, sensibility and reason," he is intuitively perceiving that the worlds of sensation and of ideas have a common origin in the "primary eidetic unity." (*Eidetic Imagery*, p. 118)

But most important of all, as studies of children and reports on primitive peoples showed, in what Jaensch was pleased to call the "unitary types," there was proof of an original "undifferentiated unity" of perceptions and memory images, which allowed him to explain how different structures of consciousness could develop with distinct propensities for "Cartesian" thought. And he went on to suggest a theory of education and to elaborate a whole typology of "eidetic" types, some with a greater gift for abstraction and others with a greater sensibility for concrete impressions.

In this way, early proto-Gestaltist researchers like Jaensch provided the apodictic ground for Ortega's "Neo-Aristotelian" analysis of the Spaniard's antipathy for the categorial level of ideation and their tendency to remain in the concrete attitude. This is why Ortega spoke in *Meditations on Quixote* of raising Spanish consciousness by training the categorial imagination through the exercise of a kind of Husserlian "free variation"—the Ortegean "meditation."

7

MEDITATIONS ON QUIXOTE:
THE CERVANTEAN PERSPECTIVE

The famous sentence in which Kant attacks the metaphysics of Descartes—"thirty possible thaler are not less than thirty actual thaler"—may be philosophically exact, but in any case it contains a candid confession of the limits of the German mind.

Ortega, *Meditations on Quixote*

The fox knows many things, but the hedgehog knows one big thing.

Archilochus

I T is tempting to conjecture that, if he had gone on to write Meditations Two and Three in the same vein as Meditation One, Ortega would have ended by suggesting that Cervantes was the originator of the doctrine of vital or historical reason.[1] But this conjecture would put Ortega in a relationship similar to the one he imputed to Heidegger with respect to Hölderlin, namely, that of using the latter as his ventriloquist's dummy. And at first such a suggestion seems absurd. Still, Ortega's use of Cervantes is a curiosity we ought to be able to explain. Julián Marías would say, of course, that Ortega was a "hedgehog" whose "one big thing" dictated that he always appear in the guise of "fox." Thus, instead of expounding his own philosophy straight out, Ortega, to be faithful to that philosophy, must appear in the humbler role of explicator of the *Quixote*. At the same time, as José Gaos observes, it was no easy thing for Ortega to appear as less than he knew himself to be, especially when this entailed being thought a dilettante. This is why, when Indalecio Prieto accused him of only dabbling in

---

[1] See n. 1, chapter 6.

politics, Ortega reacted as strongly as he did, and why his remarks included the following surreal rejoinder: "What the Deputy, Mr. Prieto,
takes for a flashy tie I have just put on, is really my own backbone shin-
ing through."[2] If Indalecio Prieto or anyone else, Ortega was saying,
would only take the trouble to look, it ought to be obvious that all his
activities and writings proceeded from a central core; and that furthermore he was indeed a hedgehog, not a fox, and much less a fox trying
to pass for a hedgehog.

At the same time, there is something pathetic about Ortega's having
to make this kind of plea at all, as, in retrospect, there is something im-
mensely sad about the preface to his collected *Works* of 1932. How are
we to explain what was no one's fault but Ortega's, for he certainly *chose*
to hide his light under a bushel? Will the timidity he has alleged, or his
being a "philosopher *in partibus infidelium*," fully explain his abnega-
tion, his philosophical asceticism? I think neither will entirely do so.
Rather, the answer lies in Ortega's character, as the following anecdote
clearly intimates. The philosopher's brother, Manuel, tells how much
The Divine Comedy meant to the young Ortega, and how he knew and
recited, among others, a dark passage from *The Inferno* about a man
condemned to sit astride the shoulders of another man, biting his neck
throughout eternity.[3] This emblematic memory would seem to bespeak
a horror of dependence; first, naturally, on his father, but also on anyone important to him. And if we add to this an uncommon worldliness
and pride, as a philosopher Ortega would certainly have wanted to
render his true originality invulnerable to the kind of envious attack he
so well describes in the *Meditations*. Therefore, in using the *Quixote* as
a shield he was able to protect himself, and veil his philosophical allegiances, notably to Scheler and Aristotle, or so he must have
imagined. Instead, as we know, his approach must be counted a tactical
error of tremendous magnitude, inasmuch as Ortega has in fact been
accused of borrowing from every German philosopher he ever men-

[2] Quoted in José Gaos, *Sobre Ortega y Gasset y otros trabajos de la historia de
las ideas en España y la América Española* (Mexico: Imprenta Universitaria,
1957), p. 125.

[3] Manuel Ortega y Gasset, *Niñez y mocedad de Ortega* (Madrid:
C. L. A. V. E., 1964), p. 85.

tioned. Whereas, on the contrary, as we have seen, the classics of Western philosophy aside, Ortega rarely mentions another philosopher
unless he has, in fact, left him far behind, and the same is true of philosophical ideas. This, it seems to me, lays the fault where it belongs, at
Ortega's own door. For his disciples have only continued in a line of
defense that he first set down.

Perhaps now that we have prepared a context, by explaining both the
purposes of the *Meditations*, together with the way in which, as well as
the degree to which, that work may be termed a philosophical one, we
can now turn to *Meditations* itself for confirmation of our claims. For if
these can be supported there, our general thesis about the early genesis
of Ortega's philosophy can certainly be sustained.

It is not our purpose in offering a reading of the *Meditations* to approximate their richness of allusive detail, nor to retrace ground already
covered by Julián Mariás' full and important commentary. Instead, we
shall be concerned to highlight and enlarge on those aspects of the
Meditations that have received less attention. Nor will it be appropriate
here to examine all the ramifications of Ortega's theory of the novel.
This is why I would prefer to call what follows "A Reading" rather than
"A Commentary."

[1]
To The Reader

This first part or prologue was to have introduced the whole series of
ten "salvations" that Ortega first projected in 1910; it is thus addressed to
readers who may possess a predilection for "free variation," a *"tessitura"*
for categorial thinking, and for idealities, such as to make them *philotheamones* (friends of seeing) in Ortega's sense, or mundane phenomenologists as we can say now. And so he begins with a personal demonstration of what this involves. The meditations are to be a series of
"salvations" whose purpose it is to raise each subject as directly as possible "to its fullest significance" (31). Imagery throughout the whole essay
is consistently "Bachelardian": heaviness denoting matter, and airiness,
ideality or imagination. In this first part, therefore, Scheler's presence is
easily decried, whose *Der Formalismus in der Ethik und die materiale
Wertethik*, Part I, had appeared in 1913. But Ortega gives his Prologue

a Platonic cast to disguise the ethical origins (and purpose) of his method. Still there are clear echoes of Scheler, when he calls for an active doctrine of love, "love for the perfection of the loved object" (32), to replace the hate that has inhabited the Spanish heart for so long. Hate separates us from things while through love we discover an essential structure of connection (33). The essays that follow will demonstrate an "eagerness to comprehend" and the need to develop "some new facets of ideal sensibility" (34) in his fellow Spaniards.

To this end, understanding (*comprensión*) is called for; understanding rather than mere knowledge (*sabiduría*). And now philosophy is introduced as "the general science of love"; if love connects, philosophy represents "the greatest impulse toward a total connectedness" (38). Delicately, Ortega begins to prepare his readers for momentous things. Instead of the "*Und-Verbindung*" approach of facts, facts, facts of nineteenth-century positivism, a holistic approach is required; the connections must be discovered in the things themselves, not in the mind of the scientist. Philosophy's highest goal is thus a hypothesis that will give "being" to "everything" as Cohen would have said, or, as Ortega now says, "to arrive at a single proposition which would express the whole truth" (39), and Ortega has the temerity in this first book to use the example of a formula that, he says, condenses the twelve hundred pages of Hegel's *Logic*. Understanding (*comprensión*) is a sudden explosion of meaning that we experience—a kind of esthetic orgasm—when we have read the *Logic* with enough thoroughness so that we fully understand the formula "The Idea is the Absolute." Ortega shows enormous assurance here, for he is implicitly suggesting a parallel between Hegel's formula and his own, and in truth, when we finally have plumbed its depths, the formula "I am I ('I') and my circumstances," does clarify the "enormous perspective of a world" (39). Moreover, since the world of values is as accessible as the material world, once we learn to perceive it, there is no need to sandbag the reader with mountains of proof. This in no way means, as we have already had occasion to show, that Ortega has written anything here for which he could not produce unimpeachable evidence (40). Unfortunately, no one has realized that this claim was literally true.

In the seventh or central section of the Preface, Ortega pauses to describe the provenance of culture. Still jousting with the nineteenth century, Ortega wants to show that culture is always conceived "in the inner spirit of an individual, mixed with his whims and humors" (43–44). Although it seems to be a hieratic, purified object, culture was once immediate, spontaneous life (43) from which the *logos* had not yet been extracted. *Logos*, we are told, is "meaning," "connection," "unity." Here Ortega avoids the idealistic overtones of Husserl's essences; his concepts or ideas are only to be found "in" language. But Spaniards have limited themselves, like windowless monads, to the concrete attitude, the mode of disconnection, eschewing the categorial attitude in which things can be easily shared; hate and envy have militated against solidarity. So now Ortega urges on Spaniards a collective-individual thematization of their spontaneous life. Indeed, this is the method Ortega himself has chosen. This is why he is offering his *Meditations, "modi res considerandi,"* as "possible new ways of looking at things." But how can Ortega do otherwise, if "the ultimate reality of the world is neither matter nor spirit, is *no* determinate thing—but a perspective" (45)? I may imagine I can choose the grandest of enterprises; *in reality,* I am like Robinson Crusoe, alone and a prisoner on the island of "my life."

Underlying this acute awareness of limitation is the notion of *aesthesis;* what Ortega commonly refers to as "way of looking at things." It has always the broad Aristotelian sense of "sensation," which, like Husserl's *Erfahrung,* means *ultimate givenness*—that beneath and before which we cannot go. *Meditations* is thus the translation, the *logos* of Ortega's own *aesthesis,* his "esthetic." By his example, then, he will show Spaniards the way to "the security, the firmness—τὸ ἀσφαλές—" of culture. Still, "everything achieved in culture, is no more than a strategic turn to bring the immediate into focus" (44). Even reason and reflexiveness are no more than second order forms of spontaneous life. Culture is only a provisional binding up of things in a hypothesis. As such, even Ortega's thesis about human life *as thesis* is culture, a strategic turn. But if Spaniards are to be raised to the creation of culture, why does Ortega also deprecate it? Inasmuch as he sees the need of an integration, a balancing of Plato's (and Marburg's) "flight in order to draw closer" and Aristotle's (and Scheler's) *aesthesis,* he is bound to reject either extreme, whether it be Spanish "impressionism" or Neo-Kantian critical philosophy. Hence his kinship is not with Don Quixote nor with Sancho but with Miguel de Cervantes Saavedra.

The three meditations Ortega will dedicate to the *Quixote* will not study the quixotism of the hero, but that of the novel; the quixotism of Cervantes (perhaps, the post-1911 *Brentanism* of Cervantes) in the book. Don Quixote is only a particular instance of the Cervantean style (52). Therefore, we must not separate Don Quixote from *his* circumstances. Instead we must make him the object of loving comprehension and discover, unveil, *his* profound meaning, his entailments with the rest of *his* "world." But this is not a scientific undertaking; *Don Quixote* is not a material but an ideal object (51). Therefore, a special hermeneutics is called for: "It does not surrender to weapons; it surrenders, if at all, to the meditative cult" (52). Since, Ortega says, in closing, he has rejected "a decrepit Spain," with these and successive meditations he fulfills a moral obligation to essay experiments in a new one (53).

[2]
Preliminary Meditation

In this part, a methodological and programmatic introduction to the *Quixote* meditations, Ortega will give a demonstration of how circumstances are *re*-absorbed and new culture comes into being. This entire part is framed by two matching descriptions of Ortega's immediate, spontaneous life. In the silence on a hillside near the Escorial, he turns away from Imperial Spain, history, tradition; instead of looking *through* the window (his life) at the garden (Spain's past), he focuses on his surroundings, the life itself, out of which a new "past" must be summoned, a new "culture" (his philosophy) raised up and secured. He will extract the *logos* from this moment of human life; and not think merely, but write the thoughts down, sharing their meaning. Now we are to see how this creative act of culture is performed, what is to be gained by it, what its limitations are, and why it has been so rare among Spaniards.

In the first four sections of this part, Ortega gives a phenomenological theory of perception that pits proto-Gestaltist phenomenological psychology against Husserl. Ortega's phenomenology of seeing uses the same circling hermeneutics he has prescribed for literary critics, since in both cases, as we now see, "selection-interpretation" is of the essence. At the same time, he makes clear that what is positivistic about Husserl is precisely his insistence on passive seeing and his demand that every-thing appear—on the surface—*essentially*. Husserl is faulted for follow-ing out Brentano's descriptive or phenomenological psychology and ig-noring the really valuable part of the latter's work, in other words, his illuminating essays in *genetic* psychology. Things *are* where they come from and this means tracing them back to the point where they surged into time. Finally, the example of "the woods" shows that we do not get to the "essence" of "the woods" *descriptively*, but by "being in the woods" ourselves and narrating the story of how we got there. At this point in his career, philosophy is showing Spain how to get out of the woods. Of course, if we insist positivistically on essences, if we reduce the world at all, as hate—what Scheler termed *"Ressentiment"*—has made Spaniards do, we are deluding ourselves with dreams of "eidetic" and "phenomenological" reductions, with "pure consciousness," when the truth is that there is no complete reduction, that instead there are focal points of attention surrounded by horizons and a shading away to indistinctness, but all necessarily there. This is why Ortega's hermeneu-tics is of necessity genetico-historical, and hence diametrically opposed to Husserl's initial approach.

There are at least two more levels on which the experience of "the woods" has meaning for Ortega. If no one had ever entered a wood before, that experience would today still be virtual, raw Being, a still unthematized part of the *kosmos noetos*, and Ortega's would be the first attempt to domesticate it. In a species of "free variation," he in fact imagines the original awe at being in a woods and how this was allayed by binding all the mysterious trees together in one generic term. In ad-dition, and equally important, the refrain "one cannot see the woods for the trees," has a second meaning. As he says, "It may be that the in-tended joke turns its point against the speaker" (61). To what joke does Ortega refer? Who is the joke finally on?

Again, the answer is Husserl. For the refrain, which states an "obvi-ous truth," supposes that while we don't see the "woods" (a concept), we *do* see the trees: they are a "surface," "patent," while the woods is "profundity," "latent." But, says Ortega, *pace* Husserl, "there are things which present only what is strictly necessary to enable us to realize that they lie concealed behind it" (62). The reverse side of an orange is never seen, but we know it exists as certainly as the front. The "orange" invites our "perceiving" hand to pick it up. Yet no one has ever *seen* an orange; and "if by seeing we understand merely a sensorial function, neither they nor anyone has ever seen an orange in their terms" (63). And this means, of course, that if we cannot *see* oranges, we can no more *see* trees. What we *see* are sensations, masses, colors, luminous points of light. This is why, "things or certain qualities of things would not exist for us if there were no other manner of seeing than the strictly passive kind of vision" (63). Ortega is saying that *things*, extension, space, form, require something more. Thus, it makes no more sense to say we *see* a "box," or a "tree," than it does to say we "taste" them. We *see* the "shape" and "color" of the orange, but we learn to see the "orange" as part of living in a world of oranges. What a "thing" is, it is in the matrix of human life.

What, then, is the lesson of the "woods?" Now we see clearly what Spaniards must do:

The woods has taught me that there is a first plane of realities which imposes itself upon me in a violent way; they are the colors, the sounds, the pleasure and the pain of the senses. Towards this plane my attitude is a passive one. But behind those realities there appear others, as the outlines of the higher mountains appear in a sierra when we have reached the first foothills. . . . But these higher realities are rather bashful and do not seize us as their victims. . . . Science, art, justice, manners, religion are orbits of reality that do not overwhelm our persons in a brutal way as hunger and cold do; they exist only for him who wills them to exist. (67–68)

Although this is a difficult leap, Ortega is saying that "faded blue" and "Justice" are different in degree, but not in kind (68). Thus when he says that a surface has two values, one material, the other virtual, he already distinguishes between two approaches to the world at hand: one, "positivistic," "impressionist," or "descriptive,"; another, "conceptual," "genetic," and historical. We must learn, as Spaniards, to exercise the second way of seeing if we are to understand the profundity of the *Quixote*. As with our experience of the woods, we also collaborate in the novel's "constitution." This is why Ortega terms the *Quixote* an "ideal woods" and a "foreshortened book" (70), by which he seems to be saying—long before Roman Ingarden—that a novel is a curious ontological hybrid.

But before we can approach "culture" or the *Quixote*, Ortega, in sections five through eight, invites us to exercise our newly acquired "active vision," in order to disengage a crippling misconception that Spaniards have about themselves; this will be the reader's first conscious participation in a meditation:

> Impressions form a superficial tapestry from which ideal paths seem to lead us toward a deeper reality. Meditation is the mechanism by which we abandon the surfaces, as if they were shores of the mainland, with a feeling of being thrust into a more tenuous element in which there are no material supports. We go forward holding onto ourselves, keeping ourselves in suspension by our own effort within an ethereal orb inhabited by weightless forms. (74)

We must fight off a sense of vertigo, and proceed in Hegelian fashion:

> In our meditation we proceed, feeling our way among masses of thoughts, separating some concepts from others, piercing with our glance the imperceptible crevice left between closely related concepts, and having put each concept in its place we stretch out imaginary springs between them so that they will not become confused again. (74)

Nineteenth-century Spain could not understand the *Quixote* or itself, because it had no sensitivity for values. It demanded that everything appear on the surface in the same way and with equal force. Positivistic, pseudo-empirical, it "flattened out" the world, at the same time priding itself on its "Latin clarity." This idea, Ortega says, is a "biased misconception" (75). There is, as Jaensch's and Scheler's work suggested, a fundamental difference between Germanic and Latin cultures, but not the one Menéndez Pelayo had in mind. Instead, Germanic culture was "the culture of profound realities," while the Latin was "the culture of surfaces." Moreover, the two kinds of culture were in fact "two separate dimensions of an integral European culture" (75). The Germanic people were the true inheritors of Greek essentialism, while the Latin cultures were really only Mediterraneans like the Romans. Nevertheless, Ortega will examine "clarity," since it is a primary characteristic of the historical nature of the Mediterranean people. What does this Mediterranean idea disguise? Nothing less than the secret of Spanish realism. "We Mediterraneans, who do not think clearly, see clearly" (83):

Nos oculos eruditos habemus: what in seeing belongs to mere impression is incomparably more energetic in the Mediterranean and for this reason people here find it usually sufficient. The pleasure of seeing, of examining, of sensing the surface of things by the pupil is the distinguishing feature of our art. It should not be called realism because it does not consist in the emphasis on the *res*, on the things, but on the *appearance* of things. It would be better to call it "apparentism," illusionism, impressionism. (84)

Spaniards pride themselves on saying with Gautier that the external world exists for them. This is certainly their forte, and in Cervantes "this power of vision is literally incomparable" (83), but they must also realize that "the imperceptible world—the deeper zones"—are also "external to the ego," in short, not *merely* subjective entities. For if Spaniards cannot develop a sensitivity for ideal objects, they run the risk that "invaded by the external, we may be driven out of ourselves, left with our inner selves empty, and thus be transformed into back doors on the highway through which a throng of objects come and go" (85). The real point of this acute diagnosis is not of course that this *may* happen to Spaniards, but that they have long been this way. Now, however, Ortega will offer a way out of the predicament.

After straightening out "this notorious controversy between Germanic mists and Latin clarity" (87), Ortega proceeds, in sections nine through eleven, to examine the nature of "profundity *in genere.*" We must know this if we are to understand the "concept" ("idea" or "notion"), since "the organ of the thinker is the concept" (87). An indication as to its nature lies in the earlier distinction between the world of pure impressions and "the latent worlds made up of structures of impressions" (87). This second world is structured, and its structure is a second-order entity, that is to say, there is "a group of things or simple material elements, plus the order in which these elements are arranged." Of course it is obvious that the elements and their order are real in different ways. In a wood a tree may be green and to my left; both are qualities of the tree, but the "being to my left" is a relative quality the tree does not seem to have when it is, in fact, not to my left. This "being to my left" is what Meinong called a "relational property," although Ortega would probably say that the quality is a "disposition" of the tree (an "aspect" of the tree), and that we may produce an idea or concept of it. At any rate, it is this *type* of quality that Ortega has been trying to isolate—like the "distance" of the second pair of sounds in "Streams and Orioles," the quality (distance) exists because I am there—for he next says that "it is this interlocking of things that forms a structure" (88). Nature is precisely such a lived complex of structures of relations. But how are these structures formed? We have already seen this with the example of the woods. By the mechanism of attention, Ortega says. It orders whatever enters our visual field, beginning with what is central and working out toward the edges: "If we continue paying attention to one object, it will become more clearly perceived because we shall keep finding in it more reflections of and connections with the surrounding things" (89). And these connections and reflections with, and of, other things are the "profundity" of anything. The "meaning" of a thing is "the highest form of its coexistence with other things" (89), and thus Ortega suggests by anticipation the horizonal "meaning" Husserl returned to late in life.

Intuition gives us "the material body of a thing" (89), but I also need to know the "meaning" a thing has. When I have the "meaning," the concept or "relationship" of a thing, as when, in addition to being "in the woods," I have the idea "woods," then I have "the ideal hollow corresponding to [the woods] within the system of realities" (92). Since the world is an infinite abundance—"an inexhaustible wellspring of realities" Ortega says elsewhere—only a madman would choose the spectre of a concept over the reality itself. At the same time, it is only by thinking a thing that it becomes secured, falls into our hands, and this is why Spanish culture, an impressionist culture in Ortega's sense, is condemned to not being a progressive culture, why it has been instead a "frontier culture," a culture of "Adams" (94–95). "Culture is not the whole of life, but only the moment of security, of certainty, of clarity" (96). The concept is not a substitute for "the spontaneity of life," but an instrument for its possession and thematization.

Thus far Ortega has shown the need for culture and the concept, as well as how they are acquired—he has made the first half of his contribution to the debate over the "Europeanization" of Spain; now in the remaining sections of this part, he moves on to a consideration of the work of art as an element of culture, and of the curious ambiguity of the *Quixote* in the field of Spanish art. Ortega begins this change of focus by warning that culture and the concept are only half the total European inheritance and must be adopted (and adapted) without abandoning "impressionism," Spain's own unique perspective on the world. His plea is for a synergistic integration or rather re-integration of the two modes, a balance that has been especially lacking in the history of Spanish art and literature. Ideally, the work of art should exhibit "a strong power of reflection, of meditation" (100), instead of being the "mere reaction of one part of life—the individual heart—to the rest of it" (100). In fact, when we confront "our most traditional works," "we find ourselves facing them as we face life itself" (100). In this respect the *Quixote* is and is not an exception. Although academic critics have not been able to show this, it is the most profound book we have, even though, or perhaps precisely because, it seems to operate wholly within the realm of "pure impressions" and to avoid "any general and ideological formulae" (102). Nevertheless, we are meant to infer, where positivistic critics have failed through a lack of sensitivity to its profundity, the *Quixote* may yet yield its secret to Ortega's hermeneutics of comprehensive openness. Nothing could be more important than to fathom this secret, since a proper understanding of Spain's destiny hangs in the balance (103). But even Spain's destiny cannot be considered in isolation; for, when

a race succeeds in developing its particular energies fully, the earth is enriched in an incalculable way: the new sensibility promotes new uses and institutions, new architecture and new poetry, new sciences and new aspirations, new sentiments and new religion. On the contrary, when a race fails, all this possible innovation and accretion remain irrevocably unborn because the sensibility which creates them is not transferable. (105–6)

This is why it is imperative to ascertain "the Cervantean way of dealing with things," to discover the secret of Cervantes' style (107). If that can be done, Spain will win for herself "a philosophy and an ethics, a science and a politics," and in the course of acquiring these will fulfill her European destiny as well.

[3]
First Meditation (A *Short Treatise on the Novel*)

As we have been warned, in this last part of *Meditations,* we are not to expect a complete elucidation of "the Cervantean way of looking at things." This meditation was to have been merely the first of three encirclements of the *Quixote,* and the most peripheral at that. In addition, the focus necessarily shifts off Spain somewhat, since the ostensible subject here is not the *Quixote* but the novel *in genere.* At the same time, this final part follows, to a large extent, the same tripartite movement as the "Preliminary Meditation." That is, it too consists of (a) a discrimination of terms, (b) the correction by replacement of a false assumption, and (c) the discovery of an *integration* or dynamic balance. The primary difference between the two arguments is that in the "Preliminary Meditation" it was imperative that Spain ensoul the concept, whereas here for the novel to become the novel it had first to absorb the innovation of Spanish impressionism.

Although his discussion of the novel ranges over the whole history of western literature, Ortega's completed argument entails a criticism of the nineteenth-century view of the arts. As becomes clear when this theme takes the center in *The Dehumanization of Art,* he considers Realism an epiphenomenon and the classical nineteenth-century novel a degenerate form. This is why the "Short Treatise" begins by suggesting that the *Quixote* seems as near to us as the works of Balzac, Dickens, Flaubert, and Dostoevsky, and ends by declaring that the *Quixote* will probably outlast them all. But what, Ortega asks, *is* a novel?

Just as, in the first third of the "Preliminary Meditation" Ortega separated the real and the ideal ingredients in perception, so here in the first six sections of the "First Meditation" he performs an analogous operation. Taking his clue from a remark in the *Exemplary Novels,* he notices that for Cervantes the term "novel" applies to two very distinct modes. On the one hand, there are the marvelous tales whose interest lies precisely in their lack of verisimilitude. On the other, the "realistic" tales whose primary interest lies in the way their ordinary subjects are depicted. Although at the outset there seems to be nothing remarkable about this distinction, it is by clarifying and refining these two modes that Ortega will arrive at his definition of the novel; not until we see them as they are "in themselves" can we come to understand that in their proper combination lies the distinguishing feature of the novel. But what, Ortega asks again, *is* a novel?

Clearly, he says, it is not the direct descendant of the epic, as many critics and novelists have contended. In fact, novel and epic are exactly opposite. But this observation allows Ortega to begin to define the novel by contrasting it with the epic genre. For one thing "the theme of the epic is the past as such" (118). By this, he means that the epic past is an absolute, ideal past as distant from Plato as from ourselves. This means that Homer was not a naïve poet but an archaist, because the Greeks could not conceive of the possibility of creating a poetic object. Because the present could never be poetic, it meant that poetic material always had to be drawn from the pre-existent store of mythology, and thus the poet's role was to evoke this ideal past for his listeners, to make it "present" for them. Curiously enough, in Homer, for example, the technique of "making things present" is so well developed that we are almost tempted to call the result Realism. But this misunderstanding only shows our nineteenth-century heritage of insensitivity. For us the real is what we see and touch, what we can sense, whereas for the Greeks the real was "the essential, the profound and latent; not the external appearance but the living source of all appearance" (124). What the epic poet is bent on doing with his epithets, and his archaic grammar, is to uproot his listeners from "everyday reality." Another sharp contrast between the epic and the novel is in the figures which inhabit them. It follows, from what he has already said, that the bard deals in unique characters that already exist in legend and mythology; in contrast, the novelist deals in types or representatives of types. In this way, by examining the epic we have gained a clearer perspective on the novel. Its theme is not the past, but the present as such; its characters are not unique and poetic per se, but are taken from our own familiar world; and, finally, we have seen that the "art" in literature is a strategy for bringing the poetic to light, but is not itself "poetic." While the strategy may be, and at times must be, realistic, we should never make a norm of Realism. On the contrary, the principal problem in esthetics—

says Ortega—is to explain how the real becomes part of the esthetic object.

The sharp opposition between epic and novel that Ortega has taken pains to expose would seem to settle the question of a genetic relationship between them in the negative. But this assumption is as false as the assumption of a *direct* genetic relationship between the two. For in sections seven through thirteen, Ortega shows that at least one essential feature of the epic survives and is passed on to the novel.

Once the Greeks ceased to believe "in the cosmogonic and historical reality of their narratives" (128), the mythical seeds of legend continued to exist "in literary memory" where they continued to offer "a poetic leaven of incalculable energy." Reappearing in the so-called Greek novel, they caused essentially historical material to burn with a marvelous flame. And so it is with all "literature of the imagination," whether tale, legend, ballad, or book of chivalry: it offers a different world from ours, governed by strange laws, where the impossible is possible and where the only law is: "adventure permitted" (129). Thus the last appearance of this world of impossibilities is the books of chivalry: "chivalry means adventures," Ortega says. And here, as in the epic, the poetic instrument is narration. This reminds Ortega of another contrast: the epic *narrates* whereas the novel *describes*. In the novel it is not *what* is described but the *way* that it is described that interests us. Neither Sancho, nor the priest, nor Madame Bovary, nor Charles is interesting; "But we would give away a kingdom for the satisfaction of seeing them captured in the confines of those famous novels" (131). This often misunderstood remark is meant to remind the reader of two things: first, Ortega's promise to consider not just Don Quixote, but Don Quixote in the whole novel; and second, that man in his "striving," and his circumstances in their "resistance," are two halves of the same ontological "event." At any rate, in contrast to the novel, the book of chivalry deals in interesting, even marvelous adventures. Although these are no longer due to divine intervention, they still retain the ability to lift us off our feet; as Ortega puts it, "Adventure shatters the oppressive, insistent reality as if it were a piece of glass" (132). Life itself is an encirclement, a prison, so that if we do not let it become a vice, there is nothing wrong with "this strong drug of the imagination" which allows "an easy escape from the heavy weight of existence" (132). However, as Ortega will soon show, in contrast to "escapist literature," a healthy respect for contingency is essential to the mechanism of the novel; it is man's destiny to "reabsorb" his circumstances, to thematize, not escape from them. Ortega next turns to the Master Pedro's puppet theater episode from the *Quixote* to exemplify the psychology of the reader addicted to escapist literature. When we read an adventure story, we are torn between following the ascensional movement of the story up "out of this world" and the downward, gravitational pull of reality. This is not what happens to Don Quixote, who commits the esthetic faux pas of taking the adventure of Gaiferos and Melisendra *as* reality: he tries to *enter* "a fantastic world . . . of adventure, of imagination, of myth" (134) and literally breaks up the show. But there is another meaning to be drawn from the scene. Just as the "Meinongian" world of the "Preliminary Meditation" contained an upper story of ideality, here in the *Quixote* there are also "new planes of reality." In the background is the puppet theater with its impossible creatures; in the foreground are the muleteers with Sancho and Don Quixote among them. They at least belong to "our world"; but *do* they? For the puppet show and the inn also exist within the larger "puppet show" of the novel, within "the hollow interior of an esthetic body" (134). Most significant in this scene, says Ortega, is the osmosis and endomosis between the antithetical continents of the puppet show and the inn, which means we must accept Cervantes' statement that his book is written *against* the books of chivalry. Cervantes' condemnation, ambiguous in any case, is esthetic, not moral. Cervantes demands "profundity" of the novel, which means the inclusion of a second dimension, not this time of ideality, but of "reality." This is "esthetic profundity," which requires "a plurality of aspects." "Now our poetry has to be capable of coping with present reality." "How could the inn and Sancho and the muleteer and the blustering Master Pedro be poetic?" (136). Don Quixote is the touchstone here. To which continent does he belong? To both. He belongs to Sancho's world, is "real," but he *wills* impossible things, adventures that are not "real." Like man, his is "a frontier nature" (136). By including an aggressive foreground of "reality" in the novel, the adventure acquires greater esthetic power, and the "real" gets accepted as "poetic" too. So that, "although the real-

istic novel was born in opposition to the so-called novel of fantasy, it
carries adventure enclosed within its body" (137). The adventure is still
"real," but only in Don Quixote's brain. Before the *Quixote*, the reader
could naïvely "live through" the imaginary adventures of literature; now
in the *Quixote* and in all realistic novels, the reader is forced to see
through the imaginary adventures to the brute reality that lies in wait
(139). This means that the novel is essentially an ironic genre, one
depicting the destruction of a myth.[4]

But now Ortega turns to another encounter of Don Quixote's: his
battle with the windmills of Criptana. We have always understood, as
readers, that things have a different meaning for Don Quixote and for
Sancho; only now Ortega explains this difference in terms of the distinction of the "Preliminary Meditation": "One is the 'sense' of things, their
meaning, what they are when interpreted. The other is the 'materiality'
of things, the positive substance that constitutes them before, and independent of, any interpretation" (141). The "meaning" of the windmills is that they are giants, and this interpretation is not different
in kind from the first appearance of giants in the world, or of a "woods"
among the trees. There never have been giants *really*, but there "are"
giants now just as there "are" chimeras and centaurs. They are like all
creations of the human spirit that come to light when we follow the interpretive directions reality points out to us. And culture belongs with
these; all are "mirages produced on matter" (141). The danger is that,
like Cohen, Husserl, or Don Quixote, we may take them for giants and
fail to see that they are only "thematized" "aspects" of the real: "Culture—the ideal side of things—tries to set itself up as a separate and self-
sufficient world to which we can transfer our hearts. This is an illusion,
and only looked upon as an illusion, only considered as a mirage on
earth, does culture take its proper place" (141–42).

This sudden reappearance of "culture" should not surprise the reader,
for after all the purpose of *Meditations* is to discover "the Cervantean
way of seeing things," and this was to be done in part to reveal how

[4] This point suggests most clearly the parallel between Ortega's view of the dynamics of the novel and his own "way of thinking," which is a self-ironizing
"rationalism" that continually undercuts itself in order to be faithful to the contours of the real.

Meditations: The Cervantean Perspective

Spain can fulfill her destiny; Ortega has already shown us that "culture" is the way, and now we are asked to consider Cervantes' contribution to the subject. In this respect, Don Quixote's meeting with the windmills is exemplary. If we take the windmills as windmills, we live "disillusioned lives," if we take them as giants we live "under a hallucination." This is because there is an "everlasting conflict" between the two: the "idea" or "meaning" struggles to free itself from matter, to be autonomous, while matter tries to reabsorb the "meaning." Obviously Ortega sees a parallel between man's struggle to raise up "fallen" reality against its wishes, and the mechanism of the realistic novel; it is not the characters that interest us per se, but their attempts to "interpret" the resisting "barbarous, brutal, mute, meaningless reality of things" (145). It is not the characters, for "the real things, the realities do not move us but rather the representation of their reality . . . the poetic quality of reality does not lie in the reality of this or that particular thing, but in reality as a generic function" (144). Any object may be depicted in the novel, but it is a novel because we are shown "the pure materiality beneath it." We are made to see in this "materiality" its final claim, its critical power before which, provided it is declared sufficient, "man's pretension to the ideal, to all that he loves and imagines, must yield." And this is the "profundity" of the *Quixote*; this is the sad, ironic message that Cervantes built into his masterpiece; and this is the warning that is Spain's contribution to Europe's destiny, what she has to offer in exchange for the concept:

It is sad that it should reveal itself to us thus, but what can we do about it! It is real, it is there: it is terribly self-sufficient. Its force and its single meaning are rooted in its sheer presence. Culture is memories and promises, an irreversible past, a dreamed future. But reality is a simple and frightening "being there." It is a presence, a sediment, an inertia. It is materiality. (145)

If this is the high point of the "Short Treatise" and of *Meditations on Quixote* as well, it is not the end. We have seen our false assumption about the relation of epic and novel corrected and refined; we have seen the similarity in the movements of the arguments in the two meditations—although in the first he stresses the "idea," whereas here the appropriate opposite term is more heavily weighted; but what we have not seen is why the novel is a degenerated form. In the remaining seven sections, Ortega develops this point by showing how, in the *Quixote*, the novel maintains a fine balance between comedy and tragedy. Implicit in what he has already said is the possibility that we may view Don Quixote's "case" in one of two ways. If we see him as a comic *poseur,* and nothing more, the novel is in danger of becoming comedy; if we side with Don Quixote and see him as a hero, we add at least enough tragedy to his story to counterbalance the incipient comedy. This means that the novel is tragic-comedy when some semblance of a balance is maintained. But this is only just managed in the *Quixote.* What makes the nineteenth-century novel a degenerate form, then, is that the century's ideals were of so little moment that their fall under the attacks of the real may fail to interest us at all. When Darwin swept "heroes off the face of the earth," there was no other protagonist left in the novel but the "environment" itself. This is how Ortega ends his "Treatise on the Novel"; he makes no recommendations for the regeneration of the novel because that is incidental to his patriotic concern. But what was promised has been accomplished: *Meditations on Quixote* is the first of Ortega's unparalleled "experiments in a new Spain" (53).

If we step back now from the picture we have completed of *Meditations* and view it in its entirety, there can be no doubt that what Ortega says there about Spain, the novel, and the *Quixote,* is in each case a reflection of his fundamental holistic philosophical thesis: that the basic reality is "human life," a dialectic of striving and resistance, of "Being-from-within" (or *Zuhandenheit*) and "Being-from-without" (or *Vorhandenheit*), of *aesthesis* (Be-ing) and *logos* (Having), and hence its name, *vital or historical reason.* Culture in Spain is to be provisionally achieved by adopting the concept, but without relinquishing Spanish "impressionism" or forgetting that culture is a fiction; the modern novel came into being through a dialectical synthesis of the marvelous and the "real"; and the *Quixote* is the masterpiece it is, not because Don Quixote is right or because Sancho is, but because Cervantes balances one against the other on the scales of his Olympian irony. In short what Ortega has done in *Meditations on Quixote* is to use the substance of his capital discovery to show how three related problems have their source in the pre-theoretical layer of human life; in other words, he has employed a mundane phenomenology, as he did from the time of *Meditations on Quixote* until his last work, *The Idea of Principle in Leibniz.*

[8]

POSTSCRIPT:
ON REMEMBERING THE PAST

*It is one of the strange facts of philosophy, that highest irides-
cence of the human spirit, that issues that at one moment seem
crucial, and about which the hottest debate rages, suddenly,
by a shift of light, seem not only devoid of point, but even
without a plain sense: we not only do not care about their
answers, but we have ceased to know what the relevant questions mean.*

J. N. Findlay

IN this chapter, by way of concluding, my aim is to offer some remarks on the willful neglect that has befallen Spain's greatest philosopher since Suárez. Although this suggestion of waywardness on his
readers' part strikes a discordant note, I only mean what is certainly
true, namely, that there are abundant reasons why Ortega's philosophy
should not continue to suffer the fate that J. N. Findlay—in speaking of
Meinong—sees as the lot of all or most philosophies.

While in the present study it was imperative to focus on and explicate
the *Meditations* itself, now that has been done a reassessment of the rest
of his work is in order. For the sorry truth is that historical and cultural
circumstances have, as Ortega feared, worked against his ever receiving
an open, unprejudiced hearing. The fortunes of Ortega's philosophy in
Spain, what with his return from exile, his founding of the Institute of
Humanities, and his death in 1955, could easily have been predicted.
Following his death, he was viciously attacked by the Catholic Right
and in recent years he has been vilified by the political left, both new
and old. Such vituperation has a paradigmatic quality about it, but at
least some fault for the shrillness of the attacks should be laid at the
door of his defenders, for ultimately they have had the charge of expounding and explaining Ortega's words. What passes all comprehen-

sion is the lack of understanding exhibited by some of Ortega's former students and colleagues. One searches their writings almost in vain for some sign of real understanding or even, in some cases, a kind word for their master and colleague. An interesting and honorable exception to this pattern of neglect is Manuel García Morente. But if he shows a real understanding of what Ortega was about, was closest to Ortega in age, and had in common with him the experience of Marburg, then it may be that one needed to see Ortega's work from the vantage point of Neo-Kantian philosophy *and* the phenomenology of Husserl's *Logical Investigations*. Younger followers and disciples like José Gaos, who came to study in Madrid in the early twenties, tended to feel that philosophy began in 1913 with the publication of Husserl's *Ideas* and ended with the publication of *Sein und Zeit* in 1927. Thus there is a special irony, of which the author himself is unaware, when Gaos tells of his own participation in Ortega's Silver Anniversary as holder of the Chair of Metaphysics at Madrid. As his part in the celebration, Gaos lectured on the master's work. As he later recalled:

In them [the series of lectures] the lecturer spoke of what he is about to set down here once again. . . . Naturally, his teacher learned of his disciple's presentation. When he heard it through he made a face, it did not please him. But before the disciple's insistence, which was both firm and respectful, he grew thoughtful and ended by being friendly. He must have sensed that his disciple was struggling for his own salvation in trying to "save" the tremendous circumstance that his teacher represented to him, and in the only way he deemed possible, by "putting in force" (*potenciar*) what was organic about his teacher's work and setting aside the adventitious.[1]

Clearly, what this anecdote preserves with photographic clarity is not Gaos' *nobilità* as apologist for Ortega, but the latter's annoyance, chagrin, and resignation at being so gratuitously misunderstood. I say gratuitously, but as we have seen, Ortega himself was also to blame.

At the same time this distance between Ortega and a typical disciple like José Gaos is emblematic of an absolute generational difference. Ortega had experienced Marburg before World War I when it was still possible to be optimistic about the achievements of Neo-Kantian Culturalism—to use Gaos' own word. Ortega, moreover, was fortunate

[1] Gaos, *Sobre Ortega*, p. 84.

Postscript

enough to have returned to neutral Spain with his optimism intact; he never experienced at firsthand the European chaos and destruction that so influenced the post-war Natorp and prepared the way for Heidegger's ascendancy as spokesman of an era. Yet there is still a crowning irony in Ortega's loss of his disciples' allegiance to Heidegger, for since 1914 he had been predicting the very European crisis to which Heidegger and Husserl would respond in 1927 and 1935. And now in a post-World War II-Cold War perspective, Ortega seems overly jubilant, optimistic, whereas the rest of Europe has long been appropriately dour. In this sense, on the surface, his career is an exact parallel to that of another "jubilant" Spaniard, his contemporary, the poet Jorge Guillén.

While large and obvious historical events—Civil and World Wars, diasporas, and exiles—provide ample opportunity for misunderstandings between colleagues and even friends, other and less unavoidable motivations must also be adduced. I refer to the perhaps unconscious mechanisms to which Ortega called attention in the opening pages of *Meditations on Quixote*. There, as the reader will recall, Ortega urges "connection" and "love" as a remedy for the ancient Spanish malady of rancor. This rancor, he says, results from a sense of inferiority that Spaniards have. Although his criticism is implicit, what he seeks to promote with "connection" and "love" is that kind of association that Max Scheler termed *Gesamtperson*, wherein members are responsible not only to themselves but also to the totality, where a "quintessential solidarity binds [them] in a community of love."[2] Although social psychology seems less than germane to Ortega's purpose in the opening sections of *Meditations*, he was only too aware of the danger inherent in a teaching situation where peers must be instructed without being made to feel their ignorance too acutely. Since, moreover, Ortega was reading Freud by 1911 and was also familiar with Scheler's *Über Ressentiment und moralisches Werturteil* when he wrote *Meditations*, it is no surprise to find him eliding the two and speaking of *rancor and repression* (*Verdrängung*). Then too, as we have suggested, Ortega may himself have been no stranger to a feeling of *ressentiment* with respect to his "fa-

---

[2] Lewis A. Coser, "Introduction," in Max Scheler, *"Ressentiment,"* trans. William W. Holdheim (New York: Free Press of Glencoe, 1961), p. 14.

thers," which is why he expected the enmity that eminence begets, and why he spoke of rancor in such ominous words as these: "It is the imaginary suppression of the person whom we cannot actually suppress by our own efforts. The one towards whom we feel resentment bears in our imagination the livid semblance of a corpse: in our minds we have killed him, annihilated him" (I, 314). There can be little doubt that Ortega expected to be misunderstood, just as there can be little doubt he was correct in suggesting in the thirties that the willful misunderstanding of his work was due to resentment bred by the intellectual life of Madrid. Then as now the Spanish intellectuals' arena was so small that second-rate minds were condemned to a daily ration of envy. And what better target for resentment than Ortega, the privately acknowledged leader of three generations of Spanish intellectuals.

Small wonder, then, that today his less generous critics continue to repeat unquestioningly that Ortega, while not exactly a plagiarist, was heavily indebted to a whole series of German philosophers. Among the men most frequently mentioned, one usually finds Cohen, Scheler, Dilthey, Husserl, Spengler, and Heidegger. Usually, on closer examination, the supposed influences prove to be non-existent. Since Ortega was in full possession of his philosophy in 1914, as a result of having made a "superpositivistic" critique of Husserl's phenomenology in the *Ideas*, it is a mystery how Spengler or Dilthey, let alone Heidegger, could have had any fundamental influence on him at all. What is more, unlike Ortega, neither Scheler nor Heidegger, for all their talk of the "logic of the heart" and "facticity," ever recognized "any restriction on the absolute power of philosophical thought."[3] As for Dilthey, even the German philosopher's closest disciples had scarcely any idea in 1914 of the full import of his work. In 1927 Heidegger claimed to be preparing the way for Dilthey with the analysis of temporality and historicity in *Sein und Zeit*, but few people understood Dilthey's importance until Georg Misch pointed it out in 1931 in his *Lebensphilosophie und Phänomenologie*.

[3] M. Merleau-Ponty, "Phenomenology and the Sciences of Man," in *The Primacy of Perception and Other Essays on Phenomenological Psychology, the Philosophy of Art, History and Politics*, ed. with an introd. by James M. Edie (Evanston, Ill.: Northwestern University Press, 1964), pp. 93–94.

Postscript

Although no less inappropriate, the suggestion of Spengler's influence is intrinsically more interesting, for one of Ortega's perennial themes was indeed a species of Occidental decline. But a proper reading of the apposite texts by Ortega—that is, *Meditations on Quixote,* the Buenos Aires lectures of 1916, *The Modern Theme,* the Buenos Aires lectures of 1928, and, finally, *The Idea of Principle in Leibniz*—shows that what Ortega had in mind was rather that crisis to which Husserl referred inconclusively in his 1935 *Crisis* lectures and notes as having overtaken European science, European man, and European philosophy.

It is worthwhile to pause over Ortega's real convergence of viewpoint not with Spengler but with Husserl on the subject of Crisis rather than Decline. This instance will serve as well as another to illustrate how a correct understanding of Ortega's *Meditations* is absolutely essential for even a minimal comprehension of the later work. In the *Meditations,* it is true, there is a certain ambiguity of structural design; but this is perhaps due to Ortega's change in orientation after he had written a first draft in 1910. And of course, as a consequence, even *The Modern Theme* itself has been consistently misread. Rather than an inept exposition of the new "vitalistic" stage in Ortega's philosophy, it is the rough equivalent of Husserl's *Crisis,* Part IIIA, in which he describes at great length his rather contradictory notions of the *Lebenswelt.*[4] Turning back from this new reading of *The Modern Theme* to the *Meditations,* the ambiguity of the latter work disappears. *Meditations* is entirely unambiguous about what Spain must acquire through intercourse with Europe; she must add an upper story of ideality to balance her inveterate "impressionism." What Spain in return will have to offer Europe is not worked out in nearly as great detail. But the Buenos Aires lectures of 1916 provide the missing step, the implied next step between *Meditations* and *The Modern Theme.* The fate of modern philosophy, as Ortega tells it, is very much what Scheler noticed and Husserl would say: a rampant positivism gained the ascendancy because of the mathematization of nature that originated with Galileo. This was what forced philosophy as metaphysics to cede its place to mathematical physics as the

[4] David Carr, "Husserl's Problematic Concept of the Life-World," *American Philosophical Quarterly,* VII (October 1970), 331–39.

centerpiece of European (Western) rationalism. Thus we have Ortega speaking against an "objectivism" in 1916 in precisely the terms that Husserl would employ twenty years later. Ortega even professes to see the rebirth of philosophy thanks to the new anti-psychologistic foundation of logic; together, Brentano and Husserl have provided philosophy with the proper objects it never had before. Yet Ortega's analysis of the European crisis differs from Husserl's in a fundamental respect. Where Husserl opposes transcendentalism to scientific objectivism and sees phenomenology as the possible and necessary redemption of Europe's *telos* of rationalism, Ortega sees Husserl's (and Kant's) transcendental subjectivity as the spiritual disease—to paraphrase Karl Kraus—for which it pretends to be the remedy.

What Ortega and Husserl do in their respective diagnoses of the crisis is to pass each other while going in opposite directions. In this respect their opposite use of the same image of a "life of depth" and a "life of the plane" from Helmholtz's work is no less instructive than their divergent opinions about Descartes. In order to portray to Spaniards the "presence" of idealities, Ortega spoke, rather confusingly, of a dimension of perspectival depth reaching beyond the "life of the surface" where Spaniards were already so much at home; Husserl, in his turn, a philosopher-logician addressing Germans, uses the same image of depth to stand instead for an ante-predicative life-world that he faults Kant for having passed over in silence.[5] And ultimately their views of Descartes exhibit the same kind of mirror-image symmetry. Both recognize an important beginning in the apodictic self-evidence of Descartes' *cogito*,[6] but Husserl feels the Frenchman gives a mistakenly psychologistic interpretation to his discovery, while Ortega, in partial agreement, comes down on Descartes for not having repudiated the transcendental subjectivity esteemed by Husserl in favor of an ontology of human life. Husserl, whose early work gave little indication that he would ever attempt an accommodation with history, was forced by an untenable situation in Nazi Germany to realize that the "neutral" scientific ideal he had always served could spin out of control. Ortega, by contrast, from the vantagepoint of a nation "that had won everything and had lost every-

[5] Husserl, *The Crisis*, pp. 119–21.   [6] Husserl, p. 77.

Postscript

thing," realized as early as 1914—and the proof lies in the interlocking arguments of *Meditations, The Modern Theme,* and the Buenos Aires lectures—that Western man was in transit through a gray area between two antagonistic value systems, the old one founded on culture and science, the new one on life enhancement, and that for precisely this reason a crisis was inevitable; from this it followed that Husserl's phenomenology was at best an epiphenomenon. While both philosophers deplore "objectivism" and give a similar account of its genesis, three important points set them neatly apart. In the first place, Ortega's entire philosophical enterprise is rooted in the life-world of which Husserl only seems to have become aware in the last decade of his life; second, Husserl never understood that Einstein's revolution in physics, far from being just an internal affair, was really a regional version of the "scientific reduction" he himself finally called for, but without seeing its negative implications for his own transcendental phenomenology. And, finally, Ortega had been a practitioner of "genetic" phenomenology even in his first book, whereas Husserl's first essays in the historical method date only from the last years of his life *after* his discovery of the life-world. This reversal of the natural order suggests that the life-world is so confused and heterogeneous a concept because, although Husserl needs it to found logic or go behind scientific objectivity, his attempt to make it a theme for transcendental subjectivity is simply another "manipulation."[7] As Ortega wrote in 1941 with reference to the *Formale und transzendentale Logik:*

Husserl attempts, especially in the book mentioned, to reach the fundament ("fundamental reflections") of knowledge by means of his phenomenology. As was to be expected, he realizes that this fundament is not cognitive, but pretheoretic, or "vital" as we might loosely put it. But, since he has discovered all this by doing phenomenology, and phenomenology has neither founded or justified itself, his whole project has no ground under its feet. (v, 546)

[7] J. N. Mohanty, " 'Life-World' and 'A Priori' in Husserl's Later Thought," in *The Phenomenological Realism of the Possible Worlds: The 'A Priori', Activity and Passivity of Consciousness, Phenomenology and Nature; Analecta Husserliana: The Yearbook of Phenomenological Research,* ed. Anna-Teresa Tymieniecka (Dordrecht: D. Reidel Publishing, 1974), III, 57.

It would be inappropriate to pause here and examine in detail the question of whether Ortega was more positivisitic and less "manipulative" than Husserl, or whether—in fact—"human life," Ortega's "fundamental (*radical*) reality," is a "metaphysical" or anthropological concept. What our examination of the Crisis writings of Husserl and Ortega was designed to show, is how whole "families" of texts will be overlooked or misconstrued unless their geneology is correctly drawn from *Meditations on Quixote*, where everything Ortega ever wrote has its key. If, however, we were pressed on the question of whether Ortega's *conceptualization* of human life is not in fact a metaphysical concept, and hence "posited" rather than "given," it would be easy to respond. As a direct result of Ortega's experience at Marburg, he soon rejected Husserl's "descriptive" approach to the "things themselves." And he did so, *in part*, because the very idea of Being, as he saw, was only a necessary fiction, a mere *hypothesis*, just as, at the other end of the scale in the ontological and epistemological primacy of perception ("seeing is the criterion of all truth," he said in 1916), there could be no "seeing" without "ideas."[8] Thus the answer would have to be that for Ortega "human life" was neither "posited" nor "given" but *thematized* as a *new* hypothesis, a new means of "giving 'Being,' " of "saving appearances." If this had been understood, if the following passage from *The Modern Theme* had been correctly read, Ortega would never have had to write "Neither Vitalism Nor Rationalism":

The taking up of a point of view implies the adoption of a contemplative, theoretical, rational attitude. Instead of point of view we could say *principle* [italics mine]. Now then, nothing could be more diametrically opposed to biological spontaneity, to a simple living of life, than the search for a principle from which to derive our thoughts and our acts. The choice of a point of view is the initial act of culture. Therefore, the new imperative of "vitalism" that is to direct the destiny of mankind has nothing to do with a return to a [primitive] way of life.

[8] "This ability of the human perceptual system to go beyond immediate data is brought out dramatically by considering cartoons. A few lines convey an entire story, with the personality of each person and his mood. It is astonishing that this is so. It is useful to think of perceptions as *hypotheses*, based upon, but not limited by, current sensory data." In R. L. Gregory, *Concepts and Mechanisms of Perception* (New York: Scribner's, 1974), p. 610.

Postscript

> It is rather a new approach to culture. *It is a consecration of life, which until now has been a zero quantity, a species of happenstance, by making it a principle and a standard.* [Italics in original.] (III, 179)

Clearly, "my life" is given to me as the "ontological" medium in which everything I can know or experience appears, but Ortega never doubted that to *speak* of "my life," to narrate it, was to raise it to the status of a *working* hypothesis. The trouble, in contrast, with Husserl's concept of the "life-world" is that it was the unconscious *hypostatization* of such a hypothesis.

Just how acutely aware Ortega was of the precarious nature of all successful attempts to rise from the concrete to the categorial attitude is made abundantly clear in his last, great work, *The Idea of Principle in Leibniz and the Evolution of Deductive Theory.* Yet the same tone of what can only be described as incipient tragedy already obtrudes itself at the close of *Meditations on Quixote,* where Ortega states the final, somber message of the *Quixote:*

> the insufficiency, in a word, of culture, of all that is noble, clear, lofty—this is the significance of poetic realism. Cervantes recognizes that culture is all that, but that, alas, it is a fiction. Surrounding culture—as the puppet-show of fancy was surrounded by the inn—lies the barbarous, brutal, mute, meaningless reality of things. It is sad that it should reveal itself to us thus, but what can we do about it! It is real, it is there: it is terribly self-sufficient. Its force and its single meaning are rooted in its sheer presence. Culture is memories and promises, an irreversible past, a dreamed future. But reality is a simple and frightening "being there." It is a presence, a sediment, an inertia. It is materiality. (I, 387)

The pessimism of this passage has never been satisfactorily explained. Julián Marías has correctly drawn attention to its apparent similarity with the Sartrean distinction between *pour-soi* and *en-soi,* but we know intuitively that this cannot be what Ortega is suggesting. What is the source of the pessimism pervading the end of *Meditations* in 1914, a pessimism all the more inexplicable since Ortega apparently had a remedy in hand? The real question, perhaps, is not what Cervantes and Ortega knew but what Don Quixote and Ortega felt; that is, Why was Ortega, beneath his jubilance, a philosopher of such high seriousness? That he *was* this, is of course difficult to see in *Meditations.* There we correctly equate Ortega with the halcyon Cervantes. Yet a strange sympathy also links both of them to Don Quixote. In fact, in Ortega's *Meditations*, that is, in *his* essay, Don Quixote is not merely the inhabitant of Cervantes' novel; he also functions much as do the waiter and Peter in Sartre's *Being and Nothingness*. It is impossible to write about being-in-the-world in the abstract and be understood.[9] We now see how no mere description such as *"res dramatica"* has sufficed to convey the magnitude of what Ortega also called an "absolute event" (VIII, 52). Likewise, his talk of being a prisoner, of being a castaway (*náufrago*), of having reached by age thirty the limits of his chain, has never been understood. Don Quixote is a tragic, and not only a tragic-comic, figure precisely because he *is* condemned to see giants and not windmills. While there never *have* been giants and it is Don Quixote's mission to "reinvent" them, the Knight is still mad, as Ortega remarks. Don Quixote's life project is predetermined by the biochemical vapors rising in his brain. It is even likely that he knows the shortness of his chain and wants to die in order to be free. This is why in *Meditations on Quixote* Don Quixote is the guardian of Ortega's own proxy of sadness.

Ortega's mundane phenomenology was designed to examine everything from theatre to eidetic imagery, but his concerns, national, and cultural, never "culturalist," came to dominate his writings to the exclusion of a philosophy of the body. This most modern philosophical "category," in some sense an existentialist evasion of history, was the point from which Ortega as a Spaniard had set out; for him, it could never be the brave new world it was for philosophers raised in the Cartesian or the Hegelian tradition. Yet a glance through *The Spectator* makes abundantly clear that Ortega did begin a "philosophical anthropology" of his own. It was a necessary part of his new philosophy; but to develop it would have been an act of philosophical self-indulgence. Nevertheless, the essays on this subject that he did write show why Ortega had abundant cause to be as sad as Don Quixote, and why he always felt himself to be, paradoxically, a "prisoner" and a "castaway." Since Ortega had taken intentionality to mean that seeing was original evidence, he was also obliged to accept the determinism this entailed.

---

[9] In addition, in a sense, the correlation is even more perfect since Ortega, too, is writing about self-negation.

Postscript

Accept, that is, perception as passive constitution, as the passive genesis of meaning, or what Merleau-Ponty, in a claimed borrowing from Husserl, called "operating intentionality."[10] This entailed, instead of an essential emptiness directed on the world, as in Sartre, a plenitude lodged at the center of consciousness, one that was not one's own, that was in a sense quite as alien as Scheler had shown. For Ortega, as for Merleau-Ponty, this pre-personal, pre-objective, operative intentionality was both an original, basic phenomenon, and "the primordial, foundational KIND OF BEING for man, with 'being' taken in the strong, metaphysical sense. Human being IS at bottom this stratum of the happening of meaning."[11] But this, as Ortega saw, was tantamount to capitulation to Bergson or to Hegel; certainly a high price to pay for outdistancing Descartes. It is no wonder, then, that Ortega vacillated between the equally unsatisfactory choices of "vital" and "historical" reason. The first dissolved man into Being and the second absorbed him into History; implicit in either case was the end of a philosophy of the subject. In the former case, because it would be exchanged for a study of genetic programing, and, in the latter, for historical biography.

As we know, Ortega preferred the latter course; this was why he gave a new and distinct meaning to biography. But, as we now see, there was a great deal of heroism and tragedy in his attempt to think together the two expressions "life" and "reason." Perhaps nowhere is the resultant feeling of awesome determinism, of destiny, so apparent as in "Request for a Goethe From Within," a letter-essay written for an editor of *Die neue Rundschau* in 1932. This essay probably contains the terrible grain of truth Ortega intended for the never-written "meditation" he referred to in 1914 as "An Essay on Limitation":

Life means being driven inexorably to realize the existential project that each one is. This project in which the "I" consists is not an idea or plan that man thinks out and freely chooses. It is prior to all ideas his mind conceives, prior to all decisions of his will. Moreover, in the ordinary way we have no more than a vague sense of it. Nevertheless, it is our authentic *Being*, our destiny. Our will

[10] Ronald Bruzina, *Logos and Eidos: The Concept in Phenomenology* (The Hague: Mouton, 1970), pp. 97–98.
[11] Bruzina, p. 99.

is free *to realize* this life-project that we ultimately are, *or not*, but it can never correct it, change it, evade it or provide a substitute. (IV, 400)

Once we have understood the enormity of the word "limitation" for Ortega, we begin to understand the desperate seriousness of his life in Spain and in exile. He could try to help others but he could not help himself. While he held in thrall the best Spanish minds of his day, with his gaze, with his words, with his very presence, he must often have wondered—and one hopes the thought gave him a terrible Yeatsian joy—how different his life might have been under different circumstances.

BIBLIOGRAPHY

I list here the books and articles to which more than passing reference is made in the text or footnotes.

Adorno, Theodor W. "Husserl and the Problem of Idealism." *Journal of Philosophy*, 37 (January 4, 1940), 5–18.

Bannan, John F. *The Philosophy of Merleau-Ponty*. New York: Harcourt, Brace and World, 1967.

Boring, Edwin G. *A History of Experimental Psychology*. 2d ed. New York: Appleton-Century-Crofts, 1950.

—— *Sensation and Perception in the History of Experimental Psychology*. New York: Appleton-Century, 1942.

Brentano, Franz. *Psychology from an Empirical Standpoint*. Edited by Oskar Kraus. Trans. Antos C. Rancurello, D. B. Terrell, and Linda L. McAlister. London: Routledge and Kegan Paul, 1973.

—— *On the Several Senses of Being in Aristotle*. Ed. and trans. Rolf George. Berkeley: University of California Press, 1975.

—— *The True and the Evident*. Ed. Oskar Kraus and trans. Roderick M. Chisholm, Ilse Politzer, and Kurt R. Fischer. London: Routledge and Kegan Paul, 1966.

Bruzina, Ronald. *Logos and Eidos: The Concept in Phenomenology*. Janua Linguarum Studia memoriae Nicolai van Wijk dedicata, Series Minor, 93. Edit. C. H. van Schooneveld. The Hague: Mouton, 1970.

Carr, David. "Husserl's Problematic Concept of the Life-World." *American Philosophical Quarterly*, 7 (October 1970), 331–39.

—— *Phenomenology and the Problem of History: A Study of Husserl's Transcendental Philosophy*. Evanston, Ill.: Northwestern University Press, 1974.

Cruz Vélez, Danilo. *Filosofía sin supuestos: De Husserl a Heidegger*. Buenos Aires: Editorial Sudamericana, 1970.

Dreyfus, H. L., and S. J. Todes. "The Three Worlds of Merleau-Ponty." *Philosophy and Phenomenological Research*, 22, No. 4 (June 1962), 559–65.

Dussort, Henri. *L'École de Marbourg*. Ed. Jules Vuillemin. Paris: Presses Universitaires de France, 1963.

Edie, James M. "Transcendental Phenomenology and Existentialism." *Phenomenology: The Philosophy of Edmund Husserl and Its Interpretation*. Ed. Joseph J. Kockelmans. Garden City, N.Y.: Doubleday, 1967.

Bibliography

Ferrater Mora, José. *Ortega y Gasset: An Outline of His Philosophy.* New rev. ed. New Haven: Yale University Press, 1957.

Findlay, J. N. *Meinong's Theory of Objects and Values.* 2nd ed. Oxford: Clarendon Press, 1963.

—— "Phenomenology and the Meaning of Realism." *Phenomenology and Philosophical Understanding.* Ed. Edo Pivčević. Cambridge: Cambridge University Press, 1975.

Gaos, José. *Sobre Ortega y Gasset y otros trabajos de la historia de las ideas en España y la América Española.* México: Imprenta Universitaria, 1957.

García Morente, Manuel. *Ensayos.* Madrid: Revista de Occidente, 1945.

—— *La filosofía de Kant: Una introducción a la filosofía.* Madrid: Librería General de Victoriano Suárez, 1917.

Gawronsky, Dimitry. "Ernst Cassirer: His Life and His Works." *The Philosophy of Ernst Cassirer.* Ed. Paul Arthur Schilpp. New York: Tudor Publishing, 1949.

Gelb, A., and K. Goldstein. "Über Farbennamenamnesie." *Psychologische Forschung,* VI (1924), 127–86, 187–99.

Gregory, R. L. *Concepts and Mechanisms of Perception.* New York: Scribner's, 1974.

Gurwitsch, Aron. *Studies in Phenomenology and Psychology.* Evanston, Ill.: Northwestern University Press, 1966.

Haber, Ralph Norman. "Where Are the Visions in Visual Perception?" *Imagery: Current Cognitive Approaches.* Ed. Sidney Joelson Segal. New York and London: Academic Press, 1971.

Heidegger, Martin. *Being and Time.* Trans. John Macquarrie and Edward Robinson. New York: Harper & Row, 1962.

Husserl, Edmund. *The Crisis of European Sciences and Transcendental Phenomenology: An Introduction to Phenomenological Philosophy.* Trans. with an Introd. David Carr. Evanston, Ill.: Northwestern University Press, 1970.

—— *Ideas: General Introduction to Pure Phenomenology.* Trans. W. R. Boyce Gibson. London: Collier-Macmillan, 1969.

—— *Logical Investigations.* Trans. J. N. Findlay. 2 vols. New York: Humanities Press, 1970.

—— "Philosophy as Rigorous Science." *Phenomenology and the Crisis of Philosophy.* Trans. with an Introd. Quentin Lauer. New York: Harper and Row, 1965.

Jaensch, Eric R. *Eidetic Imagery and Typological Methods of Investigation: Their Importance for the Psychology of Childhood, the Theory of Education, General Psychology, and Psychophysiology of Human Personality.* Trans. from 2nd ed. by Oscar Deser. New York: Harcourt, Brace, 1930.

Jones, W. Tudor. *Contemporary Thought of Germany.* Vol. I. New York: Knopf, 1931.

Bibliography

Katz, David. *Gestalt Psychology: Its Nature and Significance.* Trans. Robert Tyson. New York: Ronald Press, 1950.

—— *The World of Color.* Trans. R. B. MacLeod. London: Kegan Paul, Trench, Trubner & Co., 1935.

Kaufmann, Fritz. "Cassirer, Neo-Kantianism, and Phenomenology." *The Philosophy of Ernst Cassirer.* Ed. Paul Arthur Schilpp. New York: Tudor Publishing, 1949.

Kraus, Oskar. "Introduction in the 1924 Edition." Franz Brentano. *Psychology from an Empirical Standpoint.* Trans. Antos C. Rancurello, D. B. Terrell, and Linda L. McAlister. London: Routledge and Kegan Paul, 1973.

Kuhn, Helmut. "Ernst Cassirer's Philosophy of Culture." *The Philosophy of Ernst Cassirer.* Ed. Paul Arthur Schilpp. New York: Tudor, 1949.

Lefèvre, Frédéric. "Une Heure avec José Ortega y Gasset, philosophe espagnol." *Les Nouvelles Littéraires,* No. 339 (April 13, 1929), pp. 2, 8.

Levin, David M. "Husserl's Notion of Self-Evidence." *Phenomenology and Philosophical Understanding.* Ed. Edo Pivčević. Cambridge: Cambridge University Press, 1975.

McClintock, Robert. *Man and His Circumstances: Ortega as Educator.* New York: Teacher's College, Columbia University, 1971.

Marías, Julián. *La escuela de Madrid: Estudios de filosofía española.* Buenos Aires: Emecé Editores, 1959.

Marichal, Juan. *La vocación de Manuel Azaña.* Madrid: Editorial Cuadernos para el Diálogo, 1971.

Merleau-Ponty, Maurice. *Phenomenology of Perception.* Trans. Colin Smith. London: Routledge & Kegan Paul, 1962.

—— *The Primacy of Perception and Other Essays on Phenomenological Psychology, the Philosophy of Art, History and Politics.* Ed. with an Introd. James M. Edie. Evanston. Ill.: Northwestern University Press, 1964.

—— *Sense and Non-Sense.* Trans. with a Preface by Hubert L. Dreyfus and Patricia Allen Dreyfus. Evanston, Ill.: Northwestern University Press, 1964.

—— *Signs.* Trans. with an Introd. Richard C. McCleary. Evanston, Ill.: Northwestern University Press, 1964.

—— *The Structure of Behavior.* Trans. Alden L. Fisher. Boston: Beacon Press, 1963.

Mohanty, J. N. "'Life-World' and 'A Priori' in Husserl's Later Thought." *Analecta Husserliana: The Yearbook of Phenomenological Research.* Ed. Anna-Teresa Tymieniecka. Dordrecht: D. Reidel Publishing, 1974. III, 46–65.

Morón Arroyo, Ciriaco. *El sistema de Ortega y Gasset.* Madrid: Ediciones Alcalá, 1968.

Müller-Freienfels, Richard. *The Evolution of Modern Psychology.* Trans. W. Béran Wolfe, M.D. New Haven: Yale University Press, 1935.

Bibliography

de Muralt, André. *L'Idée de la phénoménologie, l'exemplarisme husserlien.* Paris: Gallimard, 1958.

Nelson, Leonard. *Socratic Method and Critical Philosophy: Selected Essays.* Trans. Thomas K. Brown, III. New Haven: Yale University Press, 1949.

O'Neill, John. *Perception, Expression, and History: The Social Phenomenology of Maurice Merleau-Ponty.* Evanston, Ill.: Northwestern University Press, 1970.

Ortega y Gasset, José. *Apuntes sobre el pensamiento.* 2nd ed. Madrid: Ediciones de la Revista de Occidente, 1966.

——— "Cartas inéditas a Navarro Ledesma." *Cuadernos,* November 1962, pp. 3–18.

——— "El curso de don José Ortega y Gasset," *Anales de la Institución Cultural Española.* Vol. I Buenos Aires: Institución Cultural Española, 1947.

——— "Descartes y el método transcendental." *Actas de la Asociación Española para el Progreso de las Ciencias.* IV. Madrid, 1910. pp. 5–13.

——— *Meditations on Quixote.* Ed. with an Introd. Julián Marías. Trans. Evelyn Rugg and Diego Marín. New York: Norton, 1961.

——— *Obras completas.* 6th ed. 11 vols. Madrid: Revista de Occidente, 1963.

——— *Phenomenology and Art.* Trans. with an Introd. Philip W. Silver. New York: Norton, 1975. [This volume contains translations of "Preface for Germans," "Sensation, Construction, and Intuition," "On the Concept of Sensation," and "An Essay in Esthetics by Way of a Preface."]

——— *Prólogo para alemanes.* 2nd ed. Madrid: Taurus Ediciones, 1961.

——— "Temas del Escorial." *Mapocho,* IV, No. 1 (1965).

——— *Unas lecciones de metafísica.* Madrid: Alianza Editorial, 1966.

Ortega y Gasset, Manuel. *Niñez y mocedad de Ortega.* Madrid: C.L.A.V.E., 1964.

Rancurello, Antos C. *A Study of Franz Brentano: His Psychological Standpoint and His Significance in the History of Psychology.* New York and London: Academic Press, 1968.

Salmerón, Fernando. *Las mocedades de Ortega y Gasset.* México: El Colegio de México, 1959.

Sartre, Jean-Paul. *Situations I.* Paris: Gallimard, 1947.

Scheler, Max. *Formalism in Ethics and Non-Formal Ethics of Values: A New Attempt toward the Foundation of an Ethical Personalism.* Trans. Manfred S. Frings and Roger L. Funk. Evanston, Ill.: Northwestern University Press, 1973.

——— *Ressentiment.* Ed. with an Introd. Lewis A. Coser. Trans. William W. Holdheim. New York: Free Press of Glencoe, 1961.

——— *Selected Philosophical Essays.* Trans. with an Introd. David R. Lachterman. Evanston, Ill.: Northwestern University Press, 1973.

Schérer, René. *La Phénoménologie des "Recherches logique" de Husserl.* Paris: Presses Universitaires de France, 1967.

Bibliography

Schmitt, Richard. "In Search of Phenomenology." *Review of Metaphysics*, 15 (September 1961–June 1962), 450–79.

—— *Martin Heidegger: On Being Human: An Introduction to "Sein and Zeit."* New York: Random House, 1969.

Son, B. H. *Science and Person: A Study of the Idea of "Philosophy as Rigorous Science" in Kant and Husserl.* Bijdragen Tot De Filosofie, No. 2. Assen: Van Gorcum and Comp. B. V., 1972.

Spiegelberg, Herbert. *The Phenomenological Movement: A Historical Introduction.* 2 vols. The Hague: Martinus Nijhoff, 1960.

Stériad, Alice. *L'Interprétation de la doctrine de Kant par L'École de Marburg.* Paris: V. Giard et Brière, 1913.

INDEX

Absolute knowledge, 123
Act, 84-85, 104
Act Psychology, Austrian School of, 81
"Adam in Paradise," 2, 21, 55, 26-30
Adorno, T. W., 58-59
Aesthesis, notion of, 135
Aesthetics, *see* Esthetics
Aesthetik des reinen Gefühls (Cohen), 47
Alfonso XIII, 17
"Annoyance with Orators," 36
Anthropological empiricism, 44
Anti-utilitarianism, in Scheler, 57, 75
A *priori,* 43-44, 46-47, 73
Aquinas, St. Thomas, 66, 85
Aristotle, 66, 85, 101-5
Art: as an element of culture, 142;
  nineteenth-century view of, 143; *see also*
  Esthetics
"Art of This World and the Next," 55, 75
Ateneo lecture (1915), 118, 120
Attention, mechanism of, 141
Austrian School of Act Psychology, 81
Azaña, M., 17, 21
Azorín (José Martínez Ruiz), 37

Bacon, F., 45
Being, 28, 63, 100, 105, 115, 157, 160; in
  Greek philosophy, 102-5, and having,
  113-14; for the Marburg School, 29;
  Ortega's critique of Heidegger on, 8,
  70-71, 101-2; Ortega's new notion of,
  95, 121; and thinking, 96

Being-in-the-world: Heidegger's notion of,
  86-87; Scheler's notion of, 72, 74
Berkeley, G., 45
Biography, historical, 160
Boring, E. G., 81
Brentano, F., 11, 40-42, 64-67; Husserl's
  relation to, 60, 137; Kant, Brentano
  unsympathetic to, 52; Ortega's early
  familiarity with, 56; *Psychology from an
  Empirical Standpoint,* 53-54
Buenos Aires lectures (1916), 93, 110-11,
  154

Carr, D., 92
Cassirer, E., 20, 29, 48
"Castilian Landscapes," 56
Cervantes Saavedra, M. de, 117-21, 131,
  136, 140-43, 147-49
Change, problem of, in Greek philosophy,
  103-4
Chivalry, books of, 145-46
Civic pedagogy, theory of, 21-22, 25
"Civic Pedagogy as a Political Program," 34
Clarity, of Mediterranean people, 139-40
Cognition, 79, 87, 113; of the artist, 97
Cohen, H., 19-23, 26-27, 29, 32, 36, 39,
  43-48
Color, Katz's study of, 81
Concept, 98, 102, 122-24, 140-41
"Congress for the Advancement of Sci-
  ence," 36
Consciousness, 9-12, 77, 83, 85, 96-97,
  123; different levels of, 128; Husserl's

Index

Consciousness (*Continued*)
notion of, 42, 53, 59, 61-63, 91; in new life philosophy, 94; Scheler's comments on Husserl's notions of, 62
Constancy hypothesis, 68
Constructionism, 22, 29, 90
Contemplation, 111-12
Costa, J., 35
Crisis lectures (Husserl), 64, 89
Critical philosophy, 43, 55, 79
Culture, 36-37, 98, 122-24, 135, 147, 158; Latin and Germanic, 139; how new comes into being, 136; Spanish, 141, 148-49; truth in, 124-25; value system of Western man founded on, 156; vitalism, a new approach to, 157-58; work of art as an element of, 142

Dasein, 11, 70-71, 85, 87, 99
De anima (Aristotle), 85, 103
Dehumanization of Art, The, 143
Descartes, R., 45, 155
"Descartes and the Transcendental Method," 19, 32, 65
Descriptive or phenomenological psychology, 53-55, 59, 65, 80, 110
Determinism, 159-60
Dilthey, W., 40-41, 153
Divine Comedy, The (Dante), 132
Don Quixote (Cervantes), 116-17; see also *Meditations on Quixote*

Edie, J. M., 61
Education, views on, 21-25
Egological reduction, 59, 83
Ehrenfels, C. von, 68
Eidetic imagery, 81-82, 127-30
Eidetic psychology, 81-82, 94
Eidetic reduction, 59, 62
Einleitung (Natorp), 50
Einstein, A., 156
Elementism, 90
Embodiedness, philosophy of, 126
Emotions, as a motive force, 24
Emotive apriorism, of Scheler, 73
Empiricism, 41, 44-46, 60, 79

English empiricism, 45, 46
Epic, 144-45
Epistemology, 79; Husserl's, 62; Marburg School's, 47; Neo-Kantian, 26; primacy of perception in, 157; Scheler's criticism of Neo-Kantian, 75-76; self-knowledge, 106, 117; *see also* Knowledge, theories of
Epoche, 92
Escapist literature, 145-46
"Essay in Esthetics by Way of a Preface," 78, 80, 84, 96-98, 102-3, 105-7, 113-14
Essence, 62, 90-91, 100-1
Esthetic profundity, 146
Esthetics, 26-29, 84, 135, 144-45; in Marburg School, 47; Scheler's influence on Ortega's theories of, 75; Spanish, 55
"Esthetics of Dwarf Gregorio, Wine-Skin Seller," 55
Ethics, 28; in Marburg School, 47; Scheler's theories of, 72-73; in social pedagogy, 25
Ethics (Scheler), 64, 73, 84
Europa (magazine), 32
Executivity, notion of, 97-99, 101, 105-7, 110, 123
Exemplary Novels (Cervantes), 143
Exist, meaning of term, 99-101
Existence, 99-101
Existentialism, 84, 99-101; conflict between idealism and, in Husserl, 61
Existential judgment, 76
Existential phenomenologists, 60, 88, 90
Existential proposition, 65
Experience, problem of, 46, 124
Experience and Judgment (Husserl), 64, 89, 90
Experimental psychology, 52, 64
Explanatory psychology, 82
Expression Theory of Art, 84, 97

Faro (magazine), 32
Fichte, J. G., 44
Findlay, J. N., 62, 150
First Investigation (Husserl), 94
Fischer-Trendelenburg dispute, 43
Form constancy, in Gestalt psychology, 69

Index

Forms, *a priori*, 43-44
French existentialists, 84, 99-101

Galileo, 45-46, 154
Gaos, J., 131, 151
García Morente, M., 26, 28-29, 34, 91, 93, 151
Gelb-Goldstein study of brain-injured subjects, 125
Generation of 1830, German intellectuals of the, 39-43
Generation of 1898, Spanish intellectuals of the, 16, 18, 35, 37
Genetic phenomenology, 156
Genetic psychology, 80, 83, 137
Germanic culture, 139
German philosophy, 39-42; Ortega viewed as indebted to, 153; Ortega viewed as a popularizer of, 4
Gestalt psychology, 68-69, 81
Goldstein, K., 125
Greek literature, 144-45
Greek philosophy, 102-4, 144
Gurwitsch, A., 68, 125-26, 129

Having, being and, 113-14
Hegel, G. W. F., 7, 134
"Hegel's Philosophy of History and Historiology," 71
Heidegger, M., 10-11; ontology, 86; Ortega's disagreement with, and critique of, 8, 70-71, 84, 101-2; Ortega viewed as indebted to, 153; *Sein und Zeit*, 4, 8, 11, 70, 88, 107, 153; *see also* Dasein
Historical biography, 160
Historical presentation of Ortega's philosophy, 13
Historical Reason, *see* Vital or Historical Reason
Historical reduction, 113
"History as a System," 2, 114
History of Philosophy (Bréhier), Preface to, 103-4
History of Philosophy (Marías), 2
Hobbes, T., 45
Hoffmann, H., 80-82

Homer, 144
Human life, notion of, 8-11, 51, 71, 86, 97, 105, 111, 149, 157
Hume, D., 45
Husserl, E., 50-55; Adorno on, 58-59; Brentano's influence on, 60; consciousness, notion of, 59, 91-92; contradictory aims of, 61; historicity in later works, 89; Natorp's influence on, 20; Ortega's relationship to, and critique of, 8-14, 67, 77-87, 90-91, 113-14, 136-37, 154-56; Sartre's critique of, 77; Scheler's critique of, 62-64, 75-76; *see also* Phenomenology

I, meaning of, 97-99, 160
Ideal intuition, 56, 60
Idealism, 13, 26, 34-35, 48, 55; "Essay in Esthetics" as a polemic against, 105; Husserl's, 59, 61, 83; in *Meditations on Quixote*, 122; psychological idealism in Kant, 43; refutation by phenomenological notion of intentionality, 93
"Idealism and Realism" (Scheler), 62-63, 75
Idealism of absolute consciousness, 62
Ideality, needed by Spaniards, 120-21, 125, 130, 140
Idea of Principle in Leibniz and the Evolution of Deductive Theory, The, 5, 8, 50-51, 70-71, 84, 96, 99, 101, 158
Ideas (Husserl), 53, 59-64, 88-89, 91-93; Natorp's influence on, 20; Ortega's reaction to, 77, 80-81; Sartre's critique of, 77
Ideational abilities, 125-27
"Idols of Self-Knowledge," (Scheler), 74
Image, concept of, 98, 102, 105, 110
Impressionism of Spaniards, 55, 120, 124, 140-42
Individualism, 25
Individual life, in Perspectivism, 93
Inner perception, 56
Intentionality, 159-60; Brentano's notions modified by Husserl, 59-60; Husserl's notion of, 12, 50, 95; operative, 82, 107;

Index

Intentionality (*Continued*)
phenomenological notion of, 93, 123;
Scheler on, 73
Intentionality of act, 91
Intuition, 79-80; of essences, 59

Jaensch, E. R., 81-82, 127-30

Kant, I., 22-24; epistemology, 26-27; esthetics, 27; Generation of 1830, anti-Kantianism of, 40-41; Husserl's reactions to, 61; Jaensch on spatial perceptions in, 129; study of, by the Marburg School, 43-47; Scheler's argument against, 73-74
Kants Theorie der Erfahrung (Cohen), 44, 47
Katz, D., 81-82, 127
Kepler, J., 45-46
Knowledge, theories of, 46, 86-87, 114, 123; *see also* Epistemology
Koffka, K., 69, 81
Köhler, W., 69, 81

Language, as the true locus of essences, 67
Latin culture, 139
Lebenswelt, 73, 82-83, 107, 154; *see also* Life-world
Leibniz, G. W. von, 45
Life, 28-29, 101, 111-12, 160; as the fundamental reality, 42, 51, 106, 121; Heidegger's substitution of "existence" for, 99; *potentia apetitiva* as the basis of, 85; *see also* Human life
Life enhancement, as a new value system for Western man, 156
Life philosophy, 94-95
Life-world, 91, 103, 107, 158; Ortega's system rooted in, 156; Scheler's notion of, 73
Lipps, T., 52
Locke, J., 45
Love, 134, 152
Logic: in Marburg School, 47; Natorp's view of, 52
Logic (Hegel), 7, 134

Logical Investigations (Husserl), 50, 52, 59, 61, 78, 88, 95
Logischen Grundlagen der exakten Wissenschaften, Die (Natorp), 47
Logos, 135

Man: meaning of, 24-25; relation to the world, 85
Man and People, 84, 99
Marburg School, 19-23, 31, 35, 39, 43; *a priori* as method, 47; Husserl and, 52; Kantian philosophy, 43-47; Neo-Kantian Marxism, 22; prestige of, 48
Marías, J., 2, 9, 12, 26, 84, 97, 117, 131, 158
Martínez Ruiz, J. (*Azorín*), 37
Marty, A., 65
Marxism, Neo-Kantian, 22
Matter: in Kantian epistemology, 27; meaning and, 148
Meaning, 94, 148; in *Meditations on Quixote*, 141, 147
Mechanistic view of nature, 75
Meditation, 139, 142
Meditations on Quixote, 4-8, 34, 82, 86, 99, 102-3, 112-13, 115-49, 152, 154, 157; "Essay in Esthetics," a diminutive version of, 98; Horatian creed of *dulce et utile*, 23; human life as a phenomenon, basis of thought in, 11; Perspectivist doctrine in, 93; pessimism of, 158-59; purpose of, 116, 133
Mediterranean Man, 55, 125, 139-40
Meinong, A., 54, 65, 67, 140
Merleau-Ponty, M., 69, 82, 88, 90-91, 96, 115, 126-27, 160
Metaphysics, 99-101, 154
Metaphysics (Aristotle), 101, 103
Methodological idealism, 59
Methodology of phenomenology, 50, 61
Mind, in nineteenth-century psychology, 68
Mind-body problem, 22
Modern Theme, The, 154, 157
Moral system, of Marburg School, 21-22
Morón Arroyo, C., 9, 12, 86

Movement, problem of, in Greek philosophy, 103-4
Müller, G. E., 81
Mundane phenomenology, 89-90, 149, 159; early formulation of, 107; *Meditations on Quixote* as, 115-30; as a program and method for discovering, 110-11
My life, notion of, 29, 105-6, 113, 158

Natorp, P., 19-25, 29, 32, 38-39, 45-48, 52
Natural attitude, Husserl's general thesis of the, 62-63, 85, 92; Scheler's criticism of, 75-76
"Neither Vitalism Nor Rationalism," 157
Neo-Kantian philosophy, 23, 26, 33-34, 42, 49, 50; man in, 24; social pedagogy, theory of, 24-25; Ortega's historical account of, 39, 41; *see also* Marburg School
Nietzsche, F., 18
Novel, 143-49

Objectivism, 21, 23, 155-56
Objects: man's relation to, 85; of philosophy, 110; theory of, 54
"Old and New Politics," 34, 117
"On Self-Deceptions" (Scheler), 64, 72, 84-85
"On the Concept of Sensation," 9, 78, 80-84, 107
Ontology, 8-12; Aristotle's, 103-5; Heidegger's, 86-87; Ortega's new, 95-96, 123; primacy of perception in, 157; of pure or absolute presence, 91; Scheler's, 70-72
Operative intentionality, 73, 82, 91, 107, 160
Ordinary Language philosophers, 65
Origin of our Knowledge of Right and Wrong, The (Brentano), 67
Ortega: Circumstances and Vocation, I (Marías), 2
Ortega y Gasset, J., birth and family background, 18; education, 18-21, 31-39; goal of service to Spain, 2-3; gradualists' view of development of philosophy of, 2; neglect of, 150; philosophical asceticism

of, 132; viewed as a popularizer of German philosophy, 4
Our life, notion of, 105, 107
"Our National Problems and the Youth," 15

Painting, esthetics of, 26-27
Pedagogical system, 21-25
Perception, 82; in Gestalt psychology, 69-70; in Husserl's *Ideas*, 91-92; in *Meditations on Quixote*, 136-38; Merleau-Ponty on, 88; as passive genesis of meaning, 160; in Perspectivism, 93; primacy of, 157; psychology of, 127-30; in Scheler, 72, 74
"Perception of the Other," 112
Person, Scheler's concept of the, 64
Perspectivism, 91-93; in *Don Quixote*, 118-19
Pessimism, in *Meditations on Quixote*, 158-59
Phenomenological method, 8
Phenomenological psychology, *see* Descriptive psychology
Phenomenological reduction, 90
Phenomenology, 54; Brentano's *Psychology from an Empirical Standpoint* as source of, 41; development of, 61; as an epiphenomenon, 156; *epoche*, weakest point of, 92; Husserl's claim that it is scientific, 59; Husserl sees it as redeeming Europe, 155; Husserl's separation of psychology from, 53; as an instrument, 42, 49-51; Neo-Kantian philosophy's closeness to, 50; Ortega's encounter with and relationship to, 2, 8-12, 20, 33, 37, 55-56, 84, 88; Ortega's essays on, 77-87; Scheler's view of, 71, 75
Phenomenology of inner time-consciousness, 89
Phenomenology of Perception (Merleau-Ponty), 88, 90
Philosophical anthropology, 159
Philosophical psychology, 47
Philosophy: objects of, 110; purpose of,

Index

Philosophy (*Continued*)
134; as a scientific undertaking, 19; not the supreme value, 109
"Philosophy as Rigorous Science" (Husserl), 52, 62
Philosophy of Symbolic Forms (Cassirer), 29
Physics, Einstein's revolution in, 156
Plato, 46
Poetry, 144-46
Politics, 24-25, 108
Positivism: Husserl's, 137; Marburg School's rejection of, 44; modern philosophy, ascendancy in, 154; of nineteenth-century Spain, 139
Potentia apetitiva, 85, 111
Potentiality, 103-4
Pragma, Greek notion of the, 85-86
Pragmatic philosophy, 108
Pragmatic relation of man to world, 85
"Preface for Germans," 2, 8, 14, 37-43, 49, 51, 60, 67, 84
Preface to Bréhier's *History of Philosophy*, 103-4
Pre-reflexive *cogito*, 106
Prieto, I., 131-32
Principles of Gestalt Psychology (Koffka), 69
Profundity: of *Don Quixote*, 142, 146, 148; nature of 140-41
Psychological idealism, 43
Psychologism, 44, 52, 54, 68
Psychology: Brentano's, 54; experimental, 52, 64; Husserl's separation of phenomenology from, 53; Ortega's studies in, 38; revolution in, 67-69; *see also* Descriptive or phenomenological psychology
Psychology from an Empirical Standpoint (Brentano), 41, 53-54, 56, 60, 65
Pure consciousness, 42, 53, 59, 83; Ortega's rejection of, 96, 123
Pure logic, 78
Pure psychology, 60
Pure will, 22

Radical empiricism, 79
Rancor, 152-53

Rationalism, 45-46, 155
Realism, 143-44; Ortega's critique against, 13
Realistic novel, 146-48
Reality, 27, 28, 30, 109, 146-48; Husserl's distinction between consciousness and, 91; life as the fundamental reality, 42, 51, 106, 121; in Perspectivism, 93; in Scheler, 63, 72, 73, 76
Reduction, theory of, 59, 62, 83, 90, 111, 113, 137, 156; Ortega's notion of, 107; Scheler's criticism of, 76
Relational property, 140
"Renan," 2, 23
"Request for a Goethe From Within," 160
Resistance, Scheler's notion of, 64
Rubin, E., 81, 127

Sartre, J.-P., 60, 77, 158, 160; on Husserl's intentionality, 95-96; on pre-reflexive *cogito*, 106
Scheler, M., 20, 57, 60; arguments against Husserl, 62-64, 75-76, 84; arguments against Kant, 73-74; echos of, in *Meditations on Quixote*, 133-34; *epoche*, 92; ontology in, 70-72; Ortega viewed as indebted to, 153
Scholastic philosophers, 101
Science, 28; Husserl's claim that phenomenology would be source of validity for other sciences, 78; modern created by Kepler and Galileo, 45-46; value system of Western man founded on, 156
Scientific knowledge, 47
Scientific reduction, 156
Sein und Zeit (Heidegger), 4, 8, 11, 70, 86, 107, 153
Selbstbewusstsein, 85, 105, 113
Self-knowledge, 106, 113
"Sr. Dato, Guilty of an Infraction of the Constitution," 17
"Sensation, Construction, and Intuition," 13, 33, 78-79, 107
Sensation in nineteenth-century psychology, 68

Sensationism, 22, 45, 90
Sense perception, in nineteenth-century psychology, 68
Simmel, G., 48
Social or civic pedagogy, theory of, 21-22, 25
"Social Pedagogy as a Political Program," 15, 21, 23-25
Society, 25
Society of money, Scheler on, 75
Some Lessons in Metaphysics, 13, 99-101
Space perception, 128
Spain, 2-3, 36; antipathy for ideation, 130; culture, 35, 116, 148; Don Quixote not understood in nineteenth-century, 139; education for, 24; esthetics of, 55; Europe and, 117, 120; philosophical indigence of, 7; political situation prior to World War I, 15-17; Spanish way of being in the world, 124-25; spontaneous life of Spaniards, 135
Spectator, The (magazine), 108-10
Speculative metaphysics, 44
Spengler, O., 154
Spiegelberg, H., 61, 80, 82
State, 22
Stimulus, in nineteenth-century psychology, 68
Striving, notion of, 64
Structure of Behavior, The (Merleau-Ponty), 5, 69
Stumpf, C., 52, 54, 60
Subject and objects, relations between, 85
Subjectivity, 25, 84, 97, 155
"Supplement to Kant," 71
Systematic philosophy, 49
Systematic principle of Ortega, 84

"Terrors of the Year One Thousand: Critique of a Legend," 18
"Theory of Objects" (Meinong), 65
Thinking, 105, 111, 115, 121-22; Aristotle's notion of, 104; interrelationship of, with being, 96
Thomas Aquinas, St., 66, 85

"Three Great Metaphors," 13
"Three Paintings about Wine," 75
To be, meaning of, 100
"Transcendence of the Ego" (Sartre), 77
Transcendental logic, 47
Transcendental phenomenology, 51-53; Ortega and, 58-87; Scheler's criticism of, 57, 75
Transcendental reduction, 12, 62, 85, 93, 96-97
Transcendental subjectivity, 155
Transcendental Unity of Apperception, Kant's, 29
Transcendent unity, 27-28
Trendelenburg-Fischer dispute, 43
Truth, 46, 108-9, 123-24
"Truth and Perspective," 108

"Über Selbsttäuschungen" (Scheler), 57
Umwelt, Scheler's notion of, 73
Understanding, 134
Unmediated self-knowledge, 106, 113

Vaihinger, H., 47-48
Valuation, system of, 27-28
Vital or Historical Reason, 89, 114, 149, 160; dialectical presentation of, 13; in Meditations on Quixote, 120-21; phenomenology's part in development of, 37; philosophical method of, 9
Vital utility, principle of, 110
Von der Klassifikation der psychischen Phänomene (Brentano), 56, 65, 67
Von der mannigfachen Bedeutung des Seienden nach Aristotles (Brentano), 11, 56

What is Philosophy?, 2, 13
Will, 22
World, in Scheler, 74
World of Color, The (Katz), 81
Wundt, W., 19, 38, 40-41

Zuloaga, I., 26-27